LEIBNIZ AND CHINA

Why was Leibniz so fascinated by Chinese philosophy and culture? What specific forms did his interest take? How did his interest compare with the relative indifference of his philosophical contemporaries and near-contemporaries such as Spinoza and Locke? In this highly original book, Franklin Perkins examines Leibniz's voluminous writings on the subject and suggests that his interest was founded in his own philosophy: the nature of his metaphysical and theological views required him to take Chinese thought seriously. Leibniz was unusual in holding enlightened views about the intellectual profitability of cultural exchange, and in a broad-ranging discussion Perkins charts these views, their historical context, and their social and philosophical ramifications. The result is an illuminating philosophical study which also raises wider questions about the perils and rewards of trying to understand and learn from a different culture.

FRANKLIN PERKINS is Assistant Professor of Philosophy at DePaul University, Chicago. He has published in early modern European philosophy, early Chinese philosophy, and comparative philosophy, with articles appearing in the *Journal of the History of Ideas*, the *Journal of Chinese Philosophy*, and the *Leibniz Review*.

LEIBNIZ AND CHINA

A commerce of light

FRANKLIN PERKINS

CAMBRIDGE
UNIVERSITY PRESS

PUBLISHED BY THE PRESS SYNDICATE OF THE UNIVERSITY OF CAMBRIDGE
The Pitt Building, Trumpington Street, Cambridge, United Kingdom

CAMBRIDGE UNIVERSITY PRESS
The Edinburgh Building, Cambridge, CB2 2RU, UK
40 West 20th Street, New York, NY 10011–4211, USA
477 Williamstown Road, Port Melbourne, VIC 3207, Australia
Ruiz de Alarcón 13, 28014 Madrid, Spain
Dock House, The Waterfront, Cape Town 8001, South Africa

http://www.cambridge.org

First published 2004

Printed in the United Kingdom at the University Press, Cambridge

Typeface Adobe Garamond 11/12.5 pt.   *System* LATEX 2$_\varepsilon$ [TB]

A catalogue record for this book is available from the British Library

Library of Congress Cataloging in Publication data
Perkins, Franklin.
Leibniz and China : a commerce of light / Franklin Perkins.
p.   cm.
Includes bibliographical references and index.
ISBN 0-521-83024-9
1. Leibniz, Gottfried Wilhelm, Freiherr von, 1664–1716.   2. Philosophy, Chinese.   I. Title.
B2599.C5P47   2004   2003055355

ISBN 0 521 83024 9 hardback

For my parents

Contents

Illustrations

Preface

Leibniz and China? The topic usually meets with surprise. Even when people know that Leibniz had a life-long interest in China and directed his considerable energy and political skills to encouraging cultural exchange – his "commerce of light" – the topic remains strange and peripheral to the concerns of a philosopher engaged with philosophy's history. A broader interest in the place of other cultures in early modern thought meets with greater skepticism, because it seems obvious that other cultures have no place there. The reason Leibniz's engagement with China appears so surprising and worthy of attention is its contrast with the disinterest of his contemporaries. Yet our reaction of surprise should itself be surprising and worthy of attention. In the sixteenth and seventeenth centuries, information from other cultures flooded into Europe, while Europe's economy became more and more obviously global. In this context of globalization, the odd phenomenon should not be Leibniz's writings on China but that everyone else showed so little interest in the world outside Europe. How could Descartes, so interested in the nature of "man," show no interest in the variety of human beings? How could Locke, an "empiricist," show so little interest in the experiences of non-Europeans?

Such questions seem somehow inappropriate or unfair, not the kinds of questions with which a philosopher would approach Descartes or Locke. Why? We think of our time as uniquely multi-cultural, and surely some aspects of our time are unique. For the first time, almost all cultures have some connection. We have radically fast access to almost any culture, in that, given enough money, we can fly almost any place, and we can get some limited access even faster through the internet. But if we consider our time uniquely multi-cultural because in our everyday lives we encounter people from other cultures, or because so many live in a cultural setting different from that of their parents, or because the greatest challenge of our time is how to accommodate cultural differences, then we are wrong. This illusion of uniqueness cuts us off from the guidance we could gain from history, both from the history of Europe and the histories of the rest of the world. At the same time, we strengthen the illusion that European thought is a *causa sui*, growing up of itself, without interaction with the rest of the world. This illusion of an independent Europe allows for easy distinctions between "us" and "them," "East" and "West," at the same time that it obscures the historicity of those distinctions. This illusion of an isolated Europe tempts us to explain the absence of other cultures in the writings of early modern philosophers by the absence of the rest of the world from their experience.

This book is meant to undercut this illusion, using Gottfried Wilhelm Leibniz as an example of how early modern thinkers deployed their own philosophies in understanding the place of other cultures, and how they incorporated cultural diversity into their own philosophies. Leibniz is not a typical example, standing almost alone in his recognition of the value of cultural exchange. Leibniz's vision of China developed, though, within a context of European expansion and a history of engagement with other cultures. This context must be grasped if both the uniqueness and the continuity of Leibniz's approach is to be understood. The direct goal of this book is to understand Leibniz's engagement with China, both in this context of Europe's encounters with other cultures and in the context of Leibniz's own philosophy. I hope this project also contributes to two broader goals. One is to add another small piece to a growing concern with how Europe theorized and constructed other cultures. Such a concern cannot be separated from European dominance of other cultures and the discourses of colonialism, particularly the construction of orientalism, which Edward Said (*Orientalism*) describes as forming in the late eighteenth century, and the construction of race, which Emmanuel Eze (*Race and the Enlightenment: a Reader*) attributes to the early eighteenth century. My work here differs from these histories because it addresses an earlier time and because Leibniz's writings do not fit easily into any story of the intersection of philosophy and colonialism. In its evaluation of other cultures, the early modern period is remarkably heterogeneous: when Leibniz calls for Chinese missionaries to come and teach ethics to Europeans, not everyone found his remark outrageous. Even those philosophers with little interest in other cultures explicitly claimed that all peoples have roughly equal capabilities. In the seventeenth century, we find some of the Euro-centric elements of later colonialist discourses but without the confidence in European superiority that would soon emerge, for example, in the racism of Hume and Kant. I make little attempt here to generalize about broad discourses, but the example of Leibniz at least illustrates that the discourses of European colonial dominance have both significant continuities and significant discontinuities with early modern approaches to other cultures.

With this as the goal of this book as a historical study, the other goal is more directly philosophical. Perhaps the greatest challenge of this new century is the set of issues clustered around "multi-culturalism," particularly in how to negotiate the similarities and differences between cultures and how to balance universal ethical claims with the diversity of world cultures. Yet contemporary philosophy seems particularly ill equipped to address these problems, unable even to address its own relationship to culture. Contemporary philosophers have oddly ended up in a position like that of Spinoza or Locke, happy to concede an abstract equality to other cultures but showing no interest in the thought generated by those cultures. I present Leibniz here partly as one model for a philosophical concern with cultural exchange and partly as an early but powerful voice calling for such exchange. At the same time, I hope to show that Leibniz's philosophy provides a foundation for pluralism absent in his contemporaries, and through this point to show that Leibniz's philosophy might still provide elements of a foundation for cultural exchange.

These philosophical and historical goals have required more than just a description of what Leibniz wrote about China. On one side, I have tried to show how Leibniz's engagement with China emerges from a tradition of European encounters with non-European thought. On the other side, I have tried to show that Leibniz's openness to China is not an accident of his experience or personality but flows naturally from his philosophy. In other words, the answer to why Leibniz's interest in other cultures differs from his contemporaries lies in how Leibniz's philosophy differs from his contemporaries. The first chapter of this book sets the context for Leibniz's engagement with China. It includes a discussion of the main ways European thinkers created a space for non-Christian thought and how they attempted to accommodate China in particular. Chapter 2 examines Leibniz's philosophy as it founds his approach to cultural differences, focusing on what different minds can and must learn from each other. This focus is a question of method, but it can only be understood in the broader context of Leibniz's ontology and the psychology of monads. Chapter 3 applies this broader foundation to Leibniz's particular engagements with China, focusing on his progressive vision of cultural exchange and what in particular he hoped Europe would learn. Chapter 4 examines how Leibniz thought the Chinese should be engaged and how Chinese thought should be interpreted. This progression may appear foundational, where Leibniz's political concerns derive from his epistemology, which derives from his ontology, but it would be a mistake to read it this way. Leibniz's ontology can just as easily be read as a justification for his more immediate political goals of harmonizing diverse views, as Leibniz himself lived with more concern for diplomacy than ontology. The more likely view is that all these levels – ontology, epistemology, and politics – are varying expressions of the relationship between diversity and order.

Just over twenty-five years have passed since David Mungello published *Leibniz and Confucianism: the Search for Accord*. His work was preceded by Donald Lach's translation and extensive introduction to Leibniz's preface to the *Novissima Sinica*. In the past quarter century, Leibniz's writings have become much more accessible, largely through Mungello's own work, the work of Rita Widmaier, and the translations by Daniel Cook and Henry Rosemont Jr. Other writings have become accessible as parts of broader projects, most importantly the continuing publication of Leibniz's correspondence by the Deutsche Akademie der Wissenschaften. The possibility of my writing this more inclusive study of Leibniz's engagement with China and of integrating that with his philosophy rests on the work of these scholars. Mungello's original book was animated by a conviction that accord between cultures is one of the most pressing problems of our time and that Leibniz's engagement with China has something to offer us in confronting this problem. I offer this work with those same convictions.

A wide-ranging philosophical and historical work like this would have been impossible without great assistance. This work is most directly indebted to Emily Grosholz, who first allowed me to see what was interesting in early modern thought and whose assistance went from first suggesting I look at Leibniz's writings on China to reading various versions of the manuscript. On-cho Ng, Henry Rosemont Jr., and an anonymous reader all gave me essential feedback on the entire manuscript. I am also grateful to the other members of my dissertation committee, who read an early version of much of this work, Veronique Foti and Pierre Kerszberg. I would also like to thank Charles Scott, who first drew me into philosophy and its history. This project could not have been carried out without the aid of Rita Widmaier and Herbert Breger, both of whom guided me at the Leibniz Archive and commented on parts of this manuscript. I have received beneficial comments on parts or versions of this work from Nicholas Jolley, Paul Lodge, Marcelo Dascal, and Richard Lee. The students in my graduate seminar on Leibniz also helped me to clarify many of the ideas presented here. I would also like to thank Cambridge University Press and Hilary Gaskin, Jackie Warren, and most of all Sally McCann for her careful comments on the entire manuscript. An early version of parts of chapter 2 appeared in the *Leibniz Review*. An early version of "Natural Religion and Ethics" of chapter 3 appeared in the *Journal of the History of Ideas*. Finally, I would like to thank the following for funding my research at the Leibniz Archive: Deutscher Akademischer Austauschdienst, the Penn State Institute for Arts and Humanistic Studies, and a Vassar College Faculty Research Grant.

On a personal level, my greatest debt is to my parents, who always told me to pursue what I really loved to do. I would also like to thank JungEn, who suffered through some of the difficult moments of my writing, and to thank my colleagues, first at Vassar College and now at DePaul University, for providing such a stimulating and supportive environment. Finally, I could not be where I am now without generous help in financing my college education, particularly with a Dean's Select Scholarship from Vanderbilt University and scholarships from the Richardson Foundation and the Citizens Foundation. I will always be grateful for the opportunities those scholarships made possible.

Abbreviations

A   G. W. Leibniz. *Sämtliche Schriften und Briefe.* Deutsche Akademie der Wissenschaften (ed.). Multiple vols. in 7 series. Darmstadt/Leipzig/Berlin: Akademie Verlag, 1923–.

AG   G. W. Leibniz. *Philosophical Essays.* Trans. by Roger Ariew and Daniel Garber. Indianapolis: Hackett, 1989.

AT   *Oeuvres de Descartes.* Ed. by C. Adam and P. Tannery. Rev. edn., Paris: Vrin, 1964–76.

C   G. W. Leibniz. *Opuscules et fragments inédits de Leibniz.* Ed. by Louis Couturat. Hildesheim: Georg Olms Verlagsbuchhandlung, 1966.

CD   G. W. Leibniz. *Causa Dei.* Appendix to the *Theodicy.* Cited by section number. Original text in GP VI, translation in E. M. Huggard, *Theodicy* (London: Routledge and Kegan Paul, 1951).

CSM   R. Descartes. *The Philosophical Writings of Descartes.* Trans. by John Cottingham, Robert Stoothoff, and Dugald Murdoch. Cambridge: Cambridge University Press, 1994.

CSMK R. Descartes. *The Philosophical Writings of Descartes.* Trans. by John Cottingham, Robert Stoothoff, Dugald Murdoch, and Anthony Kenny. Vol. 3. Cambridge: Cambridge University Press, 1994.

Cult   G. W. Leibniz. "De cultu Confucii civili." Cited by section. Original text in W 112–14. English translation by Daniel Cook and Henry Rosemont Jr., *Writings on China* (Chicago: Open Court, 1994).

Dascal G. W. Leibniz. *Leibniz: Language, Signs and Thought.* Ed. by Marcelo Dascal. Philadelphia: John Benjamins Publishing Company, 1987.

Discourse G. W. Leibniz. *Discours sur la Théologie naturelle des Chinois.* Cited by section. Original text in Loosen and Vonessen

(1968). English translation in Cook and Rosemont, *Writings on China.*

DM   G. W. Leibniz. *Discourse on Metaphysics.* Cited by section number. Original text in GP IV; translation in AG.

Dutens   G. W. Leibniz. *Opera Omnia.* Ed. by Louis Dutens. Geneva, 1768.

GM   G. W. Leibniz. *Die Mathematische Schriften von Gottfried Wilhelm Leibniz.* Ed. by C. I. Gerhardt. 7 vols. Berlin and Halle: Weidmann, 1849–55.

GP   G. W. Leibniz. *Die Philosophischen Schriften von Gottfried Wilhelm Leibniz.* Ed. by C. I. Gerhardt. 7 vols. Berlin: Weidmann, 1875–90; repr. Hildesheim: Georg Olms, 1978.

Grua   G. W. Leibniz. *Textes inédits.* 2 vols. Ed. by Gaston Grua. New York: Garland Publishing, 1985.

K   G. W. Leibniz. *Die Werke von Leibniz.* Ed. by Onno Klopp. Hannover, 1864–84.

L   G. W. Leibniz. *Philosophical Papers and Letters.* Trans. by Leroy E. Loemker. 2nd edn. Dordrecht: D. Reidel, 1969.

LBr   G. W. Leibniz. Reference to unpublished Leibniz correspondence, preserved in the Niedersächsische Landesbibliothek, in Hannover, Germany.

M   G. W. Leibniz. "Monadology." Cited by section number. Original text in GP VI; translation in AG.

Essay   Locke, John. *An Essay Concerning Human Understanding.* Ed. by Peter Nidditch. Cited by book, chapter, section, and page. Oxford: Clarendon Press, 1979.

Ethics   Benedict de Spinoza. *The Ethics.* Trans. by Edwin Curley. *A Spinoza Reader: The Ethics and Other Works*, Princeton, Princeton University Press, 1994. Cited by book and proposition (p), definition (d), and scholium (s).

NE   G. W. Leibniz. *New Essays on Human Understanding.* Cited by book, chapter, and section. Original text in A VI, vi; translation in RB.

NS   G. W. Leibniz. *Novissima Sinica.* Cited by section. Original text in H. G. Nesselrath and H. Reinbothe, *Das Nueste über China* (Koln: Deutsche China-Gesellschaft, 1979). English trans. by Donald Lach, in Cook and Rosemont, *Writings on China.*

PD   G. W. Leibniz. "Preliminary Discourse on the Conformity of Faith and Reason." In *Theodicy*. Cited by section number. Original text in GP VI. Translation in Hubbard, *Theodicy*.

PNG   G. W. Leibniz. "Principles of Nature and Grace Founded on Reason." Cited by section number. Original text in GP VI; translation in AG.

Remarks   G. W. Leibniz. "Remarks on Chinese Religion." Cited by section. Original text in GP II, 380–84. English trans. in Cook and Rosemont, *Writings on China*.

RB   G. W. Leibniz. *New Essays on the Human Understanding*. Trans. by Peter Remnant and Jonathon Bennett. Cambridge: Cambridge University Press, 1981.

T   G. W. Leibniz. *Theodicy*. Cited by section number. Original text in GP VI. Translation in Hubbard, *Theodicy*. Cited by section number and page in Hubbard (H).

W   G. W. Leibniz. *Leibniz Korrespondiert mit China*. Ed. by Rita Widmaier. Frankfurt: V. Klostermann, 1990.

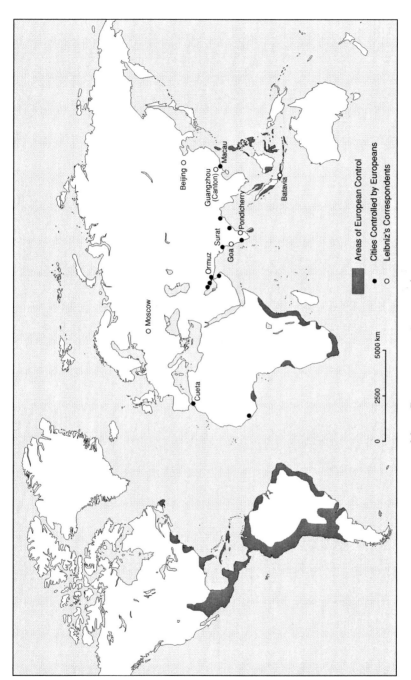

Map 1 European expansion around 1700.

CHAPTER I

Europe encounters the world

EUROPE AND OTHER CULTURES

If we insist on characterizing our age as multicultural, we should recognize it as a late phase of an age that began with increased pressure and contact with the Islamic world in the twelfth century. This pressure helped to drive the attempts to develop a sea route to Asia, which in turn led to the European "discovery" of the Americas. The history of Europe's encounter with other cultures, however, goes back much further. At no point was Europe or "the West" self-sufficient. Alexander and his troops reached India in 326 BCE. By the second century, Indian merchants traveled to Egypt and in 26 BCE a mission from Sri Lanka met with the Emperor Augustus in Rome. In the second or third century CE, Roman traders reached China, where 90 percent of Rome's silk originated.[1] Clement of Alexandria mentioned Buddhism in the third century CE, at the same time that Hippolytus discussed the Upanishads. Mani, the founder of Manicheanism, may have traveled to India and named Buddha as one of his divinities. It is difficult to judge the influence contact with Asia and Africa had on the philosophies of the Greco-Roman world, but, at the very least, this contact contributed to the development of cosmopolitan thought and the conception of a human being as a citizen of the world.

Coming into the Christian, medieval world, the distinction between Europe and non-Europe is less clear and relevant than that between Christian and non-Christian, as non-Christian cultures became the "other" to Western Christian identity. This complex relationship of indebtedness and distance had a determinative impact on Western thought, as it partly drove the attempt to distinguish philosophy from theology. Medieval thinkers from Augustine to Aquinas took philosophy as that enterprise developed in its highest form by the Greeks. For them, the attempt to validate

---

[1] Donald Lach, *Asia in the Making of Europe*, 2 vols. (Chicago: University of Chicago Press, 1965–70), vol. I, part i, pp. 11–15.

and circumscribe philosophy was at the same time the attempt to validate and circumscribe pagan thought. Later, whenever the thought of other cultures is encountered, the very same distinctions – between philosophy and theology or natural and revealed theology – are deployed, as will be seen in Europe's reaction to Confucianism. We should also note that, in general, non-Western cultures lack a clear separation between religion and philosophy. This lack is often presented as a flaw, but a more likely explanation is that the distinction between religion and philosophy is a peculiarity of a culture that defines itself by faith in certain texts that go beyond and perhaps even conflict with reason, but also valorizes the thought of a culture that lacked access to those texts. In other words, the separation of religion and philosophy – with all of its consequences for what it means to be a philosopher – results from the need to create a space for pagan thought.

The multi-cultural, cosmopolitan world of the Mediterranean fragmented and shrank with the decline of the Roman empire. Trade continued from Asia, but through intermediaries in Egypt and West Asia. The first significant break came with the Mongol empire, which at its height ran from Poland to China. Marco Polo is the most famous of those to cross the Mongol empire, arriving in China in 1275, and China under Kublai Khan was cosmopolitan enough for Polo to work in the service of the emperor. Franciscan monks established Christian communities in China and in India and a Beijing-born Nestorian Christian became probably the first Chinese to reach Europe.[2] Genoese and Venetian merchants were well-enough established in China and India by the early fourteenth century that a friar heading for China could say that in Venice he had already heard Hangzhou described by a number of people who had seen it first hand.[3] Direct contact with Asia declined with the rise of the Ottoman empire, but Chinese, Arabic, and Jewish merchants continued trading around the southern shores of Asia and the west coast of Africa. Europe remained part of this network, isolated by the monopoly held by Egypt as the connection to this world, and by the Venetians as the connection to Egypt. Intellectually, the deepest contact with non-Christian cultures came with the influx of Arabic and Greek texts into Europe. From Sicily and Spain came the influence of Islamic culture. "Arabic" numbers, coming through the Arabs from India, were introduced in 1202, and Euclid's *Elements* was translated near the end of the twelfth century. The full corpus of Aristotle had been translated by the end of the thirteenth century, as had commentaries from

---

[2] Lach, *Asia in the Making,* vol. I, part i, p. 39.   [3] Lach, *Asia in the Making,* vol. I, part i, pp. 43–44.

Avicenna (Ibn Sina) and Averroes (Ibn Rushd). These texts soon generated controversies about the relationship between theology and philosophy and the potential value of pagan thought. As time went on more and more Greek texts became available, particularly after the fall of Constantinople in 1453. The spread of these Neo-Platonic and so-called Hermetic texts raised new problems for the place of pagan thought.

Europe's contact with other cultures increased exponentially with the expansion of sea travel, led by the attempt to sidestep the monopolies on Asian trade held by the Venetians and Egyptians. Contact with Africa began with the seizing of Ceuta in Morocco in 1415, after which the Portuguese edged down the coast of Africa, in search of gold and slaves. By the 1480s, the Portuguese had direct trading relationships with the kingdoms of Mali, Benin, and Kongo.[4] In 1498 Vasco da Gama rounded the Cape of Good Hope, reached Calicut in India, and returned safely to Portugal, with a profit. In a short period of time, the Portuguese defeated Egyptian, Arab, and Indian forces, and established forts or trading posts in Sofala (Mozambique), Ormuz (Iran), Goa (India), and Malacca (Malaysia), so that, by the mid-1500s, Portugal had fifty fortified areas and approximately 10,000 people living abroad.[5] At this same time, Europeans expanded westward. Columbus reached the Caribbean in 1492; in 1521 the Aztec empire was decimated by Hernan Cortes. From strongholds in Mexico and Peru, the Spanish reached Asia from the west, founding Manila in 1571. Other nations, particularly the Dutch and English, soon joined the rush for colonies and globalized trade. France was far behind by the time Leibniz encouraged Louis XIV to invade Egypt in 1672.

Much could be said about this expansion, but we should note the extent to which Europeans were quickly in close contact with a great variety of cultures. By the time of Leibniz, hundreds of thousands of Europeans were living abroad, spread across all the continents but Antarctica. Some lived in enclosed communities, but many had close contact with local cultures, integrating themselves into established economies. The Portuguese traded slaves for gold within Africa, while other Europeans acted as intermediaries between Japan and China. Through European expansion, immense numbers of people were living between cultures: some by choice, some by force. Some cases were of extreme immersion, ranging from Indians and Africans who spent years in Europe training for service in the Church, to French

[4] David Birmingham, *Trade and Empire in the Atlantic, 1400–1600* (London: Routledge, 2000), pp. 27–47.
[5] George Raudzens, *Empires: Europe and Globalization 1492–1788* (Phoenix Mill [UK]: Sutton, 1999), p. 34.

traders living among the Hurons, to Jesuits spending their adult lives deep in China, to African slaves forced to labor in the Americas. Perhaps a symbol of this mixing of cultures is the Jesuit college in Goa, India. In 1546, the students came from eleven countries, including China, Japan, Malaysia, and Ethiopia, all being trained for service in the Catholic Church.[6]

In spite of this deep contact, goods from the rest of the world entered Europe more quickly than knowledge of the world's cultures. Even so, the contact with other cultures impacted late medieval and Renaissance thought, primarily through newly discovered Greek texts, which raised the problem of pagan wisdom and forced a clarification of the relationship between philosophy and theology. In the process of encountering the non-European world, paradigms developed for accommodating the thought of other cultures. Coming into the modern age, as knowledge of China deepened, China was encountered through "lenses" ground in these earlier encounters. The first and most important of these lenses is "natural theology," which refers to knowledge that can be had "naturally," without the aid of revelation. Natural theology originated in the classical world, as Christians used Neo-Platonic pagan writers, but it was refined as Islamic and Greek texts entered Europe from Spain. Thomas Aquinas (1225–74) provides an excellent example. As Aquinas realized, the difficulty in creating a space for non-Christian thought is its boundaries. One potential point of separation is methodology, but Aquinas rejects this division because he takes both theology and philosophy as sciences. In the *In Boethium De Trinitate*, which deals with the relationships among disciplines, Aquinas defines a science: "The nature of science consists in this, that from things already known conclusions about other matters follow of necessity."[7] Following Aristotle's *episteme*, the essence of science lies in the necessary progression from basic principles, a progression used both in theology and in philosophy. A second possible point of division is by content. In part, Aquinas accepts this point of division. The *Summa Contra Gentiles*, which directly considers philosophy as a common ground between cultures or as the means to prove truths to non-believers, begins with a division:

There is a twofold mode of truth in what we profess about God. Some truths about God exceed all the ability of the human reason. Such is the truth that God is triune. But there are some truths which the natural reason also is able to reach. Such are that God exists, that He is one, and the like. In fact, such truths about

---

[6] Lach, *Asia in the Making*, vol. I, part i, pp. 262–63.
[7] Thomas Aquinas, *Faith, Reason, and Theology*. Trans. by Armand Maurer (Toronto: Pontifical Institute of Mediaeval Studies, 1987), p. 41.

God have been proved demonstratively by the philosophers, guided by the light of natural reason.[8]

The fundamental division between theology and philosophy cannot rest on content, however, because they often treat the same topics. This overlap is clearer if we consider the division between theology and philosophy rather as between revealed and natural theology. Aquinas explains: "Hence there is no reason why those things which are treated by the philosophical sciences, so far as they can be known by the light of natural reason, may not also be treated by another science so far as they are known by the light of divine revelation."[9]

This remark suggests where the division lies for Aquinas. What defines a science is that its conclusions follow necessarily from principles, but the principles themselves can come from reflection on experience or from other sources. Aquinas argues in the *Summa Theologica* that theological science is distinct from philosophical science because its principles are not given by natural reason or experience, but by divine revelation through faith.[10] The analysis of sacred doctrine in *In Boethium de Trinitate* is the same. Philosophical science proceeds by necessity from principles of sensible things. Sacred doctrine also proceeds by necessity, but derives its principles from the divine realities themselves, through faith.[11] This separation of philosophy and sacred doctrine has powerful consequences for the encounter with other cultures, as it allows some principles of ethics, science, and theology to be discovered by any people. This application to other cultures is no coincidence; the separation itself came from a sense that the Greeks had developed philosophy further than any Christian thinker up to that point. Although Aquinas examines only the thought that grew around the Mediterranean, nothing precludes more distant cultures from developing philosophy, and natural theology became the guiding approach for the Jesuits entering China. Natural theology was not a direct threat to revealed theology, because both come from God, so that reason cannot contradict faith.[12] Philosophy assists theology by proving what it can about God and by showing the flaws in any argument against faith. The *Summa Contra Gentiles* explicitly proceeds along these two lines. *In Boethium de Trinitate* deals with the specific uses of philosophy in sacred doctrine, which are given

---

[8] Thomas Aquinas, *Summa Contra Gentiles*, 4 vols. Trans. by Anton Pegis (Notre Dame: University of Notre Dame Press, 1975), p. 63.
[9] Thomas Aquinas, *Introduction to St. Thomas Aquinas*. Trans. by Anton Pegis (New York: Modern Library, 1948), p. 5.
[10] Aquinas, *Introduction*, pp. 4–5.   [11] Aquinas, *Faith*, pp. 41–42.
[12] Aquinas, *Summa Contra Gentiles*, pp. 74–75.

as three: it can establish certain preambles presupposed by faith, such as God's existence and unity; it can clarify the contents of faith by analogy to creatures; it can argue against unbelievers.[13] The assistance of philosophy, though, comes at a cost, as the Church could maintain exclusive authority over freethinkers and other cultures only by establishing the inadequacy of natural theology, which Aquinas thus works to circumscribe and contain. In the *Summa Contra Gentiles*, he argues why some matters must be in principle beyond reason and thus are only answerable by faith. The importance of the Church and the status of other cultures depended on showing that this excess beyond natural theology was essential to religion and salvation. We can see this threat in Spinoza, who follows the form set up by Aquinas but sees what exceeds natural theology as irrelevant to true religion, thus freeing religion from the Church and from the particularities of culture. Even in those matters accessible to reason, however, Aquinas argues that we require faith, for three reasons. First, some people are unable to develop their reason sufficiently, due to lack of ability, free time, or dedication. Second, even those who can develop philosophy only do so late in life, but matters of religion must be known much earlier. Third, human reason is liable to error, so that even learned people will sometimes accept false arguments.[14] Only the third of these reasons applies absolutely to philosophy or natural theology.

For its role in freeing philosophy from theology, the doctrine of natural theology was of tremendous importance in the formation of modern thought, and it results from encounters with the non-Christian others of medieval thought. The latter point is often ignored, but not by Leibniz. In the *Theodicy*, he explicitly attributes the conflict between faith and reason to medieval thinkers accommodating Plato and Aristotle (PD 6–7). Even so, the separation of natural theology from its intercultural origins is well established in the writings of Descartes. As an approach to other cultures, natural theology was largely lost by the collapse of arguments from universal consent, which came with greater knowledge of cultural diversity. It lingers only in popular culture, as in Alduous Huxley's *Perrenial Philosophy*, or the common claim that all religions basically say "the same thing." Yet if we take natural theology more broadly as the position that reason or experience allow us all to reach certain truths about the ultimate nature of things, then we can see that natural theology remains a significant approach.

---

[13] Aquinas, *Faith*, p. 49.
[14] Aquinas, *Summa Contra Gentiles*, pp. 66–68 (book I, ch. 4); cf. Aquinas, *Faith*, pp. 66–67.

The second lens for encountering other cultures is typified in the Renaissance tradition that has become known as *prisca theologia*, or "ancient theology." As with natural theology, this approach is grounded in the early church fathers' attempts to place Christianity in relation to pagan thought. Those early fathers wished to show that the wisdom in Plato and Neo-Platonism derived ultimately from the Judeo-Christian tradition.[15] Augustine himself suggests this approach in several places, as in *The City of God*, where he writes:

Therefore, on that voyage of his [to Egypt], Plato could neither have seen Jeremiah, who was dead so long before, nor have read those same scriptures which had not yet been translated into the Greek language, of which he was a master, unless, indeed, we say that, as he was most earnest in the pursuit of knowledge, he also studied those writings through an interpreter, as he did those of the Egyptians. . . .[16]

He supports this view with similarities between Moses and Plato. As with natural theology, "ancient theology" developed rapidly with the influx of new pagan texts, coming primarily from the fall of Byzantium to the Turks. Marsilio Ficino's Latin translation of the *Corpus Hermeticum* was published in 1471. The writings of Plato, other Neo-Platonists, and many church fathers were translated around the same time. In its various forms, this tradition took in writings thought to be from Zoroaster, Hermes Trismegistus, Orpheus, Pythagoras, Plato, Dionysius the Areopagite, and various Neo-Platonists.[17] All these sources were taken as versions of Christianity, derived from Biblical truth and able to provide new perspectives on that truth. As a hermeneutic approach, these texts were read with the goal of finding hidden or "figured" Christian truths.

The plausibility of "ancient theology" depends on several mistaken assumptions. The most crucial is the origin of the texts, which were assumed to have been written over several millennia across several cultures. In fact, all of the texts are Greek in origin, with Plato's as the oldest, and the others written in the first three centuries of the common era, originating in a time with strong syncretic tendencies, and a world-view that combined Neo-Platonism, Stoicism, and various mysticisms.[18] Interpreters also

---

[15] The church fathers most often cited were Lactantius, Clement of Alexander, and Eusebius. See D. P. Walker, *The Ancient Theology: Studies in Christian Platonism from the Fifteenth to the Eighteenth Century* (Ithaca: Cornell University Press, 1972), pp. 1–4.

[16] Augustine, *The City of God*. Trans. by Marcus Dods (New York: Modern Library, 1993), VIII, xi, p. 256.

[17] Walker, *Ancient Theology*, p. 20.

[18] Francis Yates, *Giordano Bruno and the Hermetic Tradition* (Chicago: University of Chicago Press, 1964), pp. 4–6.

failed to realize the extent to which medieval Christianity had been shaped by Greek thought. The similarities between Plato and Christianity exceed what could be dismissed as coincidence, but they are explained because Christianity developed in a Platonic world, not because Plato predicted Christianity from indirect access to Moses. We would expect notable similarities between the hermetic texts, orphic poems, Neo-Platonic texts, and early Christians, because all of these express the same cultural milieu. These similarities become perplexing, though, if the texts are thought to represent diverse times and cultures. A third assumption that made this view plausible was an underlying view of history. From the perspective of the Old Testament – taken as the only perspective on ancient history – the world is relatively young and all cultures and peoples come from one origin: first Adam, then Noah. Cultural and linguistic diversity emerges even later, at the Tower of Babel. On this Biblical view of history, all wisdom comes originally from Biblical figures. History follows a path of decline and fragmentation, so that the goal in reading later texts is to recover and piece together these original truths and sometimes even this original "Adamic" language. The older the text, the closer it is to its Biblical origins, the more likely it is to contain truth.

The hermetic tradition and ancient theology declined in early modern times, particularly as the *Corpus Hermeticum* was correctly dated by Isaac Casaubon in 1614, but this tradition had a powerful influence on how Europeans first encountered some other cultures, namely, those with a supposed ancient history. The same forces that led to the value of the *Corpus Hermeticum* also led to the importance of ancient Egyptian culture, particularly the hieroglyphs, and then China. Those Europeans first interested in Chinese culture were proto-Egyptologists, like the Jesuit Athanasius Kircher, considered an authority on both Egypt and China.[19] Paul Beurrier and Gottlieb Spitzel were two other early authors who made this connection.[20] The most relevant example to Leibniz is the Jesuit Joachim Bouvet, who spent his adult life as a missionary in China and was Leibniz's main correspondent there. Bouvet first traveled to China in 1685 and was already a prominent mathematician and member of the Paris Academy of Science. In China, he mastered Chinese and Manchu and dedicated himself to

---

[19] Athanasius Kircher published *Oedipus Aegyptiacus* in 1652 and *China Monumentis . . . Illustrata* in 1667.

[20] Paul Beurrier published his *Speculum christianne religionis in triplici lege naturalii, mosaica et evangelica* in 1663, linking Zoroaster, Hermes, Orpheus, Pythagoras, Plato, and the ancient Chinese. (Claudia von Collani, *Joachim Bouvet S.J. Sein Leben und Sein Werk*, [Nettetal: Steyler Verlag, 1985], pp. 120–21.) Spizel wrote *De Re Litteraria Sinensium Commentarius* in 1661. Leibniz had a brief correspondence with both Kircher and Spizel.

the ancient Chinese classics; the Emperor Kangxi commented that he was perhaps the only Westerner to be really conversant with Chinese literature.[21] Bouvet's approach to the classics was rooted in ancient theology and hermetism, and was later known as "Figurism."[22] Following Kircher and Beurrier, Bouvet connected Egyptian hieroglyphs and Chinese characters, believing they represented the language used before the Deluge (W 73). In an essay on the classical Chinese work the *Yi Jing* (Book of Changes), sent to Leibniz and the Jesuit Charles Le Gobien in 1700, he claims that the system of this ancient book contains "many precious remains of the debris of the most ancient and most excellent philosophy taught by the first Patriarchs of the world to their descendants, since corrupted and almost entirely obscured by the course of time" (W 123). The similarity between this system and ideas presented obscurely in Pythagoras and Plato shows that they all represent the same system, a system also represented in Cabbala (W 125). A few years later, Bouvet no longer presented his work on the *Yi Jing* as a study of Chinese culture but as a study of the culture of the Patriarchs (W 125). Bouvet's claims now seem bizarre, but they make more sense within the Biblical conception of history. According to Bouvet, Fuxi, the legendary creator of the *Yi Jing*, lived 4,600 years earlier, putting him chronologically near Noah. At that time, he argues, knowledge of the creation must have been fresh and Fuxi's ideas would have been rejected had they been false (W 126). The power of Bouvet's approach depends partly on legitimate traces of monotheism in early Chinese texts, but more on the ambiguity of those texts and his ability to identify parallel patterns. A particularly ingenious example of his method is a discussion of the identity of Fuxi. Given that Fuxi's system is so similar to "our ancient authors," he is probably the same person as either Zoroaster, Hermes, or Enoch. Even the name "Fuxi" supports this connection, he says, because the character *fu* is made up of two other characters, one meaning "dog" (*quan*) and the other meaning "man" (*ren*). This name obviously refers to Hermes, traditionally pictured with the head of a dog and the body of a human being (W 125–26).

Because both natural theology and "ancient theology" allow the possibility of religious truths in pagan writings, the approaches can be difficult to distinguish.[23] Almost all in the Jesuit mission agreed that the Chinese

---

[21] Jonathon Spence, *Emperor of China: Self-portrait of K'ang-Hsi* (New York: Alfred A. Knopf, 1975), p. 75.

[22] The best work on the Figurists in China is by Claudia von Collani, particularly *Die Figuristen in der Chinamission* (Frankfurt: Verlag Peter D. Lang, 1981); and *Joachim Bouvet S.J.* For a broader view of Figurism in the Hermetic Tradition, see Walker, *Ancient Theology*.

[23] For example, Walker makes no fundamental distinction between them, and thus sees the entire Jesuit mission as based on "ancient theology." Walker, *Ancient Theology*, pp. 196–202.

had some knowledge of God, but some, such as the mission's founder Matteo Ricci, believed they had achieved this knowledge with the natural light of reason, while others, such as Bouvet, believed they had this knowledge from ancient revelation. The positions have radically different consequences. The hermetic tradition leaves one dependent on texts, making hermeneutics the main skill for finding truth. Natural theology leads in the opposite direction, allowing for freedom from history and texts through the autonomy of reason. Bouvet and Descartes could hardly be more different. As an approach to other cultures, the two views share a tolerance and respect for pagan thought, but they differ as the kinds of truths that can be discovered differ on the two accounts. Natural theology places strict limits on reason, so that things like the trinity cannot be discovered; while in the hermetic tradition, any religious details can be found in any text, as Bouvet sees the use of six lines in the symbols of the *Yi Jing* as a reference to the six days of creation (W 155). More importantly, the dependence on texts in the hermetic traditions yields an imperative to uncover and study diverse texts. Texts are all we have, so if we find some ancient texts in China, nothing could be more important than studying them. Natural theology allows for truth in these texts, but sees no necessity in studying them. In practice, early advocates of natural theology like Aquinas saw the need to study pagan thought, which exceeded what a lone independent thinker might achieve, but this dependence was rejected by early modern thinkers like Descartes. Leibniz's hermeneutics, with its focus on finding reason in various cultural expressions, is in some ways a descendant of the "hermetic" approach. This connection is not merely a coincidence. Christia Mercer shows that, while Leibniz's earliest influences rejected the hermetic tradition, they followed a related Renaissance tradition of "conciliatory eclecticism." This conciliatory eclecticism was one of the primary forces shaping Leibniz's philosophy.[24]

The third lens, unlike the first two, focuses primarily on cultural difference. Michel de Montaigne provides the best example. Montaigne shows the kind of interest in other cultures that we would expect a curious intellectual at that time to have. He made remarkably close contact with the discoveries in the Americas, noting that he long had "a man in his house" who spent ten or so years in the French colonies in Brazil, and that Montaigne himself once spoke with some native Americans through an interpreter.[25] Montaigne uses his knowledge of other cultures in several

---

[24] Christia Mercer, *Leibniz's Metaphysics: Its Origins and Development* (New York: Cambridge University Press, 2001), pp. 23–59.
[25] He mentions both facts in his essay "On Cannibals."

ways, but I want to emphasize the main use, in support of skepticism. Montaigne realized the new discoveries would radically alter the medieval world-view, and concludes that all knowledge must remain vulnerable to the possibility of future discoveries. In the midst of an argument on the limitations of knowledge, he writes:

Even if all that has come down to us by report from the past should be true and known by someone, it would be less than nothing compared to what is un-known. . . . We exclaim at the miracle of the invention of our artillery, of our printing; other men in another corner of the world, in China, enjoyed these a thousand years earlier. If we saw as much of the world as we do not see, we would perceive, it is likely, a perpetual multiplication and vicissitude of forms.[26]

One motive for this appeal to other cultures is to criticize Euro-centrism. We think that the Peruvians are such barbarians, he says, but our actions are just as barbarous, if not more. He makes this point forcefully in the essay "On Coaches," in which he describes – among other European atrocities – the noble endurance of the King of Mexico while roasted alive by the Spanish.[27]

Some of his arguments suggest a normativity in which the uncorrupted Americans are better than their European corruptors, but he explicitly puts forth a more radical view. In the essay "On Cannibals," he claims:

I think there is nothing barbarous and savage in that nation, from what I have been told, except that each man calls barbarism whatever is not his own practice; for indeed it seems we have no other test of truth and reason than the example and pattern of the opinions and customs of the country we live in. *There* is always the perfect religion, the perfect government, the perfect and accomplished manner in all things.[28]

He uses information from the Caribbean in a similar way in the "Apology for Raimond Sebond."[29] In such passages, Montaigne gives a conventional argument for skepticism based on the diversity of opinions, rightly seeing that such arguments can be strengthened by contact with distant cultures. He uses pagan Greek sources in the same way, sometimes mixing con-temporary and classical sources. We see this mix in a passage describing self-control. Montaigne begins with a classical account of man who cas-trated himself out of frustration with his impotence, and then goes on to

---

[26] "Of Coaches," Michel de Montaigne, *Complete Works of Montaigne*. Trans. by Donald Frame (Palo Alto: Stanford University Press, 1958), pp. 692–93.
[27] "Of Coaches," Montaigne, *Complete Works*, pp. 696–97.
[28] "On Cannibals," Montaigne, *Complete Works*, p. 152.
[29] "Apology for Raimond Sebond," Montaigne, *Complete Works*, p. 433.

describe the practice of *sati*, the ritual self-immolation of a woman after the death of her husband, using a contemporary source on India. He then gives another anecdote about India, describing the voluntary self-immolation of gymnosophists, this time based on Plutarch.[30] In both the structure of the argument and the use of cultural diversity, Montaigne provides an example of how encounters with the "new" world conformed to classical models. This approach to cultures is as significant for modern thought as the approach of natural theology. Montaigne's arguments about the diversity of opinions easily shifted into an argument against the existence of innate ideas, so that whether or not there are universal innate ideas became linked to whether or not cultures were utterly diverse. Locke and Leibniz split on both issues. Even more striking is how contemporary Montaigne's arguments still appear. The downfall of dogmatism and "objective truth" and the rise of cultural relativism are partly attributed to the work of anthropologists introducing the diversity of cultures. Probably the most frequent "lens" through which we now approach cultural diversity is cultural relativism, and the drive behind this approach is the same for us as it was for Montaigne – to question our own cultural presuppositions and to make us less willing to impose them on others.

All of the "lenses" we have examined integrate other cultures into preexisting arguments and models originating in the classical Mediterranean world. All might be called ways of accommodating other cultures, in that they grant at least some points of equality to the thought of other cultures. In natural theology, all have equal access to religion through reason, though Europeans have the additional advantage of revelation. In ancient theology, all have the remnants of religious truths, though the Bible perhaps has it most clearly. In skepticism, all cultures are equally uncertain and barbaric. In a stronger sense, all three can be called ways of accommodation because each sees some gain from the encounter with other cultures. They contrast the many unaccommodating ways in which cultures were encountered, ranging from indifference to condemnation to superficial use of the fortune cookie variety. As ways of accommodation, all advocate some level of tolerance and respect for other cultures, but only the hermetic tradition sees the study of other cultures as necessary. In natural theology, other cultures could help but any truths found in other cultures are equally accessible through our own use of reason. On the skeptical view, other cultures help to make the point that all views are dubitable, but we have little more to gain from them other than entertainment. Thus while all three models tolerate and

---

[30] "Of Virtue," Montaigne, *Complete Works*, p. 532.

explain cultural diversity, only the hermetic tradition values it. Ironically, this is the view that became least significant in the early modern period. This shift is reflected in practice by the contrast between the great interest in other cultures in the Renaissance and the astonishing lack of interest in early modern thought.

THE CHINESE BACKGROUND

Leibniz never went to China and he never met anyone born in China, although he spoke and corresponded with several Europeans who had lived or were living in China, almost all were Jesuit missionaries. He read a few Chinese books, selected, edited, and translated by a small group of Jesuits. China for Leibniz appeared as a formation within European culture, partly through an interpretation "manufactured" by the Jesuits, to use Lionel Jensen's term, and partly through the broader context of European encounters with non-Christian cultures, particularly the approaches of Kircher and Spizel.[31] Leibniz's work itself became a key part of the European idea of China and Confucianism. Understanding Leibniz's engagement with China thus depends more on understanding the idea of China in the late seventeenth century than on understanding a contemporary academic perspective on China. Nonetheless, to understand that seventeenth-century context, it is helpful to begin with some orientation on Chinese history and thought. This brief orientation will focus selectively on those aspects of China most relevant to Leibniz's engagement. Matteo Ricci first entered China in 1583 in the late stages of the Ming Dynasty. Ricci found a densely populated nation of nearly 150 million people, ranging from Beijing in the north, to the borders of Vietnam and Burma in the south, to the edge of Tibet in the west. In extent and population, it was more comparable to Europe as a whole than to any European nation. In theory, this large area and population was managed by a centralized government under the authority of an emperor and administered by an extensive bureaucratic hierarchy, filled largely by those who had come up through the examination system. The examination system was a kind of a civil service exam, based on the Confucian classics and a set of commentaries on them. The exam would have been open to anyone, but would have mostly drawn people from more powerful families, both because of their greater access to education and because of occasional corruption. The massive population

---

[31] Lionel Jensen, *Manufacturing Confucianism: Chinese Tradition and Universal Civilization* (Durham, NC: Duke University Press, 1997).

lived through an economy based primarily on labor-intensive agriculture, but Chinese society was in a process of increased commercialization and urbanization, with numerous large cities and manufacturing centers. With these changes came classes of educated, urban supporters of high culture and a growing number of poorer urban workers. The setting was right for a blossoming of Chinese literature and art. Mathematics and science had made relatively slow progress since the Song Dynasty (960–1279), but in their ability to solve problems and predict outcomes they were roughly on par with Europe. The Chinese still probably had a slight technological edge. Along with Confucian and Daoist temples and the religions of the indigenous hill and mountain peoples of the south and southwest, there were sinicized Buddhist temples, Tibetan Buddhist temples, a few synagogues, many mosques, and some remnants of Nestorian Christians. Even in the relatively xenophobic climate of the late Ming, China had considerable cultural and religious diversity. This tolerance for religious views went along with an absolute confidence in the superiority of Chinese social institutions and their Confucian ideology. The Chinese saw themselves as part of an unbroken tradition going back more than 4,000 years.

The Chinese social system itself was remarkably stable, supported by its historical momentum, the power and complexity of the bureaucracy, and the sheer size of the population, but the Ming Dynasty was weak. In the end, threats came through rebellions from within and invasions from without. In 1644, Beijing fell first to a rebel army led by Li Zicheng and then to a Manchu army led by Dorgon. Over the course of Chinese history, the peoples of Central Asia frequently threatened imperial power. We have already mentioned one example, the Yuan Dynasty (1279–1368), initiated by the Mongols under Chinggis Khan. During the Ming Dynasty, the Manchu people lived to the north and east of Beijing, and were united and organized under Nurhaci. Unlike the Mongols, the Manchus came from a mixed base of hunting and settled agriculture. As close neighbors of China, they had experience and knowledge of how the empire worked, and their gradual expansion allowed them to develop ways of integrating into patterns of Chinese society. With the invasion of Beijing, the Qing Dynasty was established, with Shunzhi as its emperor. His successor, Kangxi, finalized Qing control of China, which lasted until the fall of the imperial system over 250 years later. The Manchus deliberately took up traditional forms of Chinese legitimacy and maintained traditional rituals. The bureaucratic system was streamlined to allow efficient central control and to facilitate Manchu supervision, but it was not radically altered. Confucianism remained the dominant state ideology and the basis for the examination system. A few Jesuit missionaries were killed in the change of dynasty but overall they managed it well and ended up closer to the center of power even in the first year of the Qing Dynasty. It is in the reign of Kangxi, the second Qing emperor, that Leibniz first came into contact with China. In his *Novissima Sinica*, Leibniz translated and published a flattering description of Kangxi written by Bouvet.

The Jesuit missionaries associated primarily with the class of Confucian scholar officials, the *ru*, or "literati," and these served as their main source on Chinese thought. They were thus introduced to an orthodox form of what has come to be called "Neo-Confucianism," while remaining ignorant and dismissive of Buddhism and Daoism. They presented Christianity as a supplement to Confucianism, a spiritual side to complement Confucian ethics.[32] To understand Confucianism as encountered by Leibniz and the Jesuits, though, we must step back to a much earlier time, the same time that Plato taught in Greece and Buddha taught in India. The Zhou Dynasty was founded in the twelfth century BCE and, following what became a typical pattern, the power of the emperors declined over time. China fragmented more and more under weak central control until small states and leaders openly struggled against each other. This period of struggle – aptly known as the "Warring States period" – lasted until the Qin state conquered the last of its rivals in 221 BCE, founding the Qin Dynasty. The social and political turmoil of the declining centuries of the Zhou Dynasty provided the context for the birth of Chinese philosophy, as dislocated teachers traveled from state to state or withdrew to the countryside, each offering their own remedies for society's ills. It was an extremely rich and diverse time, its variety not captured by the two alternatives with which most people are familiar – Daoism and Confucianism.[33] It is difficult to apply any claim to all the thinkers of this period, but three points held generally true. One is a focus on how to live a good and fulfilling life, rather than on metaphysical and epistemological questions. Second, most thinkers saw their time as one of decline, looking to the past for models of a more stable life. Third,

---

[32] Thus Ricci writes, "One might say in truth that the teachings of this academy, save in some few instances, are so far from being contrary to Christian principles, that such an institution could derive great benefit from Christianity and might be developed and perfected by it." (Matteo Ricci and Nicholas Trigault, *China in the Sixteenth Century: The Journals of Matteo Ricci, 1583–1610*. Trans. by Louis Gallagher [Random House: New York, 1953], p. 98.)

[33] The best source for the philosophers of this period is Philip J. Ivanhoe and Bryan W. Van Norden (eds.), *Readings in Classical Chinese Philosophy* (New York: Seven Bridges Press, 2001), which contains selections from seven philosophers, along with a useful glossary and directions for further readings. For general histories of the thought of the period, see A. C. Graham, *Disputers of the Tao: Philosophical Argument in Ancient China* (La Salle: Open Court Press, 1989); and Benjamin Schwartz, *The World of Thought in Ancient China* (Cambridge, MA: Belknap Press of Harvard University Press, 1985).

most were surprisingly unconcerned with anything transcending the natural world. The assumed world-view held nature itself as the ultimate, and believed that nature had an inherent order or pattern, which is probably most familiar to us as the *dao*, the "path" or "way." The main disagreement was over what these natural patterns entailed, as Daoists tended to think education and social structure were imposed on *dao* while Confucians thought they were rooted in *dao*.

The Confucians were the most consistent supporters of the appeal toward a past golden age. Even in the fifth century BCE, the Chinese saw themselves as part of a culture developing continuously for two millennia. These past times came down through legends and stories, but also through written documents. For example, the *Shi Jing* (Book of Odes) is a collection of poems, some of which celebrate great leaders, while others are rooted in common life, containing love poems, descriptions of social turmoil, and even criticisms of war. Another of the ancient books, the *Shu Jing* (Book of Documents), is a collection of documents from transitional moments in Chinese history, drawing ethical and political lessons. All of the ancient books were written over a long stretch of time, all were organized and modified by Confucians, and all were thought to be older than they really were. As this period of ancient Chinese history was of undue significance to the Jesuits and to Leibniz, a few points must be made regarding it.

The classic books notably lack super-human figures. The heroes are extraordinary but human, which is why they served as role models theoretically attainable by anyone. For the Confucians, the great heroes were the founders of the three previous dynasties: Yao and Shun, who founded the Xia Dynasty; Tang, who founded the Shang Dynasty; and King Wen, King Wu, and the Duke of Zhou, who founded the Zhou Dynasty. Ironically, the Confucian heroes were revolutionaries. The stock villains were the inept and immoral last emperors: Jie, overthrown by Tang; and Zhou, overthrown by Wen and Wu. For Leibniz and the Jesuits, Yao and Shun were most significant, along with an even more ancient legendary figure, Fuxi. Fuxi was thought to have invented the Chinese language and laid the foundations for the *Yi Jing* (Book of Changes). These figures were so significant to the Europeans because they seemed to have lived inexplicably close to the Deluge.

A second point of interest to Leibniz and the missionaries were the suggestions of the theism in the classical texts. Two terms were of particular significance. One is *Shang Di*. The first character means "high" or "above," while the second means "lord" or "ruler." *Shang Di* then means something like "Lord on High" as it is translated by Wing-Tsit Chan, but most early translators like James Legge and Fung Yu-lan rendered it simply as "God." Chan writes that *Shang Di* probably began as a tribal Lord or deified ancestor but later developed into a "God for all."[34] Fung explains that *Shang Di* was the highest spiritual authority, presiding over a complex hierarchy of other spirits.[35] Even in the earliest texts, *Shang Di* exists as a god within the world, not as its creator. In this sense, *Shang Di* probably resembles Zeus more than "God." The second important term is *tian*, usually translated as "Heaven."[36] With the rise of the Zhou Dynasty, the concept of *Shang Di* gradually yielded to the more naturalistic *tian*.[37] The character itself shows a line above a person, representing the sky. *Tian* can refer to the sky but sometimes seems like a conscious force guiding the universe and other times could be translated as "fate," or just "the way things are." In his dictionary, Matthews still gives one meaning of *tian* as "Providence. The Supreme Ruler. God. Celestial. Divine."[38] Fung gives five senses of *tian*: 1, the physical sky above; 2, a supreme ruler, which seems to be an anthropomorphic deity like *Shang Di*; 3, fate; 4, nature; 5, the ethical principle operative in the universe. He adds that the earliest classics tend to use *tian* in one of the first two senses.[39] As with *Shang Di*, even when *tian* appears as an anthropomorphic deity, it differs from the Christian God as being within the universe. *Tian*, however, is less often a particular being but rather an aspect of the universe, an immanent order, pattern, or force. In the early texts, *tian* rewards the good and punishes the bad. Most famously, an immoral ruler was said to have lost the "Mandate of Heaven" [*tianming*], which both justified and explained the establishment of a new dynasty, which would then take up the "Mandate of Heaven," holding it as long as the emperors remained worthy. Even in such descriptions, though, it is difficult to discern if *tian* is a conscious being judging human actions or an immanent natural law, such that ethical rulers naturally tend to have flourishing states and thus to be rewarded.

[34] Wing-Tsit Chan, *A Sourcebook in Chinese Philosophy* (Princeton: Princeton University Press, 1963), p. 4.

[35] Fung Yu-lan, *A History of Chinese Philosophy*. Trans. by Derk Bodde (Princeton: Princeton University Press, 1952), vol. I, p. 31.

[36] The best discussion of *tian* is Robert Eno, *The Confucian Creation of Heaven: Philosophy and the Defense of Ritual Mastery* (Albany: SUNY Press, 1990). Ames and Rosemont have an excellent brief discussion of the complexities of the term *tian*. (Roger Ames and Henry Rosemont, *The Analects of Confucius, A Philosophical Translation* [New York: Ballantine Books, 1998], pp. 46–48.)

[37] Chan, *Sourcebook*, p. 5.

[38] Matthews, R. H., *Matthews' Chinese–English Dictionary*. Cambridge, MA: Harvard University Press, 1966.

[39] Fung, *History*, p. 31.

The third important point from this early period is the *Yi Jing* (Book of Changes), also known as the *Zhou Yi*.[40] The *Yi Jing* was written over a long period of time, mostly after Confucius, but the later Confucians, the Jesuits, and Leibniz all thought it came from this early period. In its broadest outline, it describes a dynamic universe changing according to graspable patterns. By understanding these patterns, one can act effectively. This cosmological system is described through a symbolic system of sixty-four hexagrams, each representing different moments in the developing patterns. Each hexagram divides into two trigrams, composed of three horizontal lines. The lines signify either a *yin* or *yang* force, represented by a broken or solid line, respectively. In the broadest sense, *yin* represents the tendency to yield or be receptive, while *yang* represents the tendency to act. The characters themselves represent the shaded and the sunny sides of a mountain. Comprised of six *yin* or *yang* lines, each hexagram represents a certain balance of cosmic forces with a particular tendency to change. By identifying a situation with a hexagram, one can act appropriately. The *Yi Jing* itself lists the sixty-four hexagrams along with layers of commentary, giving advice for how to deal with each particular situation, often conveying some ethical lesson. Traditionally, the eight trigrams were invented by Fuxi, combined into hexagrams by King Wen, and commented on first by the Duke of Zhou and second by Confucius.[41] The *Yi Jing* can be best considered from three perspectives. It can be taken as an early form of science, meant to describe natural laws and how human beings fit into them. It can be taken as a collection of wise sayings and advice on how to live with different situations. Finally, it can be taken as a system of divination, which is its origin and it has reappeared in popular culture. On this view, one uses a seemingly random method to determine a hexagram representing the current situation and then acts according to the advice of the commentary.

The founding document of Confucianism is the *Lun Yu* (Analects), attributed traditionally to Kongzi (Confucius) but compiled by his followers.[42] Kongzi lived approximately from 551 to 479 BCE. The *Lun Yu* is generally short on metaphysics and epistemology, focusing instead

---

[40] A good, brief explanation of the *Yi Jing* can be found in Helmut Wilhelm, *Change: Eight Lectures on the I-ching* (New York: Pantheon, 1960). The standard translation is *The I-ching or Book of Changes*. Trans. by Richard Wilhelm and Cary Baynes (Princeton: Princeton University Press, 1961).

[41] Chan, *Sourcebook*, p. 262; Phillipe Couplet gives the same genealogy in the *Confucius Sinarum Philosophus sive Scientia Sinensis* (1687), p. xviii.

[42] An excellent source on the *Lun Yu* is Ames and Rosemont, *Analects of Confucius*. The authoritative source on the authorship of the text is E. Bruce Brooks and A. Taeko Brooks, *The Original Analects: Sayings of Confucius and his Successors* (New York: Columbia University Press, 1998).

on political and ethical questions. A passage from the *Lun Yu* captures this spirit:

Zilu asked about serving ghost and spirits. The Master said, "Not yet able to serve people – how could you serve ghosts?"
"Dare I inquire about death?"
"Not understanding life – how could you understand death?" (11.11)[43]

The "master" is Kongzi. Kongzi was followed by a number of competing interpreters, the most famous of whom are Mengzi (Mencius) and Xunzi. These commentators expanded on the earlier ethics and placed it in a broader context of nature and human psychology. Confucians of the Song Dynasty set the official canon of early Confucianism as the *Si Shu* (Four Books), which included the *Lun Yu* and *Mengzi*, along with two shorter essays, the *Da Xue* (Great Learning) and the *Zhong Yong* (Doctrine of the Mean). This was the canon familiar to the Jesuits and partially transmitted to Europe through a Latin translation published in 1687.[44] The legacy of Jesuit interest in these early Confucians is shown by the fact that, until very recently, we have continued to refer to Kongzi and Mengzi by their latinized names, Confucius and Mencius.[45] The Jesuits read this early Confucian canon within the context of the ancient history projected behind it, seeing Confucius as a monotheist who believed in *Shang Di* and *tian* as two names for God. In fact, *Shang Di* is no longer significant for the Confucians of this time and only appears in their texts in quotations from the older classics. *Tian* is used more frequently but is difficult to analyze, as it appears primarily as a figurative way of speaking about the patterns or forces by which the universe changes.

Within this monotheistic context, the Jesuits and Europeans most admired Confucian ethics, which is characterized by the primacy of social relations. Mengzi names four key virtues. One is *ren* (benevolence), which includes a feeling of caring as well as benevolent actions, and originates in our natural tendency to feel compassion for someone suffering or in danger. The second virtue is *yi* (appropriateness), which refers to doing proper actions. The third is *li* (ritual propriety), which seems strangest

---

[43] Translations from the *Lun Yu* are my own, cited by chapter and passage.

[44] *Confucius Sinarum Philosophus* contained translations of the *Lun Yu*, *Da Xue*, and *Zhong Yong*, along with extensive introductory materials on Chinese thought, including descriptions of the classical books and brief sections on Daoism and Buddhism. See Mungello, *Curious Land*, pp. 247–99.

[45] Sometimes the contrast between the Jesuit presentation of Confucius and the original Chinese thinker is drawn as the contrast between "Confucius" and "Kongzi," as in Jensen, *Manufacturing Confucianism*; and Paul Rule, *K'ung-tzu or Confucius? The Jesuit Interpretation of Confucianism* (Boston: Allen & Unwin, 1986).

from a Western perspective, but is part of maintaining harmonious social relationships. The fourth virtue is *zhi* (wisdom), adequately translated as *phronesis*. Central to all of the virtues is *xiao*, usually translated as filial piety. On the Confucian model, we begin with virtuous relationships to those closest to us, our family, and gradually extend these further and further as we become more ethically developed. Also central to Confucian ethics is the cultivation of simple pleasures: "The master said, 'With coarse rice to eat, with water to drink, and a bended arm for a pillow – there is joy to be found in these. Riches and honors acquired against appropriateness [*yi*] are for me like floating clouds'" (7.16). The cultivation of simple pleasures supports dedication to public service rather than individual profit. One last virtue should be mentioned because it struck Europeans as very familiar, *shu* (reciprocity): "Zi Gong asked, 'Is there one word which one can practice all one's life?' The master replied, 'There is *shu*. What you do not want done to yourself, do not do to others'" (15.24). In politics, the primary Confucian advice to rulers was to seek virtue rather than profit and to control the people through virtue rather than violence. The Confucians left unquestioned the need for a strong central government and the hierarchies it required.

The Qin Dynasty unified China in 221 BCE, but was quickly overthrown and replaced by the Han Dynasty (206 BCE–220 CE). A transformed Confucianism became the state doctrine, where it officially remained until last century. Its main early philosophical rivals were Daoism and Legalism, but Buddhism entered China in the Han Dynasty and grew in influence until it overshadowed Confucian thought. The next phase of Confucianism came with its revival and response to Buddhism, during the Song Dynasty. Confucianism after this revival has come to be called "Neo-Confucianism," but we could refer to it in the broadest sense as the tradition of thought of the *ru*, the class of scholar-officials trained in the classical texts.[46] The particular form of Confucianism known to the Jesuits and Leibniz originated in the Song Dynasty and is referred to as *li xue*, the school of *li*, or as Cheng-Zhu Confucianism, after its main figures, the brothers Cheng Hao (1032–1085) and Cheng Yi (1033–1107), and Zhu Xi (1130–1200). Zhu Xi is probably the most influential Chinese philosopher outside the classical period. *Li xue* can be broadly characterized as the attempt to integrate a speculative, systematic metaphysics influenced by Buddhism and Daoism

---

[46] For a criticism of the term "Neo-Confucianism," see Hoyt Tillman, "A New Direction in Confucian Scholarship," *Philosophy East and West*, 42 (1992), pp. 455–74.

into the ethically and socially oriented system of Confucianism. The *li xue* thinkers claimed that the Buddhist search for enlightenment led to a selfish avoidance of social and familial duty, and their response was to integrate the search for enlightenment with public service. Their main philosophical concepts were *li* and *qi*. We have already seen in the *Yi Jing* a vision of a dynamic universe operating according to an immanent law or pattern. On a general level, *li* represents the order of this dynamic universe, while *qi* is that which is ordered, its material force. *Li* as a term is difficult to define. Karlgren's dictionary gives, "polish gems according to the grain; dispose, regulate, manage, govern; rules, laws; principle, doctrine, reason; reasonable, right."[47] *Li* is unified and is the unifying principle of the universe, but it also exists in each particular thing, as its principle or the norm toward which it tends. Thus the famous phrase – *li* is one, but its manifestations are many, the single moon has countless reflections in water. The image is strikingly similar to Leibniz's conception of monads as diverse expressions of one God, but what makes *li* difficult to grasp and makes it different from Leibniz's account is that the *li xue* metaphysics is not based on individual substances.[48] They envisioned a universe unified by *li* but containing this unified *li* in each of its moments. The concept complementary to *li* is *qi*, which means "air" or "breath," but also "energy" or "material force."[49] The concept may be familiar from Chinese medicine or exercise, where it is sometimes written as "chi" or "ki." The relationship between *li* and *qi* became one of the central problems of later Confucianism. Zhu Xi describes the relationship: "Fundamentally, *li* [principle] and *qi* [material force] cannot be spoken of as prior or posterior. But if we must trace their origin, we are obliged to say that *li* is prior. However, *li* is not a separate entity. It exists right in *qi*. Without *qi*, *li* would have nothing to adhere to."[50] The relationship between *li* and *qi* was equated by Europeans with the distinction between form and matter, but *li* is more like the natural patterns or laws by which nature operates than it is like form, and, while *li* individuates, it does so only within a greater unity, not as creating separate substances.

---

[47] Bernhard Karlgren. *Analytic Dictionary of Chinese and Sino-Japanese* (Taipei: Ch'eng-Wen Publishing, 1966).

[48] Needham notes the similarity, which he takes as evidence of influence: "The hierarchy of monads and their 'pre-established harmony' resembled the innumerable individual manifestations of the Neo-Confucian Li in every pattern and organism. Each monad mirrored the universe like the nodes in Indra's Net." (Joseph Needham, *Science and Civilisation in China* [Cambridge: Cambridge University Press, 1954–], vol. II, p. 499.)

[49] Yi Wu, *Chinese Philosophical Terms* (New York: University Press of America, 1986), pp. 70–71.

[50] Chan, 1969, p. 77.

Qi is the energy/matter of the universe, which follows the order and laws that are *li*. *Qi*, unlike the traditional conception of matter, is not passive.[51]

Out of this brief sketch of "Neo-Confucianism," a few points should be emphasized. First, the *li xue* Confucians saw their philosophy as continuous with that of the early Confucian canon, underplaying their own radicality. In so doing, they followed a Confucian pattern of establishing one's own authority by claiming continuity with the past. In ethics, this continuity can be justified, but in metaphysics and psychology, *li xue* Confucianism shows the influence of both Buddhism and Daoism. Second, although the early Confucians show some ambiguity on whether or not *tian* is a conscious force guiding the universe, the "Neo-Confucian" thinkers do not. The universe is ordered by *li* but *li* is not a separate being controlling things according to a conscious plan. *Li* is simply one aspect of the universe itself, the other aspect being *qi*. In this regard again we find a sharp distinction between Leibniz and the later Confucians, with the latter coming closer to Spinoza. Third, the driving forces behind the thought of the *ru* were social and ethical, so an account that only discusses metaphysics is misrepresentative. *Li* is not only a principle of the natural world but also a principle for ethical relationships; the ethics described in early Confucianism would be the *li* of human beings. The foundation for ethical cultivation is that each person contains this *li* but the *li* is clouded or difficult to access. The task of ethics is to purify oneself so as to realize this inherent *li*. This task is analogous to the Buddhist attempt to escape an illusory ego, but for the *li xue* Confucians, when the ego dissolves, the *li* of ethical relations remains. Thus Zhu Xi writes: "With us Confucianists, although the mind is vacuous, principle is concrete. The Buddhists, on the other hand, go straight to their destination of emptiness and void."[52] In an enlightened state with a vacuous mind, one would dedicate oneself completely and spontaneously to serving society. The final point to note is that one reason "Neo-Confucianism" is an inadequate label is that it suggests one homogeneous school of philosophy. In fact, Confucian thought developed over many centuries and included a diversity of views and conflicts.[53] The best known rival to *li xue* was Lu-Wang Confucianism or *xin xue*, the "school of mind/heart," whose

---

[51] For a fuller discussion of *li*, see Willard Peterson, "Another Look at Li," *Bulletin of Sung and Yuan Studies*, 18 (1986), pp. 13–32.
[52] Chan, *Sourcebook*, p. 648.
[53] For an excellent view of Confucian thought in the early Qing Dynasty, see On-cho Ng's study of Li Guangdi, who lived at roughly the same time as Leibniz (On-cho Ng, *Cheng-Zhu Confucianism in the Early Qing: Li Guangdi (1642–1718) and Qing Learning* [Albany: SUNY Press, 2001]). For a good introduction to a variety of thinkers from the Confucian tradition, see Philip J. Ivanhoe, *Confucian Moral Self Cultivation* (Indianapolis: Hackett Pub., 2000).

most prominent thinker was Wang Yangming (1472–1529), from the Ming Dynasty. *Xin xue* held the same metaphysics of *li* and *qi*, but emphasized the unity of *xin*, the heart/mind, with the world, by emphasizing that *xin* already contains *li*. The fact that *xin* contains *li* means that the heart/mind has an inherent knowledge of goodness. The main conflict between *li xue* and *xin xue* was on the process of ethical cultivation. While Zhu Xi focused primarily on the study of *li* as it appeared concretely in the world and in classical texts, Wang Yangming focused more on a direct attack on the ego, through selfless action and through meditation. Perhaps his most famous doctrine is the identity of thought and action, a doctrine meant to undermine what he saw as the trivial scholasticism of *li xue* in his time.

ACCOMMODATING AND REJECTING CHINA

Europe first encountered China amidst contact with many other cultures, and these encounters were structured by previous encounters and paradigms. Nonetheless, the encounter with China was unlike the others, or so it seemed to many Europeans. China appeared as a highly developed culture, like that of ancient Greece or Rome or Egypt, but, unlike those, a living culture.[54] Both Europeans and Chinese considered themselves unquestionably the only significant culture on earth, yet now each was forced to reckon with a comparable force. Both were placed in a position to learn from the other, but such learning would require yielding some of their "centrism," admitting that they were in some ways excelled by the other. In both cases, the need to accommodate the other met with mixed success, and, although both benefited, the encounter ended in mutual rejection.[55] The Jesuits succeeded astonishingly well in integrating themselves into the educated class in China, primarily because they were willing to adapt to

---

[54] Of distant cultures, China was the only one taken seriously by Europeans at the time. One possible exception is Islam, which was sometimes recognized as a living culture with high achievements, but attitudes toward Islam were more hostile than attitudes toward China. The most obvious reason for this difference is that Islam was seen as military and cultural threat. China was not. For a brief study of attitudes toward Islam in the early modern period, see Daniel J. Vitkus, "Early Modern Orientalism: Representations of Islam in Sixteenth and Seventeenth-Century Europe," *Western Views of Islam in Medieval and Early Modern Europe*. Ed. by David R. Blanks and Michael Frassetto (New York: St. Martin's Press, 1999), pp. 207–30.

[55] For the Chinese side of this encounter, see David Mungello (ed.), *The Chinese Rites Controversy: Its History and Meaning* (Monumenta Serica XXXIII. Nettetal: Steyler Verlag, 1994); Willard Peterson, "Why did They Become Christians?" In Bonnie Oh and Charles Ronan (eds.), *East Meets West: The Jesuits in China, 1582–1773*. (Chicago: Loyola University Press, 1988); and Jensen, *Manufacturing Confucianism*.

Chinese culture. Ricci was friends with leading officials in China, and his works written in Chinese were widely read. He published not only on Christian doctrine but also on such topics as friendship and geometry, translating Euclid's *Elements* into Chinese in 1611. The acceptance of the Europeans reached its height early in the Qing Dynasty, which was particularly cosmopolitan as the Manchu leaders were themselves foreigners in China. In the first year of the Qing takeover, the Jesuit Johann Adam Schall challenged the Chinese and Muslim astronomers of the court in predicting an eclipse. Schall predicted most accurately and was named head of the imperial Bureau of Astronomy. For a time he had a personal, informal relationship with the young Emperor Shunzhi.[56] Ferdinand Verbiest, a Jesuit and a correspondent of Leibniz, was named to head the bureau after a similar challenge in 1669. He developed a close relationship with the next emperor, Kangxi, whom he tutored in mathematics and astronomy.[57] Kangxi continued to have close relations with some of the missionaries, which he described in a wonderful passage:

> After the treaty of Nerchinsk had been signed with the Russians, I ordered the Jesuits Thomas, Gerbillon, and Bouvet to study Manchu also, and to compose treatises in that language on Western arithmetic and the geometry of Euclid. In the early 1690's I often worked several hours a day with them. With Verbiest I had examined each stage of the forging of cannons and made him build a water fountain that operated in conjunction with an organ, and erect a windmill in the court; with the new group – who were later joined by Brocard and Jartoux, and worked in the Yang-hsin Palace under the general direction of my Eldest son Yin-t'i – I worked on clocks and mechanics. Pereira taught me to play the tune "P'u-yen-choi" on the harpsichord and the structure of the eight-note scale, Pedrini taught my sons musical theory, and Gherardini painted portraits at the Court. I also learned to calculate the weight and volume of spheres, cubes, and cones, and to measure distances and the angle of river banks. On inspection tours later I used these Western methods to show my officials how to make more accurate calculations when planning their river works.[58]

The passage shows Kangxi's openness to learning from the Jesuits, but does not mention his learning anything in ethics or religion, that is, anything Christian. The imperial court used the missionaries as advisers and technicians, convincing them to do everything from manufacture canons to

---

[56] Dunne says that at that time Schall was one of the most influential men in China, but that is probably an exaggeration. (George H. Dunne, *Generation of Giants: The Story of the Jesuits in China in the Last Decades of the Ming Dynasty* [Notre Dame: University of Notre Dame Press, 1962], p. 348.)

[57] Jonathan Spence, *The China Helpers: Western Advisers in China, 1620–1960* (London: Bodley Head, 1969).

[58] Spence, *Emperor of China*, pp. 72–73. For an account of this encounter between China and Europe from the perspective of the emperor, see also pp. 72–84.

design dancing waterfalls. Leibniz corresponded with several of the missionaries mentioned by the emperor. In 1692, Kangxi issued his Edict of Toleration, allowing the free practice of Christianity in China. The edict was widely known and praised in Europe.

The impact of the encounter with China on Europe is difficult to assess. Perhaps the best example of the need to accommodate China was in world history.[59] In Europe, the three crucial events of world history – the creation, the flood that again reduced all human beings to a single ancestor, the dispersion of peoples and languages at the Tower of Babel – were dated according to different versions of the Bible, the main conflict being between the Vulgate and the Septuagint. The Vulgate version of the Bible, based on a translation from Hebrew texts by St. Jerome, was most common and placed creation around 4004 BCE, the flood around 2348. The Septuagint, an earlier Greek translation made from different Hebrew sources, placed these events earlier, with the creation before 5000 and the flood as early as 3617. Into this world history, the Jesuit Martino Martini introduced his history of China in 1658.[60] According to Martini's calculations, the first Chinese emperor, Fuxi, began his reign in 2952 BCE, at which time astronomy had already been developed, and the trigrams of the *Yi Jing* were created. The picture was complicated further by Chinese descriptions of a flood in the reign of the emperor Yao (2357–2257). Martini concluded that people lived in China before the Biblical flood, but he offered no explanation for how this was possible.[61] Edwin Van Kley describes the gradual shift in world history forced by this knowledge of China, as well as the particular attempts to accommodate the new chronology. The simplest response was to use the chronology from the Septuagint Bible, as the Jesuits in China were authorized to do. Alternatively, one could simply dismiss the Chinese records as false, but more creative reconciliations appeared. Isaac Vossius argued that the Biblical flood was local and that Chinese civilization survived it.[62] Others equated the most ancient Chinese emperors with the Biblical patriarchs, taking Chinese history as a version of the Old Testament, as we have already seen Bouvet attempt. Fuxi was variably considered Adam, Noah, or Enoch, the son of Cain. An important question became from

---

[59] My account is based on Edwin S. Van Kley, "Europe's Discovery of China and the Writing of World History," *The American Historical Review*, 76 (1971), pp. 358–72; and Mungello, *Curious Land*, pp. 124–32.

[60] Martinio Martini, *Sinicae historiae decas prima res a gentis origine ad Christum natum in extrema Asia, sive magno Sinarum imperio gestas complexa* (Munich, 1658). Van Kley notes that the Chinese chronology had been presented to Europe earlier, but never in a convincing way (Van Kley, "Europe's Discovery," p. 362).

[61] Van Kley, "Europe's Discovery," p. 363; Mungello, *Curious Land*, p. 127.

[62] Van Kley, "Europe's Discovery," pp. 363–64.

which of Noah's sons the Chinese developed: Shem, the oldest; or Ham, considered the ancestor of idolatrous peoples.[63] Another issue of concern was the relationship between China and Babel. John Webb, for example, believed that the Chinese were not present at Babel (they lived so far away!), and that Chinese was the language of Noah.[64] The problem of chronology illustrates the kinds of threats posed by Europe's encounter with China and the surprising range of reactions to this threat. Many thinkers were not simply hostile or dismissive, and we find people like Vossius and Webb accommodating China in startling ways. The conflict over chronology powerfully shaped Europe's approach to China. All sides took for granted the extreme antiquity of Chinese culture and the unusual thoroughness of Chinese historical records. The antiquity of these records led many to expect hidden insight in the language and ancient books of China. Bouvet represents an extreme of this expectation, but Leibniz and others followed the same principle.

The focus in accommodating China was the so-called "Rites Controversy," which developed out of the attempt to introduce Christianity into Chinese culture.[65] The Rites Controversy was one of the leading intellectual debates in Europe during Leibniz's lifetime, involving such thinkers as Pascal, Arnauld, Leibniz, and Malebranche. The controversy arose from two questions. The first was the question of rites, in particular the rites to ancestors and Confucius. If these rituals were religious, they were idolatrous, and no Christian could practice them. The question was – are these rites religious? The second issue concerned what words could be used to translate the word "God." In particular, the Jesuits used two words we have seen in the early Chinese classics, *Shang Di* and *tian*. The question was whether these terms could be used for "God." The two questions, of rites and of terms, are not necessarily linked, and seem in tension. If the Chinese had a concept of God, so that their native terms could be used, we would also expect their rituals to be religious, and thus not allowed; while if the Chinese were atheists, the rituals would be secular. The opposing position was even more problematic, forced to claim that the Chinese were materialists with no term for God, while also claiming that their rituals were religious. Most Jesuits supported accommodation on both questions, but a few

---

[63] Thus the Dominican Domingo Ferandez Navarette, against accommodation in China, considered Fuxi to be Ham, whom he also considered to be Zoroaster (Van Kley, "Europe's Discovery," p. 366).

[64] Van Kley, "Europe's Discovery," pp. 365–66.

[65] The best philosophical source on the Rites Controversy is Mungello (ed.), *Chinese Rites Controversy*. See also Rule, *K'ung-tzu or Confucius?* For a survey of the Church's decisions in the controversy, see George Minamiki, *The Chinese Rites Controversy from its Beginning to Modern Times* (Chicago: Loyola University Press, 1985).

of the Jesuits held what seems the most natural position – accommodation on rites but not on terms. Thus, for example, Nicholas Longobardi, one of Leibniz's main sources on the Rites Controversy, held that the Chinese had no conception of God, that *Shang Di* and *tian* referred to natural principles, and that the rites were consequently civil and free of religion or superstition. The way the two questions held together shows that deeper issues connect them. The Rites Controversy marks an attempt to deal with how Christianity can mix with other cultures. On one side, it asked how far the essence of Christianity could be separated from European culture. On the other side, it asked equally difficult questions about Chinese culture: is "Confucianism" a religion?; did the ancient Chinese believe in a single, personal, God? Europeans disagreed on how the Chinese beliefs should be evaluated and categorized but even more on how to strike the balance between the essence of Christianity and its European cultural forms. Thus Virgile Pinot begins his account of the controversy with the seemingly insignificant Jesuit decision to take on the garb of the *ru*, the class of Confucian officials. The Franciscans and Dominicans retained their European clothing.[66] Those who took the side of accommodation on both questions, including Leibniz and almost all of the Jesuits, were united in their more favorable view of the Chinese and greater trust of pagan thought. They were also united in practical concerns – accommodation on both questions seemed most beneficial to the acceptance of Christianity in China. In contrast, those who opposed accommodation on both questions were united in their low appraisal of the Chinese and their distrust of pagans, and often in their dislike of the Jesuits.[67] This opposing group included most of the Dominican and Franciscan missionaries operating in Asia, the Jansenists, the theological faculty of the Sorbonne, and, ultimately, the pope.

Accommodation was established as a method of the Jesuit mission in China by its founder, Matteo Ricci. Before that time, missionaries had promoted Christianity with European cultural forms, often by means of economic or military force. Such an approach was judged inappropriate in China. Ricci set the tone by integrating himself into the scholarly class. His efforts to introduce Christianity are marked by his willingness to proceed gradually and his effort to leave as much of Chinese culture as possible intact. His gradual approach even led to accusations that he was introducing

---

[66] Virgile Pinot, *La Chine et la formation de l'esprit philosophique en France (1640–1740)* (Geneva: Slatkine, 1971), p. 73.

[67] Pinot claims that the controversy would have remained an obscure theological question if the Jansenists had not seized upon it as a means of attacking the Jesuits. Pascal was one of the first to use the controversy in this way. (Pinot, *Chine et la formation*, pp. 79–80.)

a monotheistic natural theology, rather than Christianity.[68] Practical concerns motivated this approach, as the Chinese were more open to a philosophical natural theology than to the details of Christianity, and Ricci believed that the ancient Chinese had a natural theology of their own, writing:

> Of all the Pagan sects known to Europe, I know of no people who fell into fewer errors in the early ages of their antiquity than did the Chinese. From the very beginning of their history it is recorded in their writings that they recognized and worshipped one supreme being whom they called the King of Heaven, or designated by some other name indicating his rule over heaven and earth.[69]

Originally, he says, the rites were neither idolatrous nor superstitious, but their meaning declined among the common people. Given their origin, however, he believed they could be purified and left largely intact. The accommodationist interpretation of the rites can be seen in Ricci's own description:

> The most common ceremony practiced by all the Literati, from the King down to the very lowest of them, is that of the annual funeral rites, which we have already described. As they themselves say, they consider this ceremony as an honor bestowed upon their departed ancestors, just as they might honor them if they were living. They do not really believe that the dead actually need the victuals which are placed upon their graves, but they say that they observe the custom of placing them there because it seems to be the best way of testifying their love for their dear departed. Indeed, it is asserted by many that this particular rite was first instituted for the benefit of the living rather than for that of the dead. In this way it was hoped that children, and unlearned adults as well, might learn how to respect and support their parents who were living, when they saw that parents departed were so highly honored by those who were educated and prominent. This practice of placing food upon the graves of the dead seems to be beyond any charge of sacrilege and perhaps also free from any taint of superstition, because they do not in any respect consider their ancestors gods, nor do they petition them for anything or hope for anything from them. However, for those who have accepted the teachings of Christianity, it would seem much better to replace this custom with alms for the poor and for the salvation of souls.[70]

As Ricci does here, the accommodationists considered the rites merely civil, intended to honor parents, ancestors, and people of great virtue, like Confucius. Leibniz follows this interpretation, also appealing to the

---

[68] Dunne, *Generation of Giants*, p. 96. Spence notes that the Chinese themselves considered Ricci a *hui*, the word also used for Muslims and Jews. (Jonathon Spence, *The Memory Palace of Matteo Ricci* [New York: Viking Press, 1984], pp. 93–127.) For Ricci's integration of Chinese and Christian thought, see Jensen, *Manufacturing Confucianism*.

[69] Ricci, *China in the Sixteenth Century*, p. 93.   [70] Ricci, *China in the Sixteenth Century*, p. 96.

hypothetical origins of the rites. Opponents based their position largely on the fact that the rites looked religious. In addition, while the Jesuits based their views on the projected origins of the rites or on the interpretations of the intellectual elite with whom they associated, the opponents of the rites based their opinions on the practices of the common people, where belief in ghosts and spirits would have been more widespread.[71]

On the question of terms, the Jesuits themselves split. On the surface, the controversy was on an issue of translation. How could the Western idea of God be translated into Chinese? The options were to create a new word, perhaps a transliteration of a European term, or else to use and modify a Chinese word. The latter choice raised the problem of easy misunderstandings. The former choice, however, had difficulties as well. Would a novel term better avoid misunderstanding? More importantly, the Chinese were confident in their own tradition, and suspicious of anything entirely new. Again we can turn to Kangxi for a Chinese perspective:

> For even though some of the Western methods are different from our own, and may even be an improvement, there is little about them that is new. The principles of mathematics all derive from the *Book of Changes*, and the Western methods are Chinese in origin: this algebra – "A-erh-chu-pa-erh" – springs from an Eastern word. And though it was indeed the Westerners who showed us something our ancient calendar experts did not know – namely how to calculate the angles of the northern pole – this but shows the truth of what Chu Hsi [Zhu Xi] arrived at through his investigation of things: the earth is like the yolk within an egg.[72]

The use of Chinese terms established a bridge to Chinese culture. We would expect a question of translation to be settled by linguists and experts in the Chinese language; the fact that it was not shows the stakes lay elsewhere. Virgile Pinot claims that the issue shifted with Couplet's publication of the *Confucius Sinarum Philosophus*, where defense of the Jesuit position became defense of ancient Chinese thought, shifting the debate from the Jesuits to the Chinese. Arnauld responded with an attack on the Jesuits and with an attack on Chinese philosophy.[73] The question became whether the Chinese knew God under the name of "*Shang Di*" or "*tian*." It became an issue of natural theology and the possible salvation of pagans, questions debated throughout the history of the Church. Leibniz and most supporters of accommodation also supported the possibility of pagan salvation.[74] The

[71] Minamiki, *Chinese Rites Controversy*, pp. 22–23.   [72] Spence, *Emperor of China*, p. 74.

[73] Pinot, *Chine et la formation*, pp. 88–89.

[74] For a remarkable example of the tradition claiming that pagans can be saved, particularly in relation to China, see Claudia von Collani, "Das Problem des Heils der Heiden," *Neue Zeitschrift für Missions Wissenschaft*, 45 (1989), pp. 17–35, 93–109.

heart of the controversy can be seen in the Sorbonne's condemnation of the Jesuit position. Jansenist enemies of the Jesuits presented six statements to the theological faculty of the Sorbonne for condemnation, taken from two Jesuit books advocating accommodation.[75] These propositions were as follows:

(1) The Chinese have preserved knowledge of the true God from more than two thousand years before the birth of Jesus Christ.

(2) They have had the honor to sacrifice to Him in the most ancient temple in the universe.

(3) They have honored Him in a manner that can serve as an example even to Christians.

(4) They have practiced a morality as pure as their religion.

(5) They have had the faith, humility, interior and exterior worship, priest-hood, sacrifices, saintliness, miracles, the spirit of God, and the purest charity, which is the character and the perfection of true religion.

(6) Of all the nations of the earth, the Chinese have been the most constantly favored by the grace of God.[76]

These statements are so strong in their praise for the Chinese that they make Leibniz's praise seem moderate. They illustrate again the extreme variation in how Chinese culture was welcomed or condemned. All six statements were condemned by the Sorbonne on October 18, 1700.

Although it is easy to side with accommodation, the Rites Controversy raised profoundly difficult questions about the nature of religion and Chinese culture. These already difficult questions were further complicated by political and practical concerns. Some involved rivalries between factions in the Church and between national groups, particularly the Spanish and the Portuguese. Others were more fundamental. For example, a missionary effort based on the anti-accommodation position stood little chance of success. To give up the rites for one's ancestors would show the greatest disrespect, and one had to perform rituals respecting Confucius in order to become an official. We have already seen that one of Mengzi's four key virtues is *li*, ritual propriety. Forbidding a Christian from these rituals would prevent any convert from achieving government office. In spite of these practical concerns, the Church ultimately decided against accommodation, and the collapse of the Catholic mission in China soon followed. While accommodation might have helped the missionaries, it threatened

---

[75] The two books were *Nouveaux mémoires sur l'état présent de la Chine*. 2 vols. (Paris, 1696), by Louis Le Comte; and *Histoire de l'édit de la Chine en faveur de la religion chrestienne* (Paris, 1698), by Charles Le Gobien, one of Leibniz's correspondents.

[76] Pinot, *Chine et la formation*, p. 98.

the authority of the Church. The argument that the essence of Christianity could be separated from its cultural formulations could easily play into Protestant hands – if Christianity could be stripped of its Europeanism and adapted to China, couldn't it also be stripped of its "Romanism" and adapted to England? An even deeper threat follows from the praise of Chinese morals, as in the statements before the Sorbonne. The praise of a Confucian morality derived from natural theology tended to weaken both the revealed "Christian" part of Christianity and the dependence on an institutionalized Church. The anti-accommodation position could be even worse, though. What does it mean if the Chinese have such good morals, while lacking not only Christ but any knowledge of God?[77] For many opponents of the Church, the Chinese joined Spinoza as the prime examples of the "virtuous atheist."

The Rites Controversy reached its peak and end during Leibniz's life. Leibniz watched the movement against the rites with trepidation and puzzlement, although he maintained hope that Rome would come to its senses. In 1704, after seven years of investigation, Pope Clement XI issued a decree against accommodation, forbidding participation in the ceremonies for Confucius and many aspects of the rituals for ancestors. The decree was kept secret while the papal legate Charles Thomas Maillard de Tournon traveled to China to announce and enforce the decision, which he did in a mandate on February 7, 1707. He was banished from China shortly after, and the Chinese emperor initiated the policy of requiring all missionaries to have a certificate (*piao*), which could only be received by agreeing to follow the position of Ricci. Kangxi was particularly offended by the decision because he had officially endorsed the Jesuit view. He writes:

I had agreed with the formulation the Peking fathers had drawn up in 1700: that Confucius was honored by the Chinese as a master, but his name was not invoked in prayer for the purpose of gaining happiness, rank, or wealth; that worship of ancestors was an expression of love and filial remembrance, not intended to bring protection to the worshiper; and that there was no idea, when an ancestral tablet was erected, that the soul of the ancestor dwelt in that tablet. And when sacrifices were offered to Heaven it was not the blue existent sky that was addressed, but the lord and creator of all things. If the ruler Shang Di was sometimes called Heaven, *Tian*, that had no more significance than giving honorific names to the emperor.[78]

Leibniz takes Kangxi's statement as decisive for the controversy, but it was taken as interference by the Church.[79] The pope's decree against the rites

[77] Cf. Pinot, *Chine et la formation*, p. 105.   [78] Spence, *Emperor of China*, p. 79.
[79] Minamiki, *Chinese Rites Controversy*, pp. 40–42.

was published in Europe in 1709. Although other decrees followed, the decision against the rites was maintained until the twentieth century.[80] In 1724, a year after Kangxi's death, his son, Yongzheng, banished all missionaries except those needed for astronomy, ending the Catholic mission in China. Kangxi describes an earlier meeting with Charles Maigrot, another official critic of accommodation, in terms worth quoting:

Maigrot wasn't merely ignorant of Chinese literature, he couldn't even recognize the simplest Chinese characters; yet he chose to discuss the falsity of the Chinese moral system. Sometimes, as I pointed out, the emperor is addressed honorifically as "under the steps of the throne"; would Maigrot say this was a reference to a set of steps made by some artisan? I am addressed as "Wan-sui, Ten Thousand Years"; obviously that too is not literal – since from the beginnings of history to the present day only 7,600 years have passed. Even little animals mourn their dead mothers for many days; these Westerners who want to treat their dead with indifference are not even equal to animals. How can they be compared with the Chinese? We venerate Confucius because of his doctrines of respect for virtue, his system of education, his inculcation of love for superiors and ancestors. Westerners venerate their own saints because of their actions. They paint pictures of men with wings and say, "These represent heavenly spirits, swift as if they had wings, though in reality there are no men with wings." I do not find it appropriate to dispute this doctrine, yet with superficial knowledge Maigrot discussed Chinese sanctity. He talked for days, with his perverse reason, his poorly concealed anger, and fled the country when he could not get his way, a sinner against the Catholic teaching and a rebel to China.[81]

UNIVERSALS, TOLERANCE, AND THE PLURALITY OF CULTURES

By the time Leibniz began to think about Kangxi, almost two centuries had passed since Europe's expansion into Asia, Sub-Saharan Africa, and the Americas. The initial enthusiasm for other cultures settled and paradigms for approaching, accommodating, and rejecting different cultures coalesced. At the same time, the philosophical issues rooted in the contact with other cultures gained independent life. These issues manifested themselves most directly in the debate over innate ideas, which connected to questions of cultural universals and natural theology, which connected in

---

[80] For a discussion of the decrees involved, see Minamiki, *Chinese Rites Controversy*, pp. 25–76. In the twentieth century, the Church changed its position on the rites. Based on nationalist requirements in Japan and Manchukuo – the area of Northwest China captured by the Japanese – the Church decided that the Confucian and Shinto rituals were civil and could be practiced by Christians.

[81] Spence, *Emperor of China*, pp. 79–80. Kangxi gives a longer description of his meeting with Tournon, pp. 75–79.

turn to skepticism and arguments for the existence of God based on uni-versal consent. These positions can be seen as descendants of the earlier paradigms and lenses developed in medieval and Renaissance encounters with Europe's others. Spinoza and Locke address the status of other cultures more directly, but Descartes sets the context. Although the very project of proving core truths of religion through reason alone became possible only in the tradition of natural theology which emerged in a space made for non-Christian thought, Descartes severs his work from this intercultural context. Descartes' apparent disinterest in other cultures is heightened by the tendency of commentators to ignore the little interest that he has. For example, the indexes of the three volumes of *The Philosophical Writings of Descartes* contain only one citation of another culture – a reference to the Hurons of the Americas – even though the *Discourse on Method* alone contains three references to China, a reference to Persia, and a reference to Mexico. These references may seem insignificant but they mark an absence. Ignoring them gives the impression that Descartes ignores other cultures because he was unaware of them. Both Europe's history and Descartes' own references show the falsity of such an impression. When we recognize this context, we are compelled to ask why a philosopher like Descartes would show so little interest in the cultural diversity then accessible to Europeans.

The issue of cultural diversity emerges in the beginning of the *Discourse on Method*:

[T]he power of judging well and of distinguishing the true from the false – which is what we properly call "good sense" or "reason" – is naturally equal in all men, and consequently the diversity of our opinions does not arise because some of us are more reasonable than others but solely because we direct our thoughts along different paths and do not attend to the same things. (CSM iii; AT VI, 2)

A few sentences later he shows that this equality includes human beings as a species – "as regards reason or sense, since it is the only thing that makes us men and distinguishes us from the beasts, I am inclined to believe that it exists whole and complete in each of us" (CSM 112; AT VI, 2). These passages are remarkably explicit in advocating the equality of all human beings as a species. The first passage is also remarkable for its vision of something like culture: human beings differ because they apply their reason to different paths and different concerns. One would think this vision of reason as emerging through culture would lead Descartes to study all the diverse applications of reason. Such a view leads Leibniz to take China seriously, but Descartes takes it in an opposite direction, following the lead of Montaigne. Descartes repeatedly connects diversity and skepticism, noting that he might have remained content with the opinions of his teachers if he had not encountered such a diversity of opinions. He writes in a passage that echoes Montaigne:

I have recognized through my travels that those with views quite contrary to ours are not on that account barbarians or savages, but that many of them make use of reason as much or more than we do. I thought, too, how the same man, with the same mind, if brought up from infancy among the French or Germans, develops otherwise than he would if he had always lived among the Chinese or cannibals; and how, even in our fashions of dress, the very thing that pleased us ten years ago, and will perhaps please us again ten years hence, now strikes us as extravagant and ridiculous. Thus it is custom and example that persuade us, rather than any certain knowledge. (CSM I 119; AT VI 16)

Descartes comes oddly close to cultural relativism in such passages. His point is that the diversity of human culture and custom proves that culture and custom cannot be relied upon in the search for truth.

From this skeptical appropriation of diversity, Descartes astutely draws two conclusions. One is that skepticism alone cannot drive a deep interest in other cultures: "It is good to know something of the customs of various peoples so that we may judge our own more soundly and not think that everything contrary to our own ways is ridiculous and irrational, as those who have seen nothing of the world ordinarily do" (CSM I 113–14; AT VI 6). Beyond this realization of the limits of our own view, though, there is no more need to study this diversity. The second point he draws from this apparent cultural relativism is that if there is any truth, it must be sought outside the limitations of culture. His alternative route is through self-reflection and innate ideas. When he points to the value of experiencing cultural diversity, he adds that through this knowledge, "I gradually freed myself from many errors which may obscure our natural light and make us less capable of heeding reason" (CSM I 116; AT VI 10). The value of cultural diversity is to free ourselves from culture, leaving only the pure light of reason. In the *Meditations*, the method of doubt is condensed, but the *Discourse* shows that what we must doubt is not only our naïve ontology but culture itself. When we free ourselves from the culture we imbibed in our youth, we can build truths on a solid foundation, by drawing out ideas innate to each mind. Thus in the *Discourse* he says that, to free himself from his opinions, he thought it better to travel than to sit in a stove-heated room, but after nine years of sampling the diversity of human opinions, when he was ready to turn to the task of establishing truth, he retreated to Holland, where he could "lead a life as solitary and withdrawn as if I were in the most remote desert" (CSM I 126; AT VI 31).

Spinoza's approach to other cultures follows the lines laid down by Descartes but is more explicit. The existence of a universal, common human nature is central to Spinoza's political and theological writings: his political arguments will be beyond doubt, he says, if he derives them from "a general consideration of human nature."[82] In describing this common nature that allows for political science, Spinoza's focus is on our dominance by passion rather than our capacity for reason. As he puts it, "All men, Jews and Gentiles alike, have always been the same, and in every age virtue has been exceedingly rare."[83] This universal human nature functions differently in Spinoza's writings on religion and theology. The negative side of human nature explains the universality of superstition and the tendency of religion to turn into respect for ecclesiastics, but, on the positive side, we all share the ability to reach the truths of religion through reason and common innate ideas. Thus in the chapter on the vocation of the Hebrews, he writes, "in respect of understanding and virtue, that is, in respect of blessedness, God is equally gracious to all, as we have already stated and proved by reason."[84] Spinoza goes further than others in allowing the equality of other peoples because he denies special status to the Bible and Christianity. The commonality of human nature for Spinoza reveals the complex intersection between his use other cultures for European concerns. Spinoza's intent is not to show that religion is universal but to show that it is accessible to each of us without revelation or religious institutions. The claim that all peoples are equally gifted in reason, virtue, and blessedness is not meant to direct us toward a comparative study of other cultures, but rather to show that each of us needs nothing more than our own common nature supplies: "The natural light of reason enjoins nothing that is not within the compass of reason, but only what it can show us quite clearly to be a good, or a means to our blessedness."[85] At the same time that Spinoza equalizes different cultures, the condition of their equality – the universality of reason and common ideas – makes cultural diversity irrelevant. The recognition of the rationality of other non-Europeans might appear as an extension of arguments for tolerance and freedom *within* Europe, but the causality runs in the other direction. The space within Europe for an independent religion based on reason extends from the space originally created for pagan thought.

---

[82] Benedict de Spinoza, *Political Treatise*. Trans. by Samuel Shirley (Indianapolis: Hackett, 2000), p. 77.

[83] Benedict de Spinoza, *Theological-Political Treatise*. Trans. by Samuel Shirley (Indianapolis: Hackett, 1998), pp. 146; cf. Spinoza, *Political Treatise*, pp. 61–62.

[84] Spinoza, *Theological-Political Treatise*, p. 40.   [85] Spinoza, *Theological-Political Treatise*, p. 52.

Spinoza's argument has two sides: to show that all people have access to the core of religion through reason and innate ideas; and to show that most of organized religion is not part of this core. Thus Spinoza must define the essential core narrowly – "To love God above all and one's neighbor as oneself."[86] Although the Bible might lead us to these truths, its usefulness is limited because its stories are adapted to particular audiences and rely on experience, while the core truths of religion must be known from general ideas through reflection.[87] Ceremony relates only to temporal happiness and political stability; doctrines matter only as they lead to justice and charity – "faith requires not so much true dogmas as pious dogmas, that is, such as move the heart to obedience."[88] The latter claim supports a pluralistic position. The same core truths have been expressed in many ways, even within the Bible, and they could be expressed in many more ways. In fact, the truth must be accommodated to different peoples.[89] Spinoza primarily appeals for tolerance for his own thoughts about God, but this broad tolerance extends to other cultures as well, as Spinoza says directly in a letter to Jacob Ostens: "As for the Turks and other Gentiles, if they worship God by the exercise of justice and by love of their neighbor, I believe that they possess the spirit of Christ, and are saved, whatever convictions they may hold in their ignorance regarding Mahomet and oracles."[90] His insistence that all people have equal access to knowledge and virtue pushes the above statement past a conditional, suggesting that there are people in those other cultures who practice justice and charity. God is equally gracious to all, so all cultures should have had prophets to exhort them to true virtue.

Part of this argument for pluralism and tolerance is a strict separation between what is essential and available to everyone and what is inessential and dependent on culture. This separation means that, if one takes the internal path to God through reflection, worldly manifestations have nothing to add. Spinoza shows no interest in the different ways the true core manifests itself in history or culture. Like Descartes, his claims about universal human nature rely on no support from observations of the diversity of human beings. These factors are striking but not surprising in the context of Spinoza's epistemology. The height of piety, which is the practice of justice and charity, depends on intuitive knowledge of God, which is the highest degree

---

[86] Spinoza, *Theological-Political Treatise*, p. 151.
[87] Spinoza, *Theological-Political Treatise*, pp. 150–51.
[88] Spinoza, *Theological-Political Treatise*, p. 161.   [89] Spinoza, *Theological-Political Treatise*, p. 163.
[90] Ep 43; Benedict de Spinoza, *The Letters*. Trans. by Samuel Shirley (Indianapolis: Hackett, 1995), p. 241.

of knowledge (Ethics 5P32, 4P37). The desire or endeavor for this kind of knowledge is driven by rational knowledge, which is one degree lower (Ethics 5P28). Both kinds of knowledge rely on adequate ideas, defined as "an idea which, in so far as it is considered in itself, without relation to an object, has all the properties or intrinsic denominations of a true idea" (Ethics 2P40, 2P41; 2D4). By "intrinsic" he means to exclude the extrinsic relationship between the idea and its object, but he also means that the idea bears its truth as a quality of itself. For an idea to be adequate, it must be complete within our mind, based on "those things, which are common to all, and which are equally in the part and in the whole" (Ethics 2P35; 2P38). The result of these propositions is that knowledge of God must be based on ideas contained entirely within each of us and common to all people. Looking at the practices, dogmas, and symbols of other cultures would only entangle us in fragmentary, confused, disordered ideas at the lowest level of knowledge (Ethics 2P40s2). Such ideas cannot lead to true knowledge of God, nor even to the desire for true knowledge of God (Ethics 5P28).

Spinoza's epistemology and his approach to cultural diversity come together nicely in an exchange of letters with Albert Burgh. Burgh had recently converted to Catholicism and wrote an impassioned, if less than coherent, letter exhorting Spinoza to do the same. Burgh writes to Spinoza:

You assume that you have at length discovered the true philosophy. How do you know that your philosophy is the best out of all those that have ever have been taught in this world, are at present being taught, or will ever be taught in the future? To say nothing of possible future philosophies, have you examined all those philosophies, both ancient and modern, which are taught here, and in India, and everywhere through the whole world?[91]

Spinoza responds:

[Your question] I might with much greater right ask you; for I do not presume that I have found the best philosophy, but I know I understand the true philosophy. If you ask me how I know this, I reply that I know it in the same way that you know that the three angles of a triangle are equal to two right angles. . . . For truth is an index of itself and the false.[92]

If one bases religious truths on experience, miracles, and testimonies, one must confront endless obscure evidence from all the diverse world religions.

---

[91] Ep 67, Spinoza, *Letters*, p. 303 (translation modified). Shirley provides another example of the erasure of other cultures from early modern thought. His translation omits the specific reference to India, obscuring the fact that Burgh explicitly raises the problem of comparative philosophy and that he is aware that other parts of the world have philosophy.

[92] Ep 76, Spinoza, *Letters*, p. 342.

Fortunately, that is not necessary and is about as relevant to philosophy as measuring slices of pie is to geometry.

Both Spinoza and Descartes approach cultural diversity through a distinction between what is universal and important and what varies culturally and is insignificant. Spinoza differs by his greater emphasis on what all peoples have in common. John Locke maintains a similar distinction but focuses more on what varies culturally. Locke uses other cultures to make a philosophical point opposed to Spinoza, against innate principles and ideas. In this use of other cultures, Locke more closely approaches the skepticism of Montaigne, although his position is more complex because on the one side Locke is not as skeptical as Montaigne, while on the other side his tolerance has broader support than his skepticism. I will not attempt to do justice to the complexities of Locke's position here; my goal is only to illustrate one line of argument, the argument in which he consistently uses other cultures. Like Montaigne, Locke enjoys curious anecdotes about the rest of world, and his interest is primarily in the peoples of the Americas. Also like Montaigne, Locke criticizes the treatment of indigenous peoples, remarking "how easily the pretence of Religion, and of the care of Souls, serves for a Cloak to Covetousness, Rapine, and Ambition."[93] He argues that native Americans should be granted religious freedom and should be treated with love.

The similarity between Locke and Montaigne goes deeper than this shared interest in the Americas. In the "Letter Concerning Toleration," Locke makes a claim about "orthodoxy" almost identical to Montaigne's claim about "barbarity":

For it must be remembered that the Civil Power is the same every where, and the Religion of every Prince is Orthodox to himself. If therefore such a Power be granted unto the Civil Magistrate in Spirituals, as that at *Geneva* (for Example), he may extirpate, by Violence and Blood, the Religion which is there reputed Idolatrous; by the same Rule another magistrate, in some neighbouring Country, may oppress the Reformed Religion; and, in *India*, the Christian.[94]

This passage remarkably puts Europe and India on equal footing. In forcing our ideas on others, we do the same as an Indian prince does when forcing his ideas on Christians. A less tolerant response is obvious – the intolerant Christian is not like the intolerant Indian because the Christian is right. Locke's rejection of this response is rooted in skepticism – just because we

---

[93] John Locke, *A Letter Concerning Toleration*. Trans. by James H. Tully (Indianapolis: Hackett, 1983), p. 34.
[94] Locke, *Toleration*, pp. 42–43.

think we are right does not mean that we are in fact right; thus we should be reluctant to impose our views on others, just as we would be reluctant to have their views imposed on us. Locke's goal is close to that of Montaigne, but he is less concerned with tolerance of other cultures than he is with tolerance within Europe. Given this purpose, he repeats similar arguments without reference to other cultures, as when he argues that, even if there is only one way to heaven, no one can be sure which way it is.[95]

From this context, we can see how the *Essay Concerning Human Understanding* develops this skeptical support for tolerance and intersects the status of non-Christians. Locke himself sets this context in his introduction, where his goal is to examine how our understanding leads to ideas which are "so various, different, and wholly contradictory" that, if we examine the history of human opinion, we might conclude that either there is no such thing as truth, or that we humans lack the means to find it. To avoid this conclusion, he will examine the limits beyond which our knowledge is uncertain, with the practical goal of making the minds of men "more cautious in meddling with things exceeding its Comprehension" (I, i, 3–4). In drawing a limit beyond which we should be skeptical, Locke follows Descartes and Spinoza, but he leaves more knowledge on the far side of the limit. Other cultures fit into this approach by illustrating the diversity of human opinion and practices, thus undermining any easily grasped universals. This intersection of issues is clearest in the first book, directed against innate principles. Locke summarizes his argument:

There is scarce that Principle of Morality to be named, or Rule of Vertue to be thought on (those only excepted, that are absolutely necessary to hold society together, which commonly too are neglected betwixt distinct Societies) which is not, somewhere or other, slighted and condemned by the general Fashion of whole Societies of Men, governed by practical Opinions, and Rules of living quite opposed to others. (Essay, I, iii, 10, p. 72)

While Spinoza argues for cultural universals based on his access to reason, Locke argues against them, with empirical evidence of other cultures. Locke's evidence is worth reading:

In a Part of *Asia*, the Sick, when their Case comes to be thought desperate, are carried out and laid on the Earth, before they are dead, and left there, exposed to Wind and Weather, to perish without Assistance or Pity. It is familiar amongst the *Mengrelians*, a People professing Christianity, to bury their Children alive without scruple. There are Places where they eat their own Children. The *Caribes* were wont to geld their Children, on purpose to fat and eat them. And *Garcilasso de la*

---

[95] Locke, *Toleration*, p. 36.

Vega tells us of a People in *Peru*, which were wont to fat and eat the Children they got on their female Captives, whom they kept as Concubines for that purpose; and when they were past Breeding the Mothers themselves were kill'd too and eaten. The Vertues, whereby the *Tououpinambos* believed they merited Paradise, were Revenge, and eating abundance of their Enemies. They have not so much as a Name for God, no Acknowledgement of any God, no Religion, no Worship. The Saints, who are canonized amongst the Turks, lead Lives, which one cannot with Modesty relate. (Essay, I, iii, p. 71)

He continues with some stories of the Turks, and then shows that some cultures reject even the narrowest rule, that parents should protect their children.

Locke's line of argument seems odd. He rightly points out several times that even if there were universal principles, it would not prove they were innate. He gives the example of the idea of fire, which might be universal but is not innate (Essay, I, iv, 9, p. 89). At the same time, Locke is not a skeptic. He believes in true and knowable principles of religion and morality. His arguments from other cultures undermine this claim just as they undermine the claim for innate ideas. In other words, cultural universals have little direct relevance to whether knowledge comes innately or from experience. Two considerations make better sense of Locke's approach. We read his arguments as engaging in a debate about innate ideas, but he initiates this debate from within another debate, about universal consent to the existence of God. In this debate, appeals to other cultures and to innate ideas both figured heavily. This context is clear from Locke's use of other cultures, but also from his lengthy criticism of the book of Lord Herbert of Cherbury, entitled *de Veritate* and published first in 1624 (Essay I, iii, 15–19, pp. 77–80). Herbert was a Deist, and his book was one of the leading expressions of the argument for natural theology based on the universal consent of diverse cultures. Herbert himself connects universal consent and innate ideas. His five principles of natural religion – God exists, God should be worshiped, the chief element of worship is virtue, vice should be repented, reward and punishment happen in the next life – are all derived from "Common Notions" that structure experience rather than deriving from experience. His arguments in each case begin with a claim that all cultures accept the given principle.[96] Spinoza presents his arguments for common notions in this same context of cultural universals, as we have seen. The second consideration directing Locke's line of argument is his concern for

[96] For example, see Herbert of Cherbury, *De Veritate*. Trans. by Meyrick H. Carré (London: Routledge/ Thoemmes Press, 1992), p. 291, where he claims that Greeks, Romans, Muslims, Jews, the Indians of the West, and the Eastern Indians all have some sovereign deity.

tolerance. Locke wants to claim that we must remain unsure enough of our views so as not to impose them on others, but he does not want to advocate complete skepticism (or complete tolerance). These two sides of his position can be in tension, and the appeal to other cultures supports the skeptical side. A good example of this connection is his discussion of innate ideas of God. That discussion begins with an appeal to other cultures, saying that there are whole nations in Africa, Brazil, and the Caribbean with no notion of God or religion. He notes that, while these peoples lack arts and sciences, even some very learned nations like Siam and China lack an idea of God (Essay, I, iv, 8, pp. 87–88).[97] His point is to discredit the existence of an innate idea of God, but, as the discussion continues, he applies this point to tolerance. Even most Europeans lack an idea of God, he says, or they hold different and conflicting ideas. They share the same *word*, but not the same *idea*. Because we have no common, innate idea of God, we must shape it from our limited experience, and thus we should be reluctant to impose our idea on others.

In spite of their differences, the views of Locke and Spinoza hold a considerable amount in common. Both associate cultural universals and innateness. These two issues are not necessarily linked, as we have seen. Spinoza could claim that only Europeans have reflected sufficiently on their innate ideas, just as much as Locke can claim that only Europeans have reflected sufficiently on their experience. Descartes sees the separation between these issues, commenting on the same book by Herbert that drew Locke's attention:

The author takes universal consent as the criterion of his truths; whereas I have no criterion for mine except the natural light. The two criteria agree in part: for since all men have the same natural light, it seems they should have the same notions; but there is also a great difference between them, because hardly anyone makes good use of that light, so that many people – perhaps all those we know – may share the same mistaken opinion. Also there are many things which can be known by the natural light, but which no one has yet reflected on. (CSMK III 139, AT II 597–98)

The second common point between Spinoza and Locke is that both use their epistemology to support tolerance of diverse views, extending that tolerance even to non-Christians, yet neither shows serious interest in other cultures. This lack of interest follows from their philosophical systems. Spinoza maintains a strict distinction between what is important and universal and what varies and is unimportant. For Spinoza, what is important is found

---

[97] Descartes faces a similar objection to his claim for an innate idea of God in the second set of objections, in which the objector claims that the Hurons lack such an idea (CSM II 89; AT VII 124).

everywhere, including right here. Those things we could learn from cultural diversity matter little. Locke could easily take a different position, since if all of our knowledge is based on experience we should be able to learn from those with radically different experiences. That he does not take this position seems largely due to an assumed superiority of European culture, but also lies in the skeptical use to which he puts other cultures. He does not examine others in order to find truth, but rather to illustrate all the foolish and bizarre things people do.

LEIBNIZ AND CULTURAL EXCHANGE

Like Spinoza and Locke, Leibniz advocates tolerance of diverse views, but, unlike them, he establishes an imperative to learn from diversity, an imperative he follows himself. On December 2, 1697, Leibniz wrote to the Jesuit Antoine Verjus that he would like more information regarding China:

> where I take such a part, because I judge that this mission is the greatest affair of our time, as much for the glory of God and the propagation of the Christian religion as for the general good of men and the growth of the arts and sciences, among us as well as among the Chinese. For this is a commerce of light, which could give to us at once their work of thousands of years and render ours to them, and to double so to speak our true wealth for one and the other. This is something greater than one thinks. (W 55)

Leibniz is the only prominent modern philosopher to take a serious interest in Europe's contact with other cultures. Within the *New Essays*, he uses information gleaned from such places as America, the Mariana Islands, Siam, and, of course, China. Within this flow of knowledge from the world outside Europe, China held a special position. Leibniz writes, "But who would have believed that there is on earth a people who, though we are in our view so very advanced in every branch of behavior, still surpass us in comprehending the precepts of civil life?" (NS 3). Leibniz takes it for granted that China holds a wealth of new information, and that through exchange Europeans could learn at once their work of thousands of years. The importance of China to Leibniz is affirmed by its place within his body of writings. As Daniel Cook and Henry Rosemont note, Leibniz probably used the word "China" more than "monad" or "preestablished harmony."[98] Leibniz mentions China as early as 1666, when he was 20 years old, in his *De Arte Combinatoria*, in which he notes that the Chinese language is

---

[98] Cook and Rosemont, *Writings on China*, p. xi.

pictographic, rather than phonetic. One of the few books Leibniz published in his lifetime, the *Novissima Sinica*, was a collection of writings on China which he edited, published, and introduced in 1697.[99] At the end of his life, in 1716, we still find Leibniz concerned with China – his most extensive essay on Chinese philosophy was written for Nicholas Rémond and left unfinished at Leibniz's death.[100] In addition to these, Leibniz wrote two other essays directly on China, both sent to Jesuit correspondents: "De cultu Confucii civili," sent to Antoine Verjus on January 1, 1700; and a brief essay sent to Bartholomaeus des Bosses on August 12, 1709.[101] Leibniz discusses China countless times throughout his correspondence, and his efforts toward exchange with China reflect his energy and the breadth of his connections. Promotion of exchange emerges as one of his primary political and diplomatic goals, working through his relationship to the Jesuits, his role as founder and leader of the Berlin Society of Sciences, and his relationship to Peter the Great.

As with Locke and Spinoza, Leibniz's approach to other cultures and tolerance follows from his broader philosophical system. His entire philosophy can be read as a justification for his view that differences should be not only tolerated but actively understood. This view of difference is expressed in his approach to China, and also in his attempts to reconcile differences in the Church, to promote the formation of scientific societies and exchange between them, and even his reading of the history of philosophy. On one level, the foundation is in the relationship between diversity and order, or similarity and difference. For Leibniz, diversity is essential to the perfection of the world, as his criterion for perfection is "the most variety with the greatest order" (PNG 10). Such diversity is never senseless because it is always ordered; in Leibniz's philosophy order and diversity are not opposed. The most perfect possible world does not compromise between order and diversity, but maximizes them. My claim will be that, for Leibniz, no ideas are simply identical across cultures, or even across individuals, but at the same time no ideas are utterly diverse, without some ground in similarity. Thus he avoids the sharp division between the universal and the relative,

---

[99] Original text in H. G. Nesselrath and H. Reinbothe, *Das Nueste über China* (Koln: Deutsche China-Gesellschaft, 1979). English translation by Donald Lach in Cook and Rosemont, *Writings on China.*

[100] "Discours sur la Théologie naturelle des Chinois." Original text in R. Loosen and F. Vonessen, *Gottfried Wilhelm Leibniz: Zwei Briefe über das binäre Zahlensystem und die chinesische Philosophie* (Stuttgart: Belser-Presse, 1968). English translation in Cook and Rosemont, *Writings on China.*

[101] For the former, original text in W 112–14. For the latter, original text in GP II, 380–84. English translations of both in Cook and Rosemont, *Writings on China.*

thereby also avoiding Spinoza's sufficiency of lone reflection and Locke's dismissive skepticism of other cultures.

This reconciliation of order and diversity is manifested in Leibniz's concept of expression. Given the role of expression, we would expect that every monad would have at least a slightly different view of the world, allowing and even necessitating differences. At the same time, each monad expresses the same thing, providing an underlying ground for understanding, interaction, and evaluation. The maximization of simplicity and variety and the model of experience as varying expressions of the same thing relate closely, as the latter applies the former. God chose to create this world in which each monad is a different expression of the same universe precisely because it is the most perfect, i.e. it has the greatest possible combination of order and diversity. Thus one universe is multiplied infinitely by its expression in diverse monads, and a simple monad is given an infinitely diverse content. The experience of every person is grounded in a shared universe and shared rationality, yet each is limited, forming a unique perspective. We learn by reflection on our own perspective, but we can also learn from the perspectives of others, and, in practice, we *must* learn from these perspectives. Cultural differences, then, *contra* Locke, are not mere varieties of bizarre practices, because each perspective is ordered as a perspective on the same thing. Yet *contra* Spinoza, even the truths of reason are expressed in particular, limited ways by each monad, and thus can benefit from cultural exchange.

CHAPTER 2

Order and diversity in Leibniz's metaphysics

ORDER, DIVERSITY, AND PLURALISM

The challenge in examining Leibniz's interest in China and cultural exchange is to show that this interest is not accidental; to show that Leibniz encourages exchange not in spite of his philosophical system but because of it. In establishing an intrinsic connection between Leibniz's practical pluralism and his philosophy as a whole, the difficulty is in how he avoids the position we have seen in Descartes and Spinoza, that, while all cultures may be roughly equal, the study of other cultures is irrelevant to the pursuit of truth, because the pursuit of truth comes through individual self-reflection. On the face of it, separating Leibniz from this position looks impossible. Leibniz is classed as a "rationalist," best known for his advocacy of innate ideas and necessary truths, and his concern with logic, meant to facilitate the use of necessary truths. This traditional approach to Leibniz, though, typified by the Russell–Couturat line of interpretation, has been consistently undermined by recent Leibniz scholars, along three lines. One line of emphasis is on Leibniz as a more pragmatic, empirical, and fallibilistic investigator of the world. A second line shifts away from Leibniz as a logician to Leibniz as motivated by practical and theological concerns, in this case his concern with cultural exchange. The third line focuses on Leibniz as a pluralistic thinker, trying to bring different parties and schools together. These three lines of interpretation are mutually supportive and I hope my work here contributes to all three. The purpose of this chapter will be to show how the importance of exchange and the limitations of perspective emerge from Leibniz's metaphysics and epistemology. The following chapters will apply this philosophical foundation to the particular case of exchange with China.

On the surface, Leibniz's conception of expression seems particularly conducive to cultural exchange. In engaging the thought of a foreign culture, one problem is balancing similarities and differences. Without similarities, we have no point of access to the thought of the other. Without differences, we have nothing to learn. The problem is that similarity and difference seem opposed. For Leibniz, however, they are not opposed, as his well-known criterion of perfection is "the most variety with the order." Leibniz's philosophy attempts to explain the world as exactly the maximum combination of similarity and difference or order and diversity that enables intercultural philosophy. This tension between similarity and difference becomes clearer when applied to cultural exchange. If we wish not just to observe but also to engage the thought of another, then we must have some way to evaluate this thought. If we focus exclusively on differences, denying more fundamental similarities, we have no method of judging this other thought, and we have no way of evaluating what is important or of use to us. This focus on differences, a form of relativism, not only prevents us from criticizing the thought of another; it also prevents us from using that thought to criticize ourselves. If, however, we take the other extreme and focus too exclusively on similarities, we again exclude the possibility of using the other thought to criticize ourselves, because we cannot even see how this thought differs. Even worse, we run the risk of misapplying our own categories, assuming they are not ours but everyone's. This focus on a universal human nature has been attacked over and over for this very problem, as it intersects the discourses of Euro-centrism, colonialism, and racism. We can see the roots of the problem in the willingness of Descartes and Spinoza to speak for all human beings without actually studying them.

In contrast, Leibniz's metaphor of monads as varying perspectives on the same thing balances similarity and difference. Leibniz writes, "Indeed, *all individual substances are different expressions of the same universe* and different expressions of the same universal cause, namely God. But the expressions vary in perfection, just as different representations or drawings of the same town from different points of view do" (C 21; AG 33). The metaphor of monads as different perspectives on the same town captures what is needed for cultural exchange. Each monad has a unique point of view, allowing differences, but each is a point of view on the same thing, allowing similarities. More specifically, we can imagine that different people see some of the same parts of the town differently, and give different descriptions, but what these descriptions have in common is the order of events. We can also imagine that, in so far as different people see different parts of the town, they see some relationships that others did not see. Finally, we can imagine that some of these relationships correspond to relationships that others saw. For example, we might see different traffic intersections, yet we would see the same relationships or patterns. Similarly, monads in distant parts of the world could make the same conclusions about bodies or minds, even though they never experienced the same bodies or minds. From our own limited perspective, we can come to some truths about the whole, but we gain the most knowledge of the whole by drawing on other perspectives. That is, we make the most progress by bringing different people together and understanding their views, as in cultural exchange.

This metaphor, though, remains indeterminate and we must more precisely determine what different perspectives have in common and how they differ. The metaphor seems to describe well our expression of the universe and the contingent, existential truths that follow from it. Regarding facts about the world, we must gather perspectives and exchange information. But the metaphor seems incomplete if taken as a model for how *intelligent* monads or minds relate. The answer to what each perspective on the city has in common is only part of the answer of what each intelligent monad has in common. We must still account for necessary truths and innate ideas, which seem free of perspective. The claim I will argue throughout this chapter is that the metaphor of perspectives on a city still applies to intelligent monads, and that the use of innate ideas and necessary truths does not diminish the need for cultural exchange. This argument is one about scientific method in the broadest sense, but before turning directly to method and epistemology, we must place minds in their ontological context, to show the order of the universe. After this order is established, we can ask the more central question, how does each monad access this order and what can one monad learn about it from another?

Leibniz's criterion of perfection includes diversity and leads directly into an appreciation for cultural variety. The threat to this appreciation is our access to universal, necessary truths, a threat also implicit in the criterion of perfection, as order. An opposition between order and diversity may intially seem misplaced. The opposite of diversity is not order but uniformity; the opposite of order is not diversity but chaos. Order requires diversity – a homogeneous mass would not properly be described as ordered. Nonetheless, order requires some uniformity. A dictionary provides an example. A dictionary appears to be ultimately diverse – it contains words for literally all kinds of things – yet it has a tight order. In each element, there is something uniform which allows all to participate in one scheme. Each of the items is a word, participating in one rather uniform alphabet, and each item participates in one ordered scheme. Given the word "China," we can determine exactly where it fits and which words surround it. The dictionary could be more diverse if it were less ordered. For example, it could be ordered by several randomly distributed schemes – some alphabetically, some by subject, some by how much they appeal to me.[1] The dictionary could be more diverse if it held words, but also pictures, sounds, and things themselves. A maximally diverse group would seem to be one in which each item was utterly disparate from the others, subsumed either under no over-arching scheme or under an infinite number of diverse schemes. We can thus see that, in so far as order requires uniformity, it opposes diversity. This connection between order and uniformity appears in Leibniz's various formulations of harmony as the maximization of order and variety: "unity in variety," "diversity compensated by identity," and variety "reduced to a unity, symmetrical, connected" (A VI I, 484–85).[2]

To maintain the importance of diversity, the challenge is to make the order of the universe inseparable from its diversity, and grasped only through its diversity. I believe this is Leibniz's position. The first question to be addressed, though, is, what is the order of the universe? The answer can be divided into two aspects. First, everything is determined by causes, or everything has a reason. Thus, everything is part of a universal causal order. Second, this universal order has an original unity in God, its creator. Thus every monad has a determining causal relation to God and to every other monad. Both levels of order coalesce in the principle of sufficient reason, that "nothing takes place without sufficient reason, that is, that nothing happens without it being possible for someone who knows enough things to give a reason sufficient to determine why it is so and not otherwise" (PNG 7; AG 210). That everything has a reason does not in itself mean that everything is in order, but the principle of sufficient reason claims that for any event there is a determinative reason "why it is so and not otherwise." Given a particular space/time context, exactly one event is possible. Since the same claim can also be made for each event in the context – as the context itself is determined by a broader context – every event is exactly situated across space and time. This order is explained by a more fundamental order in God. In "On the Ultimate Origination of Things,"

---

[1] An apt illustration of such diversity is given by Foucault's reference to a passage from Borges: "This passage quotes a 'certain Chinese encyclopaedia' in which it is written that 'animals are divided into: (a) belonging to the Emperor, (b) embalmed, (c) tame, (d) sucking pigs, (e) sirens, (f) fabulous, (g) stray dogs, (h) included in the present classification, (i) frenzied, (j) innumerable, (k) drawn with a brush, (l) et cetera, (m) having just broken the water pitcher, (n) that from a long way off look like flies.'" Michel Foucault, *The Order of Things* (New York: Vintage Books, 1970), p. xv.

[2] Cited in Donald Rutherford, *Leibniz and the Rational Order of Nature* (Cambridge: Cambridge University Press, 1995), p. 13. Rutherford defines order: "for things to exist as ordered is for them to be subsumed under a law, rule, or principle, according to which they can be understood to be at once distinct and yet related" (p. 33).

Leibniz uses the example of a copied geometry book. We could explain the existence of the present book with reference to the one before it, and the existence of that with the one before it, and so on, but even if we could accept that the chain of such causes were infinite, there would still need to be a reason why the book was the way it was. Leibniz writes, "For in eternal things, even if there is no cause, we must still understand there to be a reason" (GP VII, 302; AG 149). In the "Monadology," Leibniz emphasizes that the chain of contingent causes not only regresses infinitely into the past but involves infinite present causes, mostly insensible (M 36; AG 217). As we can conceive other possible worlds or other chains of causes, there must be some reason why this particular chain exists.

The principle of sufficient reason forces us to seek an ultimate origin outside the chain of worldly causes, leading to God. Leibniz gives several versions of this proof from the principle of sufficient reason (e.g. GP VII, 302–05; AG 149–52; cf. M 36–41, AG 217–18; T 7). One point to note in these arguments is that the interconnection of things requires that there be *one* ultimate reason for their diversity. Thus all reasons for individual things reduce to one reason, God. The first appearance of the relationship between diversity and unity, then, is between the diversity of the creation and the unity of the Creator. A more fundamental appearance of this relationship is between the unity of God and the diversity of God's ideas, a relationship reproduced in the unity of our mind and the diversity of conscious experience. Because the diverse reasons reduce to one unity, the claim that the principle of sufficient reason is true is the claim that the universe is utterly ordered. The belief that all events have a determining cause based on natural laws is not unusual or unfamiliar, but, for Leibniz, a strong analogy between human beings and God makes the order of the universe accessible. A God who creates a universe *ex nihilo* extends its order to everything that exists, while the very name of "Creator" posits something analogous to a mind, analogous to what we ourselves experience in our own creative acts. As Leibniz often writes, an effect must express its cause: "For the effect must correspond to its cause; indeed, the effect is best recognized through a knowledge of its cause" (DM 19, AG 53; see also DM 2, AG 36). In creation *ex nihilo*, the order that results from the cause extends to every aspect of the creation. Creation provides a tremendous unity and uniformity to things, in contrast, for example, with a Manichean conception of the universe. It also contrasts the traditional Chinese conception of the world, which found a fundamental order or pattern in the *dao* or *tian*, but never saw this order as having an intentional unity. Thus the Chinese never raised the problem of evil and the doctrine of creation was one of the main obstacles for Chinese conversion to Christianity.[3] Leibniz sent his binary arithmetic to China to illustrate creation from nothing.

Since the order of the universe expresses God, we can move in knowledge from one to the other, providing the entry point for positive knowledge of God and for natural theology. At the same time, the more we determine the qualities of God, the more determinate our knowledge of the order of creation becomes. Leibniz makes the following inference: because God is perfectly wise, perfectly good, and perfectly powerful, this world must be the best possible. Leibniz here argues in a circle. Because we know from experience that something exists, we know there is a perfect God, and because we know God is perfect, we know that what exists is the best possible. How we access the order of the universe and its Creator will be the main question of the following sections, but we can note already that Leibniz believes we can access not only the order of nature but also something of God's intentions. The use of final causes illustrates one application of this analogy in making sense of the order of the universe. In defending final causes, Leibniz reacts against the tide of his time with uncharacteristic harshness: "I advise those who have any feelings of piety and even feelings of true philosophy to keep away from the phrases of certain extremely pretentious minds who say that we see because it happens that we have eyes and not that eyes were made for seeing" (DM 19; AG 52–53).[4] Leibniz considers such an elimination of final causes positively dangerous for the love of God, but final causes serve more than to "elevate our mind." In the essay "On Nature Itself," Leibniz broadens the importance of final causes, saying, "final causes not only advance virtue and piety in ethics and natural theology, but also help us to find and lay bare hidden truths in physics itself" (GP IV, 506; AG 157). Leibniz gives examples of how final causes can suggest where to focus investigations, naming anatomy and optics, as well as the discovery of his own principle of conservation of force (DM 21, 22; AG 53–55). At other times, he uses final causes as additional support for his arguments. Giving his view of the omnipresence of organic life in

---

[3] For a broader discussion of this point, see Jong-Su Ahn, *Leibniz's Philosophie und die chinesische Philosophie* (Konstanz: Hartung-Gorre Verlag, 1990), p. 180.

[4] The analogy and use of final causes was attacked by many of Leibniz's contemporaries, most amusingly by Spinoza, who saw it as one of the main prejudices holding people back from the truth. See, for example, Spinoza's *Ethics*, Part I, Appendix and Descartes' "Principles of Philosophy," 28 (AT VIII, 15–16; CSM I, 202). At the same time, Nicholas Jolley points to a counter-trend of applying the claim that we are made in the image of God, claiming that Leibniz carries the analogy furthest. (Nicholas Jolley, *The Light of the Soul: Theories of Ideas in Leibniz, Malebranche, and Descartes* [Oxford: Clarendon Press, 1990], pp. 149–52.)

nature, Leibniz writes, "it is consistent with neither order nor with the beauty or reasonableness of things for there to be something living, that is, acting from within itself, in only the smallest portion of matter, when it would contribute to greater perfection for such things to be everywhere" (GP IV, 512; AG 163). Another concrete example of how we can judge God by our own ideas of perfection is Leibniz's argument that non-Christians and the unbaptized are not necessarily condemned to Hell. Damning of the innocent contradicts God's perfection.

One of the more significant ways we make use of final causes is in morality. For Leibniz, morality requires that we act as we think God wants. Our moral duty is to regard the past with acquiescence to God's will and the conviction that what has happened is ultimately for the best. He continues:

Toward the future, however, he [the moral person] struggles with the highest enthusiasm to obey God's mandates, either expressed or presumed from the public consideration of the divine glory and benevolence. And when in doubt he does that which is more prudent, more probable, and more conducible; just as a lively and industrious man, full of enthusiasm, acts to make his things good, if a great prince has destined him to negotiate with another. (A VI, 4, 2379; cf. GP II, 136; L 360)

Our relationship to what God wants is analogous to our relationship to what our boss wants, when she goes on vacation and leaves us in charge. This process may sound too "religious" for Leibniz, but it is mediated by the criterion of perfection, which is independent of God's will. To use final causes is to approach nature and human society with the assumption that whatever happens happens in the most perfect possible way and that our role is to increase the world's perfection, maximizing harmony and diversity.[5] The use of final causes requires that we access the fundamental order of the universe.

In conclusion, the claim that the universe is utterly ordered, that everything has a place and a reason, is the claim that the principle of sufficient reason is true. The sufficient reason and the entire source of order is God. If we want to know the details of this order, how we access it, and how our access compares to that of others, we must turn next to Leibniz's conception of God. We can, however, already make two preliminary conclusions

---

[5] Not to labor the point, but the pressing need for a theodicy depends entirely on the belief that God must be justified to *human* ideas of justice. In an early theodicy directed more specifically at Hobbes, cited by Patrick Riley, Leibniz states his goal – "to make it clear that we have good and true notions of these attributes of God, or – what is the same thing – that we have reason to attribute justice and goodness to him, which would be groundless if those words signified nothing when one applies them to God" (Grua II, 495; Patrick Riley, *Leibniz' Universal Jurisprudence*, Cambridge, MA: Harvard University Press, 1996, p. 96).

regarding cultural exchange. First, we are all part of the same order and the same plan. In itself, this provides little detail, as my pen and your shoes are also part of this same order, and we have little in common with them. We can add, though, that, as we come to know this order, we come closer together. Our views are not ultimately irreconcilable. The second conclusion is that the differences between our views are not disorders or flaws; there must be a sufficient reason for these differences, and it must be an indispensable part of the best possible world that, at least at this time, we have cultural differences and even conflicts. These two conclusions, regardless of the actual structure that enables comparative philosophy, set the task in a positive context. I believe this basic context makes Leibniz so enthusiastic about cultural exchange.

THE ORDER OF GOD

The need for a sufficient reason for the order of the universe leads to the order implicit in God. This shift is required by Leibniz's conception of a sufficient reason and his conception of God. To say that the world has the order it has because God willed it that way is not to give a sufficient reason. It only raises the question, why did God will it this way? Leibniz's ability to provide an ultimate sufficient reason hinges on his arrangement of the three traditional aspects of God – will, understanding, and power. Leibniz expresses these, "God has *power*, which is the source of everything, *knowledge*, which contains the diversity of ideas, and finally *will*, which brings about changes or products in accordance with the principle of the best" (M 48; AG 219). In Leibniz's arrangement, understanding is the foundation, God wills according to his understanding, and God acts according to his will. The crucial distinction is between understanding and will. In addressing the empirical evidence which Manicheans put forth as demanding the existence of two gods, one good and one evil, Leibniz answers that in a sense there are two principles, but they are not *ultimately* two. Rather, the two principles are both God: one his understanding; one his will (T 149). Similarly, the distinction between matter as the source of evil and God as the source of good is collapsed into God, with understanding taking the place of matter (T 335, 380).

Leibniz puts forth a many-pronged argument for this precedence of the understanding. Only his account, he says, can reconcile the seeming imperfections we experience with the fact that God must create the best possible world. Only his account gives sufficient foundation to eternal truths. Leibniz adds that, if God creates the criterion of goodness, it makes no sense to praise him, since he would be equally good no matter what he did. The heart of Leibniz's argument, however, is his conception of will. He writes, "The will consists in the inclination to do something in proportion to the good it contains" (T 22; H 136). Most errors about the will come from misconceiving the will as a faculty for choosing inclinations, when the will is really itself an inclination. Locke makes the same point particularly well when he defines the will as the power of preferring and liberty as the power of acting on a preference, concluding: "*Liberty is not an* Idea *belonging to Volition*, or preferring; but to the Person having the Power of doing, or forbearing to do, according as the Mind shall chuse or direct" (Essay II, xxi, 10; 238). More specifically, Leibniz argues against a conception of will as emerging from indifference. His argument comes down to the principle of sufficient reason, that there must be "reason sufficient to determine why it is so and not otherwise" (PNG 7; AG 210). The will cannot incline one way or another without a reason to determine it. In addressing the problem of Buridan's Ass, he admits that if all the inclinations were equally divided for and against an action – an impossible situation – the ass could not act. He applies this story to God's choice for creation: if two worlds were equally most perfect, God could not choose between them, and could create nothing at all. Leibniz's conception of a "free" will directly opposes indifference: "to be morally necessitated by wisdom, to be obliged by the consideration of good, is to be free" (T 237). The result of Leibniz's conception of the will is that it cannot precede the understanding. To will is to be inclined toward the best, for God, or toward what seems the best, for us. Without something existing as the best, there simply can be no will. The attempt to put will before understanding or to make them simultaneous, according to Leibniz, is based on a misunderstanding of the will.

Thus the ground for the order of God and of the universe is not God's will but God's understanding, which establishes a realm of necessary relations. God has no choice about what is contained in his understanding. In a letter to Magnus Wedderkopf, Leibniz writes:

What, therefore, is the ultimate reason for the divine will? The divine intellect . . . What then is the reason for the divine intellect? The harmony of things. What is the reason for the harmony of things? Nothing. For example, no reason can be given for the ratio of 2 to 4 being the same as that of 4 to 8, not even in the divine will. This depends on the essence itself, or the idea of things. For the essences of things are numbers, as it were, and contain the possibility of beings which God does not make as he does existence, since these possibilities or ideas of things coincide rather in God himself. (A II, i, 117; L 146)

This necessity imposed by God's intellect serves Leibniz both as an explanation of evil and as a basis for necessary truths. What does this realm of God's understanding entail? Possibilities. All possibilities in all possible combinations are utterly determinate in God's understanding. God does not have a vague concept of me in which I could do one thing or another. Rather, God has an idea of the me who is actually here, but also a different idea of someone much like me, but having chosen to wear different shoes (assuming that were possible). There are thus an infinite number of Franklins, each slightly different. This determinateness is crucial to Leibniz's explanation of why some people receive grace while others do not. If Judas did not sin, he would not be Judas. The only question is, why did God choose to create this particular Judas? (DM 30; AG 61). The content of God's understanding is determinate and incomprehensibly immense. Everything not internally contradictory is possible and thus exists in the mind of God. Since everything not in contradiction with itself exists in the mind of God, God has many ideas whose opposites also exist in his mind. These are things that could be or could not be. The fact that all possibilities cannot be actualized together leads to a class of necessary truths implied by ideas themselves or by rules of compossibility. For example, given the definition of a substance, a substance can begin and end only by miracle, cannot have parts, and cannot interact with other substances. These truths are necessary because they are implied in the very concept of substance, and for their opposite to be true would be a contradiction. Such truths can be limited in range, but they are necessary. It is impossible for something to be a substance and to be divisible, and this truth applies with necessity to every possible world, yet some possible worlds might not contain substances at all, in which case this truth would not apply. In other words, it would not be impossible for something like a substance to be divisible. It just would not be a substance; it would be an aggregate. It is impossible for something to be divisible *and* to be a substance. In this way, the rules of compossibility open a realm of necessary truths reducible to identities.

The order of God's understanding serves several functions for Leibniz. Because its order is necessary, God's understanding can be the ultimate sufficient reason without itself needing a reason. In addition, God's understanding grounds the necessary truths minds rely on. Leibniz even uses the existence of necessary truths as proof for the existence of God. After showing that there must be necessary truths, he writes, "But existing things cannot derive from anything but existing things, as I already noted above. So it is necessary that eternal truths have their existence in a certain absolute or metaphysically necessary subject, that is, in God, through whom those things which would otherwise be imaginary are realized" (GP VII,

305; AG 152; see also M 43; AG 218). Besides responding to the claim that necessary truths are ultimately arbitrary, Leibniz grapples with their onto-logical status. If truths are necessary, they cannot be mere imaginings or rules abstracted from experience but must have some ontological status. But how can necessary truths exist outside of actually being thought by us? The answer is that they exist as actually thought by God. It is in this sense that without God there would be no eternal truths, as well as no possibilities, even though these truths do not depend on God's will (see CD 9; or T 181).[6]

The necessity of God's understanding also grounds the existence of evil. Leibniz suggests this connection when he says that God's understanding and will take the place of the Manichean principles of good and evil. The essence of creatures is necessarily limited metaphysically, and this limita-tion is manifested in intelligent beings partly as moral evil. Where does this necessary imperfection come from, since it imposes even on God? Leibniz writes, "The necessity, that is to say, the essential nature of things, would be the object of the understanding, in so far as the object consists in eternal truths. But this object is internal and is found in the divine understand-ing. . . . It is *the region of eternal truths* which takes the place of matter" (T 20). He continues, "And as this immense region of truths contains all possibilities, it is necessary that there are an infinity of possible worlds, that evil enters into many of them, and that even the best of all contains some. It is this which determines God to permit evil" (T 21). Everything that is not in itself contradictory – everything that is possible – exists in the un-derstanding of God. Evil is not internally contradictory, therefore it exists in the understanding of God. Ultimately, evil does not exist in the mind of God, as it is a privation and nothing. In context, Leibniz is speaking of what appears evil to us, in his terms, physical and moral evil. If we were to rephrase his claim more carefully, we could say that every possible universe contains limitation, and in some of these universes, including this most perfect one, these limitations manifest themselves as physical or moral evil. The existence of evil goes back to the rules of compossibility, over which God has no choice. The limits of compossibility mean not all possible things can exist together, requiring a choice by God, with the consequence that

---

[6] This status of eternal truths complicates the question of Leibniz's nominalism. Benson Mates avoids the full weight of the existence of abstract entities by claiming that ideas are in God only as dispositions or capacities. Thus the objects of geometry only *potentially* exist in the mind of God. I am claiming rather that ideas at all times exist in the mind of God, as *actively* understood. In this sense, the abstract objects of geometry, for example, have a permanent existence (Benson Mates, *The Philosophy of Leibniz: Metaphysics and Language* [New York: Oxford University Press, 1986], pp. 245–46).

this is not the only possible world but the best of many possible worlds.[7] They also allow Leibniz to claim that this existing world is the best *possible* world, excluding other worlds which an imaginative critic might suggest, as impossibly compatible with other things that are good and existing. The goods of this world cannot be separated from its evils. That is just the way things are, necessarily.

A few remarks should be made about the divine understanding. The first difficulty is in conceiving an understanding that understands without an external object. Nonetheless, there is no free-floating realm of ideas to which God's understanding relates. We must take seriously Leibniz's argument that the existence of necessary truths proves God's existence, excluding the possibility that these truths have a basis outside God. We could say that, just as God has an idea of the things he will create before he has created them, he has ideas of things that he will never create and thus do not exist, never will exist, and are only things in a peculiar sense. The second question that follows from this is the relationship between God's understanding and the ideas of possible things. This question is important, as Leibniz says that intelligent monads express God's understanding. We can look at some of Leibniz's statements in the *Theodicy*. In section 191, Leibniz writes, "This so-called *fatum*, which binds even the Divinity, is nothing but God's own nature, his own understanding [*la propre nature de Dieu, son proper entendement*]" (T 191; H 246–47). Later, he writes that God's will does not produce necessary truths, "for they are in the ideal region of the possibles [*dans la région idéale des possibles*], that is, in the divine understanding [*dans l'entendement divin*]" (T 335; H 327). In the appendix, "Causa Dei," he equates "in a state of pure possibility [*in statu purae possibilitatis*]," "in the Region of Eternal Truths [*in Regione Veritatum aeternarum*]," and "ideas held in the Divine Intellect [*ideis Divino intellectui observantibus*]" as if they are synonymous (CD 69). These statements are somewhat ambiguous, but they suggest that the divine understanding is not a faculty that does something with the ideas of possibilities, but is rather the totality of these ideas. This interpretation is supported by the lack of alternatives. As preceding the will and thus preceding power, understanding also precedes action. The understanding seems then to be simply a content, the sum mental existence of all that is possible.

In connection to cultural diversity, we can already see that there are universal truths that apply across cultures, based on God's understanding. The laws of geometry, what is entailed in certain concepts like "substance,"

7 Cf. *Ethics*, 2P16.

and even rules of virtue, are universally true, so that all people from all cultures can be held to this same core of rules. The next question is, what access do we have to these rules? We will examine this question as we examine what it means to "express" these truths, but Leibniz thinks we have at least some access to them, shown by the fact that we can prove God exists *because* we know there are necessary truths. God's understanding orders all possible worlds, and this order determines the order in which we live. That is, given that a monad's identity binds it to one particular world and that each possible world exists complete in God's understanding, the entire order of this world is contained in God before creation. That is why the question – why am I the way I am? – is answered by God's understanding, not God's will. Nonetheless, our world differs from all others because it is most perfect. The order in which we live, then, can be recognized more determinately in relation to God's will. Rules of necessity structure the order of every possible world, but our world is also structured by rules of perfection. A full account of the order of this particular world thus requires a discussion of God's will and the principle of perfection.

The criterion of perfection, to which God's will is drawn, is implicit in the necessities of God's understanding. In the *Theodicy*, Leibniz uses the example of geometry to describe this inherent fitness. If God decreed to make a sphere, but had no reason to make it a particular size, there would be no sufficient reason to determine his will. If, however, God decreed to create a line connecting a point to another line, he would be determined by "the nature of the thing" (T 196; H 249) to create a perpendicular line. Why? As we saw in the letter to Magnus Wedderkopf, there is no reason because it could not be otherwise – "What then is the reason for the divine intellect? The harmony of things. What the reason for the harmony of things? Nothing" (A II, i, 117; L 146). Leibniz formulates the criterion of perfection in two ways, which ultimately reduce to one.[8] The first is efficiency (M 58; AG 220; T 204; H 255; DM 6; AG 39). The most perfect is the greatest effect with the slightest cost. On one side is an ideal of order, simplicity, and uniformity. On the other is an ideal of variety, productivity, and phenomenal richness. Leibniz supports this criterion by analogy with criteria we generally accept: one who acts perfectly is like a geometer, who can find the best construction for a problem; like an architect, who makes the best possible use of his resources; like a householder, who uses

---

[8] In my account of perfection, I mostly agree with Rutherford, who gives a more detailed discussion, extending it to the maximization of happiness and justice (Rutherford, *Rational Order*, chs. 1–3). Where I perhaps disagree is on the primacy of what is "most pleasing to reason" in determining the best possible world. For clarification of this point, see n. 29 of this chapter.

his resources so that all is productive; like a machinist, who acts in the least difficult way; like an author, who includes the greatest number of truths in the smallest volume (DM 5; AG 38–39).[9] Within this list, we can make a distinction between efficiency as a means of maximizing production and efficiency as an aesthetic principle. Here, Leibniz sides with the aesthetic criterion regarding creation:

> It is true that nothing costs God anything – even less than it costs a philosopher to build the fabric of his imaginary world out of hypotheses – since God has only to make decrees in order that a real world come into being. But in matters of wisdom, decrees or hypotheses take the place of expenditures to the extent that they are more independent of one another, because reason requires that we avoid multiplying hypotheses or principles, in somewhat the same way that the simplest system is always preferred in astronomy. (DM 5; AG 39)

Here, according to the nature of things in God's understanding, simplicity and efficiency are simply good. The second formulation of perfection is the maximization of being, or the creation of as much as possible. Leibniz supports this formulation in "On the Ultimate Origination of Things." He begins, "we must first acknowledge that since something rather than nothing exists, there is a certain urge [*exigentiam*] for existence or (so to speak) a straining [*praetensionem*] toward existence in possible things or in possibility or essence itself; in a word, essence in and of itself strives [*tendere*] for existence" (GP VII, 303; AG 150). This urge for existence has an affinity with Spinoza's conception of being and *conatus*, as well as Leibniz's own view of the connection between a monad's being and its force. Leibniz supports the connection between being and perfection from the fact that things actually exist. It would not be contradictory, and thus impossible, for there to be nothing, so there must be some reason why things exist. Whatever the specifics of this reason, it must be better to exist than not to exist. Thus the maximization of *perfection* becomes the maximization of *existence*; the world God creates "is the one through which the most essence or possibility is brought into existence" (GP VII, 303; AG 150).

How do we get from the maximization of being to the need for the simplest means? In other words, how do we get from the greatest variety to an all-pervasive order? If means are scarce, then the connection follows. If we make use of a limited capacity, we must use it as efficiently as possible,

---

[9] Rescher distinguished three basic versions of the analogy. The first is from art, particularly the mix of order and variety in music and architecture. The second is from statecraft, where the mix is between lawfulness or order, and freedom. The third is from science, where a simple hypothesis explains a variety of phenomena (Nicholas Rescher, *G. W. Leibniz's Monadology: An Edition for Students* [Pittsburgh: University of Pittsburgh Press, 1991], p. 207).

and this involves order. We can fit more in a box when it is organized and each thing is accommodated to every other, than when we simply throw them in, as illustrated by anyone packing in a rush. Leibniz uses a similar example, speaking of games in which a board must be filled as solidly as possible, which can only be done by following a certain order (GP VII, 303–04; AG 150–51). In the "Ultimate Origination . . ." the need to actualize as much as possible moves directly to the need in practical affairs to make best use of resources. In the case of God, "time, place, or in a word, the receptivity or capacity of the world can be taken for the cost" (GP VII, 303; AG 150). He explains further, "there would be as much as there possibly can be, given the capacity of time and space (that is, the capacity of the order of possible existence)" (GP VII, 304; AG 151). In a similar argument in the "Principles of Nature and Grace . . . ," Leibniz says that God will create the most beings "that the universe can admit" (PNG 10; AG 210). Contrary to the statement in the "Discourse on Metaphysics" that "nothing costs God anything" (DM 5; AG 210), these statements suggest that things do "cost" God. God cannot simply do anything; he must at least follow the necessities of divine understanding, including rules of compossibilty. Because all things are not compossible, there is something like a capacity of the world or of possible existences.[10]

As Voltaire nicely illustrates, the problem with the claim that this world is the best possible is that we experience bad things. In explaining these experiences, Leibniz fills in more details about the criterion of perfection. The positive tactic Leibniz uses to explain the perfection of the world we experience is the need for variety in the most perfect possible world. Maximization of being is taken as the maximization of varieties of beings. In speaking of what brings us pleasure, he writes, "Pleasure does not derive from uniformity, for uniformity brings forth disgust and makes us dull, not happy: this very principle is a law of delight" (GP VII, 307; AG 153). In the *Theodicy*, Leibniz makes fun of those who demand that each thing be perfect, and thus the same: "To multiply one and the same things only would be superfluity, and poverty too. To have a thousand well-bound Vergils in one's library, always to sing the airs from the opera of Cadmus and Hermione, to break all the china in order only to have cups of gold, to

---

[10] Rutherford makes the claim that any world must have a spatial-temporal order, so the capacity of any world is limited by space and time. God's task in creating the world is then to determine the best way to fill time and space, which is to maximize order. We could also say that the order of succession and of coexistence limit what can be created. This limitation is a manifestation of the basic need to order all things so as to avoid conflict and realize the maximum possibilities and at least appears to us in the form of time and space (cf. Rutherford, *Rational Order*, pp. 189–90).

have only diamond buttons, to eat nothing but partridges, to drink only Hungarian or Shiraz wine – would one call that reason?" (T 124; H 198). An argument underlies these examples. Given the identity of indiscernibles, no two things can be exactly alike. God is perfect, and therefore anything else created must differ from God and therefore be less perfect. In the same way, creatures only differ from one another in degrees of perfection. If the best possible world has the most existing things, then it will also have the greatest variety of degrees of imperfection.[11] Thus inequalities in perfection are not disorders – no one accuses God for not making all ants peacocks (T 246). Leibniz's more common tactic defends the perfection of the world with skepticism about experience, emphasizing the limits of our perspective. Leibniz writes, "But we cannot see nature's order, because we don't occupy the right point of view, just as a perspectival painting can best be seen from some positions, but does not show itself properly if seen from the side."[12] Perfection lies in the whole that we never see. Emphasizing skepticism of experience raises various tensions for Leibniz, as it seems that the less we are able to judge the goodness of the world, the less we are able to employ final causes.

THE CREATION

The single order that proceeds from God thus has two sources. The first source of order comes from the necessity of God's understanding, applies to all worlds, and allows us to use necessary and universal truths. The second source follows from the goodness of God's will and the principle of perfection. Because this is the best possible world, we can to some degree use final causes and we can expect ultimate justice. Before addressing how monads access this dual order, it is necessary briefly to sketch the structure of the world God chooses to create, so as to establish the environment in which monads seek to learn from other cultures. Anything that exists must either be a true unity or be reducible to a true unity, that is, a simple substance. Leibniz takes this claim as a necessary part of the order imposed on any possible world by God's understanding. Since something does in fact exist (a fact that depends on God's will), there must be simple substances, which must be true unities and must found the composites we experience. As simple substances, monads can have no parts (M 1; AG 213). They cannot be extended, for everything extended in space is divisible (M 3; AG 213). Monads also cannot interact, for they have no parts that could

---

[11] Cf. Rutherford, *Rational Order*, pp. 25–26.
[12] Quoted in Rescher, *Leibniz's Monadology*, p. 202; cf. T 128; H 201.

be given to another monad, nor do they have doors or windows through which they can take parts into themselves (M 7; AG 213–14). Consequently, anything that happens or will happen to a monad must already be contained within it. Leibniz claims that each monad contains the entire universe, past, present, and future. Lacking interaction, monads can begin and end only supernaturally, by a direct act of God (M 6; AG 213). This indestructibility contrasts aggregates, which are made and unmade by the arrangement of their parts. As the real constituents of the universe, simple substances ground all experience. Since we experience change, there must be a principle of change within these monads. At times, Leibniz speaks as if this force or change were the most fundamental aspect of the monad. In "The Principles of Nature and Grace . . ." Leibniz begins by defining a substance as "a being capable of action" (PNG 1; AG 207), and in the essay "On Nature Itself" he writes, "the very substance of things consists in a force for acting and being acted upon" (GP IV, 508; AG 159). The experience of change also requires some multiplicity of qualities. Monads thus must be both simple and qualitatively complex. This requirement seems difficult, but Leibniz takes a readily available model – consciousness. Leibniz writes – "We ourselves experience a multitude in a simple substance when we find that the least thought we ourselves apperceive involves variety in its object" (M 16; AG 215). Any particular apperception already involves a multiplicity and, in a broader sense, consciousness itself is simple, forming a unity out of multiplicity. On this model, Leibniz says that all simple substances consist of perceptions and the tendency of these perceptions to change, which he calls appetite (M 15; AG 215). As characterized by perception and force or action, every substance in a sense lives. The ontology of monads is very simple – monads are only perception and the tendency of these perceptions to change or unfold. A monad is thus not a thing that has perceptions – it is a unity of perceptions; it is consciousness. I emphasize this point because it means that everything in a monad, including reason and innate ideas, must be either perception or appetite. Leibniz uses "perception" in a broad sense, and in distinction to apperception or conscious awareness (M 14; AG 214–15). Even the monads that make up a stone have perception, but this perception is utterly confused and does not reach consciousness. In animals, this perception is conscious and accompanied by memory, and in rational beings, it is self-conscious and accompanied by reason (M 25, 29; AG 216–17).[13] Leibniz designates the latter monads as minds.

---

[13] For a subtle account of the details and ambiguities of the distinction between animals and rational beings, see Mark Kulstad, *Leibniz on Apperception, Consciousness, and Reflection* (München: Philosophia Verlag, 1991).

The fact that monads do not interact suggests an immediate problem – how can the same Leibniz who considers monads "windowless" also privilege cultural exchange? The short answer is that as the entire universe is contained in each monad, other cultures must be there as well. To make sense of what this containment means, the transposition of the universe into the monad can be seen as a kind of phenomenological reduction, much like that established through Descartes' method of doubt. All problems and distinctions remain, but now as phenomena of monadic consciousness, cut off from judgments about ontological status. Everything we now think of as out in the world becomes part of the monad. The monad does not need windows – everything is already on the inside. This reduction explains why Leibniz so often continues to talk as a Copernican speaks of the rising sun. For example, all that we usually discuss as causality remains, but as a phenomenon within monads, just as the distinction between knowledge from experience and knowledge from reflection remains, as a phenomenon within monads. Finally, all that we would characterize as cultural exchange remains, but as a phenomenon within monads. To make this reduction plausible on Leibniz's terms or our own terms is too difficult in this context, and it should suffice to note that I will follow Leibniz's lead in speaking of cultural exchange as a Copernican speaks of the rising sun. Nonetheless, one point should be emphasized. Leibniz concurs with Spinoza in claiming that substances cannot interact and that if "things" interact they must be modes of one substance rather than separate substances. For Spinoza, this claim means there can be only one substance. For Leibniz, it means that the entire universe must exist within each substance. Leibniz's point in saying that monads are windowless is not to exclude contact with others but to show that we do not interact with others as separate things reaching in and out of windows. We are already implicated in a world with others and my identity as a substance cannot exclude any of the world I interact with.

It could be that other cultures exist only as modes of my monad. I can never get outside of myself in order to know what exists. Leibniz himself writes, with reference to Saint Theresa, that it could be only he and God exist (DM 32; AG 63–64). A universe of one monad or even of several isolated, unrelated monads would be possible, but not most perfect.[14] Leibniz coordinating substances through preestablished harmony: "That is, we must say that God originally created the soul (and any other real unity) in such a way that everything must arise for it from its own depths

---

[14] Rescher rightly points out that, while substances must necessarily be monads, monads do not necessarily have to relate to one another (Rescher, *Leibniz's Monadology*, p. 200).

[*fonds*], through a perfect *spontaneity* relative to itself, and yet with a perfect *conformity* relative to external things" (GP IV, 484; AG 143; see also M 78; AG 223). Preestablished harmony depends directly on two factors. The first is that each simple substance contains and unfolds everything that will ever happen to it. The second is that this internal development coordinates with all others. Leibniz again uses the model of conscious perception. Each monad is an expression of the same whole, and is thus coordinated with others, just as several people viewing a city from slightly different perspectives have coordinated views of it (M 57–58; AG 220). God does not simply order every single thing to every other, which would violate the efficiency his perfection implies. Every monad is coordinated with every other because each monad is a variation of the same universe (M 78; AG 223). This provides a simple means of creating great diversity (M 58; AG 220). Preestablished harmony means that people from other cultures are not merely modes of my unfolding monad; they exist as monads in a universe full of monads, each of which expresses that entire universe.

Beyond the problem of the status of cultural others, the question of what it means for a monad to have a culture remains. We usually consider cultural differences to arise because members of certain groups have more interaction with each other than with other groups. This cannot be the case for Leibniz, since the same universe is contained in every monad, and monads interact no more with their "neighbors" than with any others. To account for culture we must address perspective and embodiment. Although each monad expresses the same universe, monads differ because each contains that universe in a different way, from a different perspective. Perspective is usually taken as limitation in what each monad experiences or "sees," but it must also include how each mind makes sense of those experiences, so that for a mind to have a perspective is also to have culture. To understand perspective and embodiment, we must first note that because of preestablished harmony, monads are related in spite of their non-interaction. Leibniz writes, "But in simple substances the influence of one monad over another can only be ideal, and can only produce its effect through God's intervention, when in the ideas of God a monad rightly demands that God take it into account in regulating the others" (M 51; AG 219). Because what unfolds in this monad coordinates with what unfolds in all the others, the condition of any given monad is determined by all others. Given rules of compossibility, it may be the case that an increase in my perfection requires a decrease in the perfection of another monad, and vice versa. These relations allow Leibniz to talk about causality. Leibniz uses several sets of terms, but his account of causality depends ultimately on how the perfection of two monads compare regarding a particular event (cf. M 49–52; AG 219). A thing is said to act on another in so far as it is more perfect, which is to say that God adjusts the other monad to it, which is to say that the reason for the event is more clearly represented in the active monad. When someone's perfection requires a decrease in my perfection, that unfolds in my monad as an action by the other upon me. This ordering becomes extremely complex, as I am simultaneously acting and acted upon at all times. Simplicity or order is provided to this complex network of relations by the organization of the infinity of monads into systems of bodies and composite substances. The status of bodies is complicated by Leibniz's account of space, but at the very least we can say that a body is a hierarchy of monads, in which the lower levels are ordered to the higher levels. The mind is the most perfect monad in human beings and thus God generally orders the actions of the rest to be accommodated to it. I experience this relationship as control over my body.

This first level of bodily organization underlies a monad's ordered relationship to the universe and its perspective because the mind relates to the rest of the universe according to the body. Thus, although each created monad represents the whole universe, it more distinctly represents the body, which is particularly affected by it. And, just as this body expresses the whole universe through the interconnection of all matter, the soul represents the whole universe by representing this body (M 62; AG 221). The basic structure of this relationship depends on the fact that the body is related to the whole universe and is modified by events in every other part of the universe, though its relationship to these parts is not of the same strength or distinctness. The body is more directly or strongly impacted by bodies "closer" to it (M 61; AG 221). This relationship is best represented metaphorically by a spatial continuum – the further events are from the body, the less the body senses them.[15] The other factor conditioning this relationship is that, even though the body is infinitely connected to the universe, the mind cannot clearly apperceive an infinity of perceptions at once. The graduated presence of the whole universe in the body is condensed or blurred in the apperception of the mind according to hierarchies depending on the body. Distant perceptions fade into confusion. Leibniz's well-known example is the roar of the sea. The motion of every single wave affects and modifies the body, and thus the body perceives every wave, but these sounds are so confused that all we consciously recognize is the roar

---

[15] Given Leibniz's account of space, however, the causality here may be reversed. Our perceptions are not of differing degrees of clarity centering around the body because of the body's position in space; rather, space is a phenomenon representing this relationship of the body to the rest of the universe.

of the sea. What appears distinctly in our experience depends on both the position and the structure of our body, so that some kinds of bodies, namely those with sense organs, concentrate perceptions to make certain aspects of experience more distinct (M 25; AG 216). Our own unique view depends on what in particular comes out of our vague awareness and into our conscious attention, or what moves from perception to apperception. In conclusion, the organization of our mind and other monads into a body organizes the relationship of our mind to the rest of the universe. As created minds always have bodies or always dominate hierarchies of other monads, our relationship to the universe is always through embodiment (M 72; AG 222). This embodiment of every perspective is central to Leibniz's account of cultural exchange, as our perspectival experience of the universe limits and particularizes our innate ideas. Embodiment creates differences between monads, requiring exchange, but it also founds the commonality of a culture. The embodiment of a monad's perspective means that, even without interaction, each monad reflects the monads nearest to it more clearly and holds a similar perspective on the rest of the world. Thus a group of monads "near" each other reflects the universe in more similar ways, generating similarities within cultures and differences between cultures.

TWO TRUTHS — ONE CONSCIOUSNESS

God's understanding, will, and power come together to create an ordered and diverse world, organized by necessity, perfection, and space and time. As embodied, every monad holds a determinate place in that order. The presence of order, however, means little without considering our access to this order. The metaphor of monads as diverse perspectives on a town has already been raised, along with the question, what is common to each perspective and what varies. The metaphor describes well our access to created things. Each monad is "spatially" located in an infinite field of monads. The action of any monad affects every other monad, but "closer" monads are affected more intensely, giving us a spatially oriented perspective. But this metaphor seems misleading as a metaphor for intelligent monads or minds. The explanation of monads as different perspectives on the same thing captures our access to the existential realm, but where is our access to necessary truths? This question is primarily one of scientific method in the broadest sense, yet it must be approached from its roots in Leibniz's ontology. Two distinct kinds of things can be distinguished in Leibniz's ontology. The first are the contents of God's understanding. In this realm are found the ideas not only of all existing things but also of all possible things, and thus also all rules of possibility and necessity. The second ontological realm is that of existing, created things. These two ontological realms have a complex relationship. God's understanding contains ideas of things that do not and never will exist, as incompatible with the best possible world. It also contains claims that are universal, true of every particular experience and any possible experience. In contrast, the created world is contingent, entirely actual, and always particular. Leibniz's distinctive account of knowledge can be traced to the intersection of his ontology based on two distinct realms of being with his psychology based on the simplicity of monadic consciousness. The position of relations and general ideas in this ontological scheme should be noted, as Leibniz's distinction of two ontological realms allows him to give a particular account of their existence. Leibniz follows a nominalist position in denying that general ideas or relations exist in the stronger sense of existing, but they have real ontological status in the mind of God. Thus Leibniz writes, "The reality of relations is dependent on mind, as is that of truths; but they do not depend on the human mind, as there is a supreme intelligence which determines all of them from all time" (NE II, 30, § 4; I RB 265). If relations and general ideas are grounded in the mind of God, then they cannot be arbitrary, nor simply grounded in words, nor a result of our limited capacity to perceive and keep track of individuals (NE III, 3, § 12; RB 292). This status of relations and general ideas is crucial because the realm of created things for Leibniz is minimal. There are only simple substances. Much of what we experience consists in well-grounded phenomena. The most visible consequence of Leibniz's account of relations, then, is that relations are not arbitrary. A second consequence is that human thought, depending on general ideas, has constant recourse to the realm of ideas, and thus to God.

God's understanding and this particular world are two discreet orders in which monads come to knowledge. Through God, though, these two realms relate. God's understanding contains the ideas of all possible things, which include the ideas of all existing things as a subset. Existing things thus have a dual existence: as ideas in God's understanding and as existing things. Moreover, as the rules of possibility and the criterion of goodness are included in the ideal realm, the choice of this particular world for creation is included in the ideal realm itself. The existential realm can be exactly deduced from the ideal realm, which is only to say that God knows what to create by considering his understanding alone. For this reason, "all contingent propositions have reasons to be one way rather than another or else (what comes to the same thing) that they have *a priori* proofs of their truth which render them certain and which show that the connection between subject and predicate of these propositions has its basis in the natures of both" (DM 13; AG 46). We can apprehend contingent truths "either by experience, that is, *a posteriori*, or by reason and, that is, by considerations of the fitness of things which have caused their choice" (PD 2; H 74). The distinction between necessary and contingent truths, consequently, is not the same as the distinction between truths based on God's understanding and those based on the creation, because all truths are based on God's understanding. Rather, the distinction between necessary and contingent truths is, on one side, between truths whose opposites are contradictory and truths whose opposites are possible (but not compossible with the world God chooses to create), and, on the other side, between truths which are capable of finite analysis and those which require infinite analysis (DM 13; AG 44–46; M 31–33, 36; AG 217). These distinctions are the same because truths whose opposites are contradictory are capable of finite analysis, ultimately yielding an identity or contradiction, while those whose opposite is possible and whose truth is based on God's choice of the best possible world require a consideration not only of the totality of the infinite existing world but even of the infinite number of infinite alternatives.[16] The result is that existential truths have a dual existence and we can consider them from either realm.

As the creation is a product of God's understanding, we can reciprocally learn about God's understanding from considering the existing realm, most importantly by establishing possibility, but the relationship between the ideal and the existential realms is not reciprocal. The existential realm follows with certainty – although not with necessity – from the ideal. Facts about the ideal realm, in contrast, can only be established with probability from the existential realm. Necessary truths can never be established by induction from existing things: "however many instances confirm a general truth, they do not suffice to establish its universal necessity; for it does not follow that what has happened will always happen in the same way" (RB 49). Leibniz gives the example of the daily rising of the sun, noting there may be a time when the sun no longer exists (RB 49–50), and the example of the King of Siam, who did not believe that water could have the form of ice, since no one in his kingdom had ever seen ice (NE IV, 9, § 1; RB 433–34). Conclusions from experience are always provisional – we never know if we are in the position of the King of Siam.

---

[16] Cf. Rescher, *Leibniz's Monadology*, p. 133.

Leibniz's method and the relationship between necessary truths and embodiment is further complicated by the ontology of a monad. Preestablished harmony and the fact that nothing new ever enters a monad demand that the objects of our knowledge have a *triple* existence. Things exist in God's understanding along with the ideas of other possible things; they exist in themselves as created by God; and they exist within each mind. The entire universe is contained in each monad in the form of perception. In the same way, necessary truths must not only have a real existence in the understanding of God but also some existence within each monad. Leibniz makes this requirement clear in addressing Malebranche. Even if we do perceive necessary truths or ideas in God, he says, these ideas must have some effect on us, and we must have "not little copies of God's [ideas], as it were, but affections or modifications of our mind corresponding to that very thing we perceive in God" (GP IV, 426; AG 27). Leibniz's remarks are favorable to Malebranche, and this passage implies that it is no less true that we perceive ideas in God than that we perceive things existing out in the world. Leibniz's response to Malebranche applies just as well to all perception. In the "Discourse on Metaphysics," Leibniz clarifies this account with reference to his conception of a substance. Because a substance contains from the beginning everything that will ever happen to it, if our perception of an idea in God has some effect on our mind, then this effect is contained in us from the beginning, and in this sense we can say that we have the idea in ourselves (DM 29; AG 60). So the problem is that necessary truths exist in God's understanding and must exist within each monad, and the question remains, where in a monad are the necessary truths? We can already see how the answer will direct Leibniz toward pluralism. Given the ontology of a monad, necessary truths must be within the perception of each monad. Given the unity of consciousness, the perception of necessary truths will have to be seamlessly integrated with our embodied perspective on the created universe. Nonetheless, because this is such an essential point, a few alternatives should be considered.

Necessary truths might derive from what is common to every perspective, or what is present equally in every part of the universe. Spinoza grounds adequate knowledge in this way, writing: "Those things, which are common to all, and which are equally in a part and in the whole, cannot be conceived except adequately" (2P38).[17] In Leibniz's terms, we might say

---

[17] Spinoza himself applies this proposition to the question of other cultures, writing in the corollary "Hence it follows that there are certain ideas or notions common to all men; for . . . all bodies agree in certain respects, which . . . must be adequately or clearly and distinctly perceived by all" (*Ethics*, 2P38C).

that something present in every perspective could be adequately known from any perspective, but, although our perspective on the universe might give us near-universals, no matter how many times a truth is reinforced in our perspective of the city, we cannot presume that it is necessary, because our view is always limited. Whatever is constant in our perspective could be like the constant liquidity of water in the perspective of the King of Siam. The same applies to self-reflection. That is, there might be universal and necessary conditions of all experience, but self-reflection cannot recognize necessary truths for the same reason that experience of the outside world cannot – such experience only provides instances, and we can never know that what is true of our mind is necessarily true. Necessary truths are more than psychological constants and cannot be established through self-observation. Leibniz says explicitly that necessary truths cannot come from induction (e.g. RB 49), but several factors support this claim. Leibniz does not take the structure of our minds as a necessary structure for all minds. Our mind might, after death, be elevated to a level of knowledge now inconceivable. The existence of spirits with radically better understanding has the same effect, putting into question any psychological necessities we now experience (NE IV, xvii, § 16; RB 490).

It seems, then, that the metaphor of differing perspectives on a town provides an inadequate or incomplete account of the epistemological condition of an intelligent monad. To account for necessary truths, then, we might step outside the metaphor of perception. We might say that perception is like a perspective on a town, but that there is another non-perceptual aspect of our knowledge that founds necessary truths, namely, innate ideas. According to Leibniz, however, a monad's *only* qualities are in its perceptions, as we have seen. In the "Principles of Nature and Grace," he writes that a monad can be distinguished from another only by its internal qualities, "which can be nothing but its *perceptions* (that is, the representation of the composite, or what is external, in the simple) and its *appetitions* (that is, its tendencies to go from one perception to another) which are the principles of change" (PNG 2; AG 207). Appetition itself is immanent in perception, as Leibniz calls it the tendency for change in perception. Since a mind moves toward what seems best, appetition can only be our tendency toward the best perception, and its path thus is determined by perception. In a letter to Burcher DeVolder, Leibniz writes, "I recognize monads that are active per se, and in them nothing can be conceived except perception, which in turn involves action" (GP III, 256; Rescher, 1991, 80). Finally, the reason Leibniz claims that monads never stop perceiving is that, without perception, a monad would have no qualities and would thus not exist

(M 21; AG 216). This would not be the case if, beside perceptions, monads had other qualities, like extra-perceptual innate ideas.

Our access to necessary truths thus cannot lie outside of perception. The difficulties that an account of the knowledge of a monad faces can be summarized in five points:

(1) There are two ontological realms, one of ideas in God's understanding, and one of created beings.

(2) The monad has access to both necessary truths and to existential truths.

(3) Necessary truths cannot be induced from our experience of existing things, or derived from existential truths.

(4) Existential truths (except the existence of God) cannot be finitely derived from necessary truths or from the realm of ideas.

(5) All qualities of a monad are present in its perception, and the monad has no qualities beyond its perception.

From these five points, it follows that:

(6) A monad must have direct access to both necessary truths and existential truths.

(7) This access to both realms must be contained in one unitary perception.

An intelligent monad must be a two-fold reflection or expression, reflecting the realm of existing things and reflecting God's understanding. Both the created universe and the understanding of God are reflected or expressed in the monad, and are actually present in perception at any given moment. The metaphor of perspectives on a city only tells half the story, that of our reflection of the universe. This partial story for us is the whole story for non-rational monads.

This account may sound strange and too theo-centric, but Leibniz says directly that intelligent monads have this dual expressive nature. In the "Discourse on Metaphysics," he writes, "although all substances express the whole universe, nevertheless the other substances express the world rather than God, while minds express God rather than the world" (DM 36; AG 67). In the "Monadology," he writes, "souls, in general, are living mirrors or images of the universe of creatures, but minds are also images of the divinity itself, or of the author of nature" (M 83; AG 223). In the "Principles of Nature and Grace," he writes that a rational soul differs from other monads because, "It is not only a mirror of the universe of created things, but also an image of the divinity. The mind not only has a perception of God's works, but it is even capable of producing something that resembles them, although on a small scale" (PNG 14; AG 211). A rational monad expresses, perceives, or mirrors the mind of God in the same way that it and all other monads express, perceive, or mirror the created universe. The passage from the "Discourse" says this directly. The other two passages mentioned, admittedly from a later point in Leibniz's philosophy, are somewhat inconclusive because, in both, Leibniz shifts terminology from being a mirror to being an "image." To say that human beings are an "image of God" naturally connects to a common place of Christian theology and to a broad, indeterminate meaning. To be an image of God can easily mean only to be like God, and Leibniz sometimes says that we are the image of God in that we are capable of knowledge and in that we are able to act purposively, not necessarily that our mind is literally an image or reflection of the ideas in the mind of God. A consideration of knowing and action, however, reveals that these claims reduce to a reflection of God's understanding. In a passage in the "Causa Dei," Leibniz examines this resemblance more precisely: "The remains of the Divine image consist in both the innate light of the intellect and also in the inherent Liberty of the will" (CD 98). We imitate God because we have innate ideas and a will. Our knowledge, however, the "innate light of the intellect," is just our apperception of ideas, while free will is just appetition, immanent in perception. Thus we are an image of God, in that we have an understanding which expresses the understanding of God, and we have a principle of appetition which is a fallible version of God's. Taking Leibniz's terminology seriously, to be an "image" is more determinate than to be like, and has the same sense of expression with which Leibniz describes our relation to existing things. Leibniz uses "image" to describe both relationships, and uses image and mirror as if interchangeable, saying *"miroirs vivans ou images"* (M 83; AG 223). The relationship between our ideas and those of God is more explicit in Leibniz's earlier writings. In the "Meditations on Knowledge, Truth, and Ideas," Leibniz writes that our ideas must be "affections or modifications of our mind corresponding to that very thing we perceived in God" (GP IV, 426; AG 27). In the "Discourse on Metaphysics," he writes that "the essence of our soul is a certain expression, imitation or image of the divine essence, thought, and will, and of all the ideas comprised in it" (DM 28; AG 59), and that the mind expresses "God, and with him, all possible and actual beings" (DM 29; AG 60). A later explicit statement is in the *New Essays*, where Leibniz writes that "the soul is a little world where distinct ideas represent God and confused ones represent the universe" (NE II, i, § 1; RB 109).

Taking necessary truths as expressions of the structure of God's understanding also explains the normative role Leibniz grants ideas. In the "Discourse on Metaphysics," Leibniz makes a distinction between notions or concepts, and ideas: "Thus, the expressions in our soul, whether we conceive them or not, can be called ideas, but those we conceive or form can be called notions, concepts" (DM 27; AG 59). More often Leibniz draws a distinction between having an *idea* of a thing and merely thinking of a thing (GP VII, 263; L 207). This distinction has important consequences. If all mental events are ideas, then to say that a thought is an idea is trivial – all thoughts are ideas. If, however, ideas are a subset of thoughts, to say that a thought is an idea can have some normative value. Ideas differ from mere notions because they must be possible, i.e. not self-contradictory. Leibniz writes, "Now, it is evident we have no idea of a notion when it is impossible. And in the case where knowledge is only suppositive [when its possibility is not proven], even when we have the idea, we do not contemplate it, for such a notion is only known in the way in which we know notions involving a hidden impossibility [*occultement impossibles*]" (DM 25; AG 57). Some ideas are simple and intuitively known as possible, so that we immediately recognize them as ideas. More often, analysis is required in order to re-cognize that something is possible, so that we must examine our notion in order to ascertain if it is an idea. For this reason, Leibniz says that Descartes assumes we have an idea of God, by which he means that Descartes assumes that God is possible. For Descartes, whether or not we have an idea of God is a phenomenological question and can thus be made from the condition of complete doubt. For Leibniz, self-observation can tell us that we have a notion of God, but can never tell us that this notion is an idea, or, what is the same thing, that this notion expresses something possible. The way we distinguish between ideas and concepts is logical, but the distinction between them is deeper than this method of recognition. The fundamental difference between ideas and concepts is that ideas express something real, even if not created. Ideas express possibles in the mind of God. Thus, in the *New Essays*, Theophile says that intelligible ideas do not refer to existing things, but that "all intelligible ideas have their archetypes in the eternal possibility of things" (NE IV, iv, § 5; RB 392).[18] Later Theophile adds that it is in God that one finds "the pattern [*l'original*] for the ideas and truths which are engraved in our souls" (NE III, xi, § 14; RB 447). That the object of our ideas is God's understanding explains why, in the *Theodicy*, Leibniz says that without God geometry would have no *object*, rather than just saying that geometry would not be possible or have no necessity (T § 184; GP VI, 226), and why, in the "Causa Dei," he says that the mind of God contains all possible objects of the understanding (CD § 13; GP VI, 440). In conclusion, if a notion expresses something possible, then this notion

18 Translation modified.

expresses something real in the mind of God, and this notion is truly an idea; if a notion expresses something impossible, it expresses something with no reality at all, and is not an idea. A real idea is an idea with a real object, as we would expect, but this object can be ideal rather than created.

The initial metaphor of monads as reflections on the same city now must be modified with the addition of access to necessary truths, and this modification seems to strike a blow to what was appealing for an understanding of cultural exchange – the model of perspective. It seems that our access to existing things is limited and perspectival, and regarding knowledge of contingent existences we have much to learn from other cultures, which see this universe from different sides. Regarding knowledge of necessary truths, though, we all have access to God. If our access to the mind of God is not limited and perspectival, then we have little to learn regarding necessary truths from other cultures, and there is no difficulty in using these truths to judge other cultures. The danger of the "centrism" we hoped to avoid is clear. There is a sense in which this account agrees with Leibniz's actual practice regarding other cultures. Leibniz does not doubt that substances cannot interact nor that God exists. These are universal truths that not only apply to anyone but can be discovered by anyone. In this respect, he approaches the position of Descartes and Spinoza. Nonetheless, Leibniz's account is more complex because our access to the ideal realm is also limited. Returning to our metaphor of the city, we should not assume that a mind has on one side a perspective on the city and on the other a totality of necessary truths common to everyone. The metaphor is better reconceived with monads having an expression of the city and an expression of another realm, both merging into one unified perspective. The question of what the perspectives of different monads have in common is thus not answered by saying that what they have in common is the realm of God's understanding – rather the question is doubled, to what is common to our perspective on the city and what is common to our "perspective" on God.

THE PROBLEM OF INNATENESS

The threat to Leibniz's pluralism and what brings him nearer to the position of Descartes and Spinoza is a monad's access to necessary truths, which derive from innate ideas, which express the structure of ideas in the understanding of God. Innate ideas stand at the center of Leibniz's methodology and epistemology. The fact that these ideas are innate in itself suggests that they will have little connection to cultural exchange. If they are innate, we can find them in ourselves, which is exactly the point made by Descartes and Spinoza. The challenge then is to show how innate ideas and necessary truths remain central to Leibniz's method while keeping him open to cultural exchange and the need to consult other perspectives. I will show this by showing how innate ideas emerge into apperception only within an embodied perspective on the universe. Strictly speaking, since monads do not interact, all perceptions and ideas are innate. As we have seen, though, the distinction between experience and self-reflection remains as a monadic phenomenon. Leibniz feels comfortable with this distinction, particularly in the *New Essays*, but it can make his meaning unclear, as all perceptions are innate but some are innate in a stronger sense. He addresses these two senses in the "Discourse on Metaphysics," where he argues that, metaphysically speaking, no ideas come from outside. In concession to Aristotle, though, we can in a popular sense say that some ideas come from the senses, although we can in no sense say that all ideas do (DM 27; AG 59).

The term "idea" in Leibniz's time is used with notorious ambiguity and different shades of meaning, as Nicholas Jolley nicely brings out in *The Light of the Soul*.[19] Robert McRae analyzes the doctrines of ideas in the seventeenth century, arguing that Descartes' use of "idea" yielded three interpretations: an idea is an object; an idea is an act; an idea is a disposition.[20] He attributes the latter view to Leibniz. McRae's account provides an adequate starting point, because Leibniz differentiates his conception of an idea from two alternatives which roughly correspond to those McRae proposes. Against Arnauld and Locke in the *New Essays*, Leibniz denies that an idea is merely an act, form, or part of thought. He writes, "If ideas were only the forms or manners of thoughts, they would cease with them; but you yourself have acknowledged, sir, that they are the inner objects of thoughts, and as such they can persist" (NE II, ix, § 2; RB 140). In the preface to the *New Essays* he writes, "This is how ideas and truths are in us – as inclinations, dispositions, tendencies [*habitudes*], or natural potentialities [*virtualités naturelles*], and not as actualities [*actions*]" (RB 52; cf. NE I, i, § 26; RB 86). Leibniz's connection of ideas and truths in this passage is relevant, as the normative value of ideas directs Leibniz to reject identifying ideas with thoughts. Leibniz opposes his conception of idea to Locke's by making ideas permanent in us and by making ideas a narrower

---

[19] Jolley, *Light of the Soul*.
[20] Robert McRae, " 'Idea' as a Philosophical Term in the Seventeenth Century," *Journal of the History of Ideas*, 26 (1965), pp. 175–90.

subset of notions or mental acts, so that ideas retain a normative force. Malebranche's account of ideas opposes Locke's on the same ground, but Leibniz distances himself from Malebranche as well, rejecting the claim that ideas exist outside our mind, as we have seen.

Leibniz does not merely provide an alternative to Locke and Malebranche, but tries to unite the two, retaining the normative power of Malebranche's account and the naturalism of Locke's account. The question then is, what is the position of ideas in consciousness? Ideas are neither mere acts of the mind nor things existing outside the mind. McRae's answer is that they are "dispositions," with a disposition being something in us, but not a thought that would come and go. In this choice of terms, McRae follows Leibniz himself, who calls an innate idea "a disposition, an aptitude, a preformation" (NE I, i, § 11; RB 80). Later he says that they "are merely natural tendencies [*habitudes naturelles*], that is dispositions and attitudes, active or passive" (NE I, iii, § 20; RB 106). The problem is that habits, dispositions, and aptitudes all seem to have extra-perceptual existence. Leibniz's most common metaphor for innate ideas – veins in marble – also suggests that innate ideas are outside perception. The latter is, however, a metaphor, and the question is how strongly to take it. A block of marble is used metaphorically by Leibniz in another telling sense – as an example of a being by aggregation, thus not a real substance. The metaphor of veins in marble, or spatial patterns in an aggregate, can only be loosely applied to a simple being that has no parts, is a true unity, and is not extended.

Leibniz's use of "habits," "dispositions," and "aptitudes" to describe innate ideas must be taken in a peculiar sense that can place them within a unitary substance whose only qualitative differentiation is its perception. The problem remains that ideas are something existing in us that does not fluctuate with our acts of thought, yet they can only exist in our perception, which seems to say that they only exist as acts of thought. Leibniz, though, has an explanation for how innate ideas could be perceived by us always while being only occasionally recognized: the distinction between perception and apperception. The distinction between perception and apperception founds the metaphor of perspective: the entire universe exists in each monad as perceived, but only partly apperceived. That portion which is apperceived establishes our perspective. Similarly, although we do not *apperceive* all necessary truths, we might *perceive* them all, giving us something like a perspective on God's understanding. Such a perspectival access to the stock of necessary truths would maintain the importance of cultural exchange. On this account, ideas would exist in our perception, sometimes coming into apperception in fleeting acts of thought.[21] We could also put this distinction into terms of potentiality and actuality. The entire universe is actually perceived in each monad at all times, but this universe is only potentially apperceived. Similarly, God's understanding is actually perceived as a stock of innate ideas, which are potentially apperceived. The process of learning consists in actualizing potential apperceptions, but these potential apperceptions exist as actual perceptions. Given Leibniz's theory of monads, a disposition can only exist as perception or appetition or both.[22] Because appetition is immanent in perception as the tendency of perceptions to change, there seems to be no alternative to making innate ideas perceptions.

This view of innate ideas existing in a monad as actually perceived (but not apperceived) goes against the standard interpretation of innate ideas as dispositions. The standard account would have monads consist of perceptions, appetites, and dispositions, while my account reduces dispositions to perceptions. The problem is that an unconsciously perceived idea does not sound like a "disposition." We must be careful, however, with Leibniz's terms. As far as I know, he never defines disposition. More importantly, he doesn't simply call innate ideas "dispositions." Each time he lists several different words, at one point or another using: *inclinations, dispositions, habitudes, virtualités naturelles, aptitudes, préformations*. At the very least, Leibniz is dissatisfied with the available terms. This dissatisfaction weakens how much we can rely on any one of the terms. Finally, if we consider the way that appetite and perception relate, that appetite is always toward what seems the best, and that innate ideas are our closest relationship to God, we can conclude that the mind must have an active tendency toward these perceived but un-apperceived innate ideas. This status of innate ideas is supported by their analogy with memories, which consist in actual present traces of the past. In the *New Essays*, Theophile gives this interpretation of memory directly: "there are dispositions which are the remains of past impressions, in the soul as well as in the body, but which we are unaware of except when the memory has a use for them" (NE II, x, § 2; RB 140).

---

[21] This is the conclusion that C. D. Broad also reaches. C. D. Broad, *Leibniz: An Introduction* (Cambridge: Cambridge University Press, 1975), pp. 134–35.

[22] Broad suggests a third view, when he writes, "It is a dispositional proposition that, if and only if at any time its temperature should be at or above 1062° C, it would then be liquid" (Broad, *Leibniz: An Introduction*, pp. 20–21). Broad later says, however, that all dispositional properties must reduce to non-dispositional ones. In addition, such dispositional properties seem to come only from the limitations of our perspective. Since the entire future of a monad is determined, it only has determinate properties, such as, at time *t*, this bit of gold reached a temperature *x* and became liquid. Finally, it is difficult to see how such a hypothetical proposition would constitute something present in a monad as a disposition.

A soul cannot lose its past: "It retains impressions of everything which has previously happened to it, and it even has presentiments of everything which will happen to it, but these sentiments are mostly too minute to be distinguishable and for one to be aware of them" (NE II, xxvii, § 14; RB 239).[23] Thus memories are perceptions of past events remaining in the present, and the ability to remember is the ability to apperceive these weak perceptions. Innate ideas have exactly the same status. Such a status may not seem like a "disposition," but, in the above passage on memory, Leibniz calls memories "dispositions" which are remains of past impressions.

Going beyond the vague term "disposition," we can say that innate ideas are perceptions or expressions of God's ideas, in the same way that confused notions are perceptions or expressions of God's creation. In the same way that, given preestablished harmony, my perception of anything I will ever perceive is contained in me from the start, so my perception of possibles, of ideas, is contained in me from the start. Finally, in the same way that, while I perceive all existing things, the task of learning is to bring these perceptions into apperception, so I perceive all ideas, and the task is to bring them into apperception. This is precisely how Leibniz describes our relationship to innate ideas. Ideas are in us "not always so that we apperceive them, but always in such a way that we can draw them from our own depths and render them apperceivable" (NE IV, x, § 7; RB 438).[24] The key point in the account of innate ideas, as Theophile tells Philalethe, is "I cannot accept the proposition that *whatever is learned is not innate*" (NE I, i, § 23; RB 85). Given the distinction between perception and apperception, it is possible to learn – to bring into apperception – what we already perceive.

These innate ideas lie in the vague recesses of every mind, away from conscious attention. They emerge into apperception through self-reflection. Leibniz's statements about innate ideas and self-reflection are sometimes contradictory and are certainly unclear.[25] These difficulties, though, come not from inconsistency in Leibniz's account, but from the use of the same ambiguous terms for several different distinctions. The confusion comes because Leibniz discusses ideas coming from self-reflection in two senses. One sense is through a process of *a posteriori* self-observation. Some ideas

---

[23] Translation modified. RB translates "*sentiments*" as "states of mind," which suggests that memories are states rather than actual perceptions.

[24] Translation modified.

[25] Jolley, *Light of the Soul*, p. 185. Jolley notes that the doctrine of self-reflection is adequate as an attempt to justify Leibniz's claim that we can know that the mind is a substance, but that it fails as a theory of ideas acquisition. It is this latter charge against which I want to defend Leibniz. For a more detailed response, see Franklin Perkins, "Ideas and Self-Reflection in Leibniz," *Leibniz Society Review* (1999), pp. 43–63.

only come to mind through certain experiences, as I might never think of a large animal with a trunk unless I encountered a description of it, or the King of Siam never thought of ice until Europeans told him about it. Other ideas only come to mind through the experience of being a mind, as for example, the idea of perception. This sense of self-reflection is the same sense that Locke uses. Leibniz refers to it when he has Theophile ask, "I would like to know how we could have the idea of being if we did not, as beings ourselves, find being within us" (NE I, i, § 24; RB 85–86). Here he must be speaking in the same sense that he could ask, how could I ever have an idea of a chiliagon if it had never been suggested to me by some experience? This *a posteriori* self-reflection has some privileges over other kinds of experience. The self is a universal object of experience – everyone has the experience of a being, whereas not all have the experience of ice. Leibniz also gives special status to our experience of our self as a primitive truth that is not necessary but is certain. Thus the claim that I exist is certain, though not necessary. Finally, Leibniz connects distortion or perspective with existence in space. Our direct, non-spatial access to our self either means that it is not perceived in space because it is particularly clear, or it is particularly clear because it is not perceived in space. When Leibniz talks about innate ideas and self-reflection, though, he usually intends those ideas which come *a priori* through the understanding, as, for example, the idea of a triangle. These ideas are in us only because we express the mind of God. Necessary truths about possibles are known analytically through reflection according to the principle of non-contradiction. They are thus known *a priori*, without experience. In fact, they can only be known *a priori*, since instances from experience can never generate necessary truths. In a sense, these ideas cannot be known through cultural exchange, but even this seemingly obvious claim is more complicated than it seems.

EXPRESSIONS OF TRUTH

What emerges thus far is that each mind has a unique perspective, a seamless mix between necessary truths based on innate ideas and experiences based on our embodied expression of the universe. This perspective is like the tip of an iceberg, though. It dips off gradually into unconscious, unrecognized perceptions, in two directions. One leads into our unconscious expression of the universe, into what Leibniz calls minute perceptions. The interconnection of things requires that all perceptions have some effect on apperception, and Leibniz says frequently that all thoughts and perceptions do have some effect (e.g. NE II, i, § 15; RB 116). His examples usually involve many perceptions building up into an apperception, as the unrecognized perceptions of individual waves build into the noticeable roar of the sea. More often, however, these perceptions mix and conflict and never reach apperception, effecting us as inclinations, passions, and instincts. This effect is best seen in Leibniz's argument that no decisions come out of indifference: "that is why we are never indifferent, even when we appear to be most so, as for instance over whether to turn left or right at the end of a lane. For the choice that we make arises from these insensible stimuli, which mingled with the actions of objects and of our bodily interiors, make us find one direction of movement more comfortable than the other" (NE II, xx, § 6; RB 166). All actions we do not consciously consider, including custom and habit, follow from the interaction of innumerable perceptions that result from our expression of the universe (NE II, i, § 15; RB 115–16). Our perspective also dips off gradually into our unconscious stock of innate ideas. Leibniz describes the effect of these unrecognized ideas in ways remarkably similar to how he describes minute perceptions of the universe. Thus in the *New Essays*, he writes:

As for your point that there is not universal approval of the two great speculative principles which are the best established of all: I can reply that even if they were not known they would still be innate, because they are accepted as soon as they are heard. But I shall further add that fundamentally everyone does know them; that we use the principle of contradiction (for instance) all the time, without paying distinct attention to it; and that the conduct of a liar who contradicts himself will be upsetting to anyone, however uncivilized, if the matter is one which he takes seriously. Thus, we use these maxims without having them explicitly in mind. (NE I, i, § 4; RB 76)

This passage affirms that innate ideas exist in our perception even before we become aware of them, and that they exert an unconscious influence on our perspective. In another passage, he continues, "For general principles enter into our thoughts, serving as their inner core and as their mortar. Even if we give no thought to them, they are necessary for thought, as muscles and tendons are for walking" (NE I, i, § 20; RB 84).

These passages already suggest how these two aspects of consciousness – our expression of the universe and our expression of necessary truths – merge together into a perspective, but how this perspective forms must be examined in more detail. The first question is what it means for a mind to express each of these realms of being. The second question will be how the two expressions condition each other. For the first question, we can begin by noting the similarities of the two relationships. In both cases, there is a mix of limitation and of universality. This mix is implied in the very concept of expression, which Leibniz uses to describe so many relationships, as in an early description, "Quid Sit Idea":

That is said to express a thing in which there are relations [*habitudines*] which correspond to the relations of the thing expressed. But there are various kinds of expression; for example, the model of a machine expresses the machine itself, a projective delineation on a plane expresses a solid, speech expresses thoughts and truths, characters express numbers, and an algebraic equation expresses a circle or some other figure. What is common to all these expressions is that we can pass from a consideration of the relations in the expression to a knowledge of the corresponding properties of the thing expressed. Hence, it is clearly not necessary for that which expresses to be similar to the thing expressed, if only a certain analogy is maintained between the relations. (GP VII, 263–64; L 207)

Leibniz gives many other examples of expression. An idea expresses its object (GP VII, 263; L 207). The perception of a monad expresses the universe, and the understanding of a mind expresses God's understanding. Every effect expresses its cause (DM 28; 59). The senses and secondary qualities express their objects, and express the body (NE IV, vi, § 7; RB 403). Definitions express the essence of what they define (NE III, iii, § 15; RB 294). Paintings express the cities they represent (NE III, iii, § 15; RB 294). What do such dissimilar relationships have in common? Two things need not be similar but their internal relations must be analogous. Most of Leibniz's detailed discussions of expression come in discussions of the relationship between secondary qualities and existing things. Leibniz writes that the resemblance is not perfect but is a relation of orders, as an ellipse resembles the circle whose projection it is: "there is a certain precise and natural relationship between what is projected and the projection which is made from it, with each point on the one corresponding through a certain relation with a point on the other" (NE II, viii, § 13; RB 131). In the *Theodicy*, Leibniz says that the representation has a natural relationship to what is represented. If this representation is imperfect, then it suppresses something in the object, but, no matter how imperfect the representation is, it can add nothing to what is represented (or else it would be not just imperfect but false), nor can it suppress everything in what is represented.

An expression is thus in one way exact: it reproduces an order exactly and adds nothing new, so that it is fully grounded in what is expressed. In another way, the expression is imperfect: it suppresses some things, and may have no direct resemblance to what is expressed. In the "Discourse on Metaphysics," Leibniz writes that a monad can be said to express the universe even though it is dissimilar, as long as it is proportional (DM 14; AG 47). In the "New System," Leibniz says that the soul represents the universe in a very exact manner, although more or less distinctly (G IV, 484; AG 144). In the *New Essays*, ideas from the senses express figures and motions exactly, though not distinctly (NE IV, vi, § 7; RB 403). An expression is not a compromise between something consistent and something varied, leaving something vaguely consistent. Rather, one aspect of the expression is varied, but the other is exact, and knowledge is rooted in this element that remains exact. Leibniz gives a good example of this relationship when he answers Philalethe's puzzle: if a blind man who had felt a cube and a sphere and then later gained sight could tell from sight which was which. Leibniz says that, if he knew that one was a sphere and the other a cube, the formerly blind man could tell which was which, because of the similarity of the internal relationships in both the felt cube and the seen cube (NE II, 9, § 9; RB 136–37). The "felt" cube is expressed by the "seen" cube, or, rather, both are expressions of the same relationships between monads. On this broad definition, Leibniz can use expression in so many ways: a pain can be said to express a pin, and the idea of a circle can be said to express a circle, even though a full description of these two relationships would show them to be quite different. An effect expresses its cause, because, given the principle of sufficient reason, there is a reason in the cause for everything in the effect and, in this sense, the effect reproduces an order from the cause. We can also say that the connection of words and symbols expresses their objects. Finally, we can say that our perception expresses the world and our understanding expresses the ideas of God. What does this mean for the question of what we have in common? There should be an exact relationship between the orders or relationships within each monad and those in every other. These relationships are common to all monads, while how distinct these relationships are and what relationships are more or less distinct varies from monad to monad. We can now turn more specifically to the two kinds of expression.

The way a monad expresses the universe is easier to approach, as Leibniz describes it with the now familiar metaphor of perspectives on a town. We have already noted several aspects of this relationship, for example, that the expression is both quantitatively (temporally) and qualitatively (spatially) limited, and that the monad expresses the universe according to the position of its body. Our question is, what do monads as expressions of the universe have in common? Since expression implies a correspondence of order, one answer is that each expression has in common an exact relationship to the order of relations in the existing world, although what aspects of this order we apperceive varies. Our bodily–spatial relation to the universe provides for differences, since what is closest to me differs from what is closest to you, but it also provides a second answer to what different expressions have in common, since some things are close to all of us. For example, we all experience what it is to be a mind, to have a body, to have a culture. These two answers, that we express the same overall order and that some things we express are present in all perspectives, roughly correspond to the two kinds of experiential knowledge Leibniz distinguishes: that based on the senses; and that based on intuitive knowledge.

Leibniz calls the latter primitive *a posteriori* truths, corresponding to identities, which are primitive *a priori* truths. The primitive *a posteriori* truth that I exist is of the highest evidence, is immediate, and cannot be proven by any other proposition (NE IV, vii, § 7; RB 411). Like identities, such immediate truths are equally clear and can be made no more certain (NE IV, ii, § 1; RB 367). The experiential truth Leibniz intends is the truth of our own existence, as established by Descartes, but there are also immediate phenomenal truths about our consciousness, such as "I think A," or "when I think A I think B" (NE IV, ii, § 1; RB 366). We also have immediate knowledge of what we have just thought:

> But a present or immediate memory, the memory of what was taking place immediately before – or in other words, the consciousness or reflection which accompanies inner activity – cannot naturally deceive us. If it could, we would not even be certain that we are thinking about such and such a thing; for this too is silently said only about past actions, not about the very action of saying it. But if immediate inner experience is not certain, we cannot be sure of any truth of fact. (NE II, xxvii, § 13; RB 238)

These immediate existential facts are certain, but not necessary. How many existential facts can be thus proven is unclear. We have seen that the immortality of the soul follows necessarily from the definition of a simple substance, but the existential truth that I am a simple substance is not necessary and depends on experience. I think Leibniz would claim that along with the fact that I exist, it is also immediately certain that I am a simple substance.[26] Thus while we could not establish the necessary existence of simple, undying substances, their existence could still be absolutely certain.

These truths of immediate experience relate to cultural exchange by providing some existential universal truths, particularly about our own mind. Not all people explicitly recognize their existence, but this seems to be close to a universal truth. We should note, however, that even these immediate truths of experience take us beyond our expression of the universe alone.

---

[26] Leibniz suggests this point in his discussion of identity in the *New Essays*, esp. NE II, xxvii, § 89; RB 236–37.

All apperception depends on our expression of the mind of God. Knowledge from experience is always a mix of our expression of the universe and our expression of possibles. This mix is involved even in what Leibniz calls the immediate truths of experience, and it is even more prominent in the third kind of knowledge of existential truths, that coming from the senses. If we wanted to consider a monad as solely an expression of the universe, we must consider it in terms of perception or dim awareness, the kind of immediate perception we imagine animals to have. Perhaps when we are most deeply absorbed in an experience and unaware of what is happening we only express the universe. In any case, as we have seen, these unconscious perceptions are not irrelevant. Leibniz differs greatly from Descartes or Locke, for whom, if something is not consciously thought, it is not part of the mind. The main effect of our expression of the universe taken alone is the foundation it provides for the senses that rise to the level of apperception and the determination of the unconscious inclinations which guide our behavior. These inclinations act not only when our conscious judgment is indifferent; they compete with and hinder our judgment, much as we now conceive of the unconscious. Thus one effect of our expression of the universe on our expression of ideas is the interference coming from inclinations grounded in the unconscious.

How a monad expresses the structure of God's understanding, or how it expresses its stock of innate ideas, is more difficult to explain. All possible things are contained in the mind of God, and thus, as expressions of God, we contain both necessary and contingent truths *a priori*. Contingent truths, however, cannot be clearly and distinctly known by finite beings, leaving us dependent on experience. Take the idea of a horse, which is in us *a priori*. We have first the problem of how we could ever come to think of this idea without the experience of a horse. What would bring that idea into apperception, other than some particular, contingent experience? More importantly, ideas brought into apperception from experience cannot be known clearly and distinctly, which means that they can never be known *a priori* to be possible, which means we can never know if they are contained in us as expressions of God. In other words, we cannot know if the notions coming from experience are really ideas. For these reasons, our expression of God primarily concerns our access to necessary truths. One task of learning is to bring our innate, perceived ideas into apperception, determining if our notions are really ideas by determining if they are possible. We determine if our notions are possible *a priori* by analyzing complex ideas into their parts. This reduction is necessary because, until a notion has been fully analyzed, it might contain a hidden contradiction. In the "Meditations on

Knowledge, Truth, and Ideas," Leibniz describes the *a priori* determination of the possibility or reality of an idea in terms of reduction to simple, clear, and distinct ideas. An idea is clear when we can recognize it, and distinct when we can give some criterion by which to recognize it (GP IV, 422–23; AG 24). A simple idea, an idea without parts, which is known clearly and distinctly, is known to be possible (GP IV, 423; AG 24). A complex notion must be not only clear and distinct, but also adequate: "When everything that enters into a distinct notion is, again, distinctly known, or when analysis has been carried to completion" (GP IV, 423; AG 24). When everything involved in a distinct idea is reduced to simple, clear, and distinct ideas known to be possible, then the composite idea is also known to be possible. Thus "whenever we have adequate knowledge, we also have *a priori* knowledge of possibility, for having carried an analysis to completion, if no contradiction appears, then certainly the notion is at least possible" (GP IV, 425; AG 26). At other times, Leibniz formulates this process in terms of reduction to simple identities, since to reduce a proposition to a simple identity is to show that the predicate is contained in a clear and distinct knowledge of the subject.

Through analysis into simple ideas or identities, we can determine the universality of an idea *a priori*, which again seems to undermine the importance of cultural exchange. If a notion is impossible or necessary, it is impossible or necessary for everyone – God or angel, European or Chinese. In this way, we can determine the universality of notions without examining other cultures. How these notions are manifested in the world or among other peoples is irrelevant to their universality, which is the point drawn by Spinoza. For Leibniz, however, our access to these necessary truths is limited, which is why we *express* them rather than *re-present* them. Taking space and time as either symptoms of, or reasons for, the limitation of our expressions, the difference between our expression of the mind of God and our expression of the universe is that the latter is limited through time and distorted with space, while the former is only limited through time. Both are necessarily limited – we cannot apperceive all that we perceive in either case – but our expression of existing things is necessarily limited, whereas our expression of the ideal realm can be perfect. Not that we can apperceive all the necessary truths we perceive, but when we know a necessary truth clearly and distinctly, we know it perfectly. Leibniz writes in the *New Essays* that truth consists in the relationships among ideas such that one is contained in the other and that these relationships are common to God, angels, and humans. Thus "when God displays a truth to us, we come to possess the truth which is in his understanding, for although his ideas are infinitely more perfect and extensive that ours they still have the same relationships that ours do" (NE IV, v, § 2; RB 396). In the *Theodicy*, he explains, "All reasonings are eminent in God, and they preserve an order among themselves in his understanding as well as in ours; but for him this is just an order and *a priority of nature*, whereas for us there is *a priority of time*" (T 192). The distinction between the order of nature, which is the same for all rational beings, and the order of discovery, which varies, also emphasizes the temporal limitation of our access to necessary truths (NE III, i, § 5; RB 276). Even so, syllogisms are infallible (PD 27) and reason cannot err when it does its duty. (PD 64) These descriptions of the relationship between the connection of ideas in God's understanding and their expression in finite minds illustrate the earlier definitions of expression. Our ideas differ from God's, at least because we experience our ideas through time, but one aspect of the expression is perfect: the order among God's ideas is exactly the same as the order among ours, so much so that we can obtain "*indubitable* connections of ideas and *infallible* consequences" (PNG 5).

What makes our relationship to necessary truths an expression rather than an exact copy, then, is not the certainty with which we apperceive these truths, but the limited number of such truths which we bring into apperception. Our reason is like a drop to God's ocean (PD 61), or a ray of God's light (GP IV, 480; AG 140). It takes time to apperceive truths, so that what we can apperceive is always limited by what we have time for. Thus, we cannot *a priori* learn contingent truths with certainty, because contingent truths depend on God's choice of possible worlds, which depends on knowing and balancing an infinite amount of factors, which would require infinite time and is thus incompletable. Leibniz gives another version of this infinite progression in regard to our explanations of existing things, saying that we might someday understand what causes underlie a rainbow, but then we would have to understand what causes underlie those causes, and then what underlies those, and so on, following the infinite divisibility of matter (NE II, xxiii, § 12; RB 219). This temporal limitation applies to all creatures: angels may grasp in one glance what takes us much effort, but even they have the pleasure of discovering new truths (NE IV, xvii, § 16; RB 490). Beyond the temporal limitation of our access to necessary truths, the very condition of their infallibility seems to limit their scope. For truths to be known as necessary, they must be reducible to identities, to statements that say nothing new. Thus although we can know necessary truths with certainty and apply them universally, they seem of limited use. In the *New Essays*, Philalethe makes this charge, and Theophile answers by broadening the scope of identities to include all necessary demonstrations

(NE IV, ii, § 1; RB 361–67; NE IV, xvii, § 4; RB 478–83). The logic of geometry thus becomes a subdivision of a broader logic derived from identities (NE IV, ii, § 12; RB 370–71). Leibniz believes that much can be so demonstrated. He gives a list in the *New Essays*, writing that much can be proven

> about the nature of substances, about unities and multiplicities, about identity and diversity, the constitution of individuals, the impossibility of vacuum and atoms, the source of cohesion, the law of continuity and the other laws of nature; and above all about the harmony amongst things, the immateriality of souls, the union of soul with body, and the preservation after death of souls and even of animals. (NE IV, iii, § 18; RB 383)

The most important demonstrative truths are the foundations of natural theology – the existence of God and the immortality of the soul. These truths seem distant from a simple A = A, but how they could derive from identities can be understood with reference to the earlier discussion of necessary truths. Some truths are necessary in that their opposite in itself is contradictory, but others are necessary in that their definitions imply certain conditions of compossibility. Thus if simple substances exist, they can only be destroyed by miracle, because indestructibility is contained in the very concept or identity of a simple substance.

Thus many things can be demonstrated about ideas using identities, but these truths about ideas lead to a further question. How do we match necessary truths about ideas to existing things? This question arises because the ideas of actually existing things are only a tiny subset of the ideas in God's understanding. So I might derive necessary consequences from a real idea only to find this idea was not part of the best possible world. That is, the idea might correspond to something in God's understanding but not to anything in the created world. The use of ideas depends on establishing some connection to the things of this created world. Leibniz lists three modes of access to existential truths: "we have an intuitive knowledge of our own existence, a demonstrative one of the existence of God, and a sensitive one of other things" (NE IV, iii, § 21; RB 387). Only the second kind of knowledge is derived from our access to necessary truths or our expression of the ideas of God. God is the only necessary being, meaning that only the idea of God necessarily implies his existence. Without any recourse to our expression of existing things, we can know with certainty that God exists. We might expect Leibniz to use this one bridge between necessary and existential truths as an Archimedian point, in order to prove other necessary, existential truths, but he does not. From the necessary existential truth that God exists, we can conclude a few general things about God's attributes and about the world, for example, that it is the most perfect possible. These general truths can guide our understanding of the world, as in the use of final causes, but we can establish no particular existential truths from consideration of God's attributes alone. Thus the weakness of necessary truths – that they have no connection to existing things – is only overcome within the realm of ideas in the case of the existence of God. All other existential truths will require some recourse to experience.

In conclusion, our expression of the ideas of God is perfect in that, through proper analysis, we can attain certain and universal truths, but is imperfect in that we can bring these truths into apperception only through time. Because of this temporal limitation, we cannot discover all necessary truths, but must follow an order of discovery which progresses infinitely, and we cannot discover *a priori* existential truths, which would require infinite analysis. The temporal limitation of our expression of God's understanding thus leads to two questions: which of the infinity of necessary truths do we bring into apperception (what determines the concrete order of discovery for any particular mind); and how do we match the ideas from which we can draw necessary conclusions to our concrete experience of the world? The answer to both of these questions depends on our expression of the existing universe. In this way our temporally limited access to necessary truths links to our spatially limited access to existing things. The use of necessary truths is influenced by culture; reason is always embodied.

MUTUAL CONDITIONING

Even without examining how our expressions of God's ideas and the created world mutually condition each other, we can see that they must. We experience a seamless mix of these two kinds of knowledge, and Leibniz distinguishes them logically, not phenomenologically. As we have seen, we cannot distinguish between ideas and notions through our immediate experience of them. We distinguish them only through logical analysis. The greatest puzzle arising from the interpretation of Leibniz so far is – how do two radically different sources of knowledge meld into one seamless experience? Leibniz does not answer this question phenomenologically, but he does give explicit and concrete reasons for how the two expressions condition one another. This conditioning is important, because our expression of the universe is more perspectival, while our expression of the mind of God is more universal. If these two expressions are always blended, then our expression of the universe will be less diverse and our expression of God will be less common. This mutual conditioning allows Leibniz to avoid the two extremes of skepticism and innatism, and opens Leibniz to cultural exchange.

Within this mutual conditioning of the two expressions, the dependence of our expression of the universe on our expression of God is stronger, as we can see in Leibniz's attempts to distinguish minds from other monads. Leibniz repeatedly connects expressing God with consciousness and freedom, and with the ability to know the self, immaterial things, and necessary truths. The order of dependence among these terms is difficult to determine, with no simple hierarchy among them. Some faculty of abstraction is necessary if not for consciousness at least for any self-recognition. To know the self as a distinct thing, we must abstract it from its concrete situations over time. For this reason, knowledge of the self also depends on memory (DM 34; AG 65–66). The ability to reason in turn demands self-consciousness, as we must consciously observe some method. Even when we are unaware of innate ideas, they structure our actions and perceptions as a kind of instinct for consistency. Another way to illustrate this dependence on ideas is to consider that, as expressions of the universe, we express only actual particulars. Any step out of particulars depends on our expression of possibles. In this sense, knowledge of our self requires us to see the self as transcending the particular situations in which we find it, or to see that our same self could be in other possible situations. In the same way, freedom and the ability to create depend on being able to consider multiple possibilities. We can thus see the extent of our dependence on innate ideas – in so far as we think, or are self-conscious, or make choices, we lean out of our immediate experience of the universe and draw on the realm of possibles and our expression of God's understanding. As this expression is more universal than our spatially limited expression of the universe, thought itself is more universal than pure experience. Thought draws on what is true of all possibilities, anywhere in the world. Thus through reflection we share a world with other people. This point is significant because through science and knowledge we come more and more to a common ground, and engaging in any thought takes a step toward this common ground. The dependence on possibles and necessary truths leads to some commonality between cultures, but the dependence of our use of innate ideas on our embodied expression of the universe is at least as important for the value of cultural exchange. As our expression of the universe is spatially limited, cultural limitations come to infect our access to necessary truths in so far as our access to innate ideas is conditioned by our expression of the universe. The existence and depth of cultural limitations drive the need for cultural exchange, so the greater the cultural limitations on our access to necessary truths, the greater our need for cultural exchange. I will examine four ways in which our access to innate ideas is conditioned by our expression of the universe.

The most intimate dependence of our expression of ideas on our expression of the universe is the dependence of thought on signs. Leibniz's conception of signs and their use is a complex topic beyond the scope of this book.[27] All I will establish is the limited claim that our ability successfully to reason or use necessary truths depends on the systems of signs available to us. Different cultures might have different systems of signs, and we could possibly improve our systems – and our access to innate ideas – through cultural exchange. This application is affirmed by Leibniz's own actions, as one of his main concerns in cultural exchange, with China in particular, involves language and his attempts to create a philosophical language. Leibniz states clearly that our ability to reason is limited by limitations in the systems of signs available to us, but what best establishes this point is Leibniz's intense drive to find adequate signs, and in particular his repeated claims of the value of a "characteristic," which he defines as "the art of using signs by means of a certain kind of exact calculus" (GP VII, 205; Dascal 182). I will take but one example, in which Leibniz is seeking a new system for symbolizing geometrical figures. The details of the problem do not matter here, but rather how he characterizes the need for this system of symbolization. He writes, "The reason why the linear analysis has not been devised up to now is, undoubtedly, the fact that no Characters directly representing themselves have yet been discovered. For without characters, it is hard to disentangle oneself amid a multitude and confusion of things" (GM V, 141–68; Dascal 170). He continues, saying that this method of symbolization would allow problems of optics, kinematics, mechanics, and anything else depending on the imagination to be solved infallibly, and ease the invention of new machines as well. He concludes, "And, finally, only when we shall be able to elicit from data, safely and quietly, by means of an infallible art, all that others can abstract from the same data only through the power of their wit and imagination, there will be some hope of penetrating nature's secrets" (GM V, 141–68; Dascal 171). Leibniz's claims here are mild compared with what he claims for some of his other characteristics, but they show that, regarding both geometry and penetrating the secrets of nature in general, our limited progress is due directly to our

---

[27] An excellent study on Leibniz and the use of signs, which I have relied on here, is Marcelo Dascal, *La Sémiologie de Leibniz* (Paris: Aubier Montaigne, 1978).

lack of suitable sign systems. In particular, in reasoning without suitable signs, we must consider too many things at once, so that our progress is limited and we must rely on "wit and imagination." The characteristic would aid us in all areas of investigation, including mathematics, squarely in the realm of necessary truths.

That signs can help with reasoning is clear, but the extent to which reason depends on signs is more difficult to assess. Sometimes Leibniz makes the strong claim that all thinking depends on signs. In the *New Essays* he writes, "I am convinced that created minds and souls never lack organs and never lack sensations, as they cannot reason without symbols" (NE II, xxi, § 73; RB 212). In an early essay he writes, "All human reasoning is performed by means of certain signs or characters. Indeed, it is neither possible nor desirable that the things themselves or even the ideas of them be always distinctly observed by the mind" (GP VII, 204; Dascal 181). At other times, though, Leibniz says that most – not all – thinking requires signs. In the "Discourse on Metaphysics," for example, Leibniz writes that intuitive, non-symbolic knowledge is "extremely rare" (DM 24; AG 56; cf. GP IV, 423–24; AG 25). In the *New Essays*, he says that we often reason about things like God, virtue, and happiness, in words or symbols, but that this way of reasoning is bad, because it renders these topics vague and ineffectual. Instead, we must make these ideas more vivid by "getting through to the senses of the words or symbols" (NE II, xxi, § 35; RB 187). These contradictions could reflect an uncertainty about the role of signs for Leibniz himself, but they also reflect conceptions of the need for signs coming from two different sources.

One reason Leibniz says all thinking requires signs is the preestablished harmony between mind and body. This harmony requires that for any change in the mind, there must be a corresponding change in the body. In other words, any change in the mind has some expression in the body, just as any change in the body has some expression in the mind. In one passage in the *New Essays*, Theophile concedes our dependence on experience, saying, "For it is an admirable arrangement on the part of nature that we cannot have abstract thoughts which have no need of something sensible, even if it be merely symbols such as the shapes of letters, or sounds" (NE I, i, § 5; RB 77). The reason he gives is that without such "sensible traces," the preestablished harmony between body and mind would be violated. In a letter to Bayle, Leibniz says that any change in the mind must be accompanied by a corresponding change in the body. Then he adds, "This applies even to the most abstract reasonings, because of the characters which represent them to the imagination" (GP IV, 559; L 577). An immediate question appears from this reasoning, however. Are the changes in the body signs that represent the ideas somehow, or are they merely corresponding changes in the body, for example, a change in the state of our brain? That is, is the sign of the idea of a tree the letters "t-r-e-e," or an image of a tree, or is it the firing of some particular electron in my brain when I think of a tree? In these two passages, Leibniz concludes for the former, but preestablished harmony in itself does not require this conclusion, and the claim that for every thought there is a change in the state of our body is a more reasonable claim. Nonetheless, in these passages, Leibniz moves from preestablished harmony to the need for signs in thinking. Two points follow from this argument. First, Leibniz makes the strong claim that *all* mental acts are accompanied by signs. Second, Leibniz says that all thinking is accompanied by signs, not that all thinking *depends* on signs. Not only does he not explicitly say that our use of ideas depends on these imaginings, his emphasis on preestablished harmony suggests that, while they correspond, they are independent.

The other argument Leibniz uses for the dependence of thought on signs comes directly from the limits of human knowledge. In this case, thinking not only accompanies signs but depends on them. On the one hand, we can rarely grasp ideas completely, since most ideas have too many component parts. On the other hand, we can only handle a small chain of reasoning at once, so that we cannot keep track of complex chains. In both cases, our knowledge is symbolic, depending on signs. These signs are not necessarily the signs of a formalized logic, but go much deeper, to words and even thought itself. We can see this connection in Leibniz's distinction between intuitive and blind or symbolic knowledge in the essay "Meditations on Knowledge, Truth, and Ideas." We have intuitive knowledge when we analyze a notion into its component parts, and we can grasp all of these components at once. All other knowledge is symbolic. The extent of our dependence on signs becomes clear when we see what Leibniz means by components. Leibniz uses the example of our thought of a chiliagon:

And so when I think about a chiliagon, that is, a polygon with a thousand equal sides, I don't always consider the nature of a side, or of equality, or of thousand-foldness (that is, of the cube of tenfoldedness), but in my mind I use these words (whose sense appears only obscurely and imperfectly to the mind) in place of the ideas I have of these things, since I remember that I know the meaning of those words, and I decide that explanation is not necessary at this time. (GP IV, 423; AG 25)

The component parts of the notion "chiliagon" are not only side, equality, and thousandfoldness, but also the components of each of these notions, the components of those components, and so on, until all the notions involved are reduced to simple ideas. For knowledge of the chiliagon not to be symbolic, we would have to so reduce all these parts, and grasp the completed analysis at once. Our thought could make almost no progress if we always had to take the time to reduce our ideas to their simplest components. Any progress in thinking thus depends on the correct use of symbols. Even if we had the leisure, it would be impossible fully to analyze most notions and grasp that full analysis at once. Most notions are just too complex. So in most cases intuitive knowledge is not only inconvenient but impossible.

The example of the chiliagon indicates what kind of symbols we depend on – in this case, the symbols are words. The problem is not just that we think in words, but that in these cases we merely think in words. When we think of a "side" of a chiliagon without considering its component parts, we have merely the word, without the idea that should accompany it. Leibniz makes this connection to ideas himself, continuing from the above passage: "From this it already follows that we don't perceive ideas of even those things we know distinctly, unless we make use of intuitive thinking" (GP IV, 424; AG 25). Earlier we noted that Leibniz draws a distinction between having an idea of something and merely having a notion or concept of that thing. Now it seems that notions are word-based signs. In experience, there is no difference between having a notion of something and having an idea of something, which is why in the same passage Leibniz says that we often think we have the idea of something when we really do not. Consequently, there is no immediate experiential distinction between thinking in signs and thinking in ideas – a strange conclusion. The fact that our notions are symbols emphasizes the extent of our dependence on signs, and, if these notions are words, our dependence on signs is a dependence on our concrete position in the universe and our reflection of the universe. Words are part of language, language part of culture, and if our use of necessary truths is conditioned by words it is conditioned by culture.

Leibniz makes this dependence on appropriate signs clear in his essays on the need for discovering good sign systems. These early essays should not be taken as definitive statements on the nature of knowledge, since the details of Leibniz's position frequently changed, but they can be taken as examples of our dependence on signs. For example, in an essay from 1671–72 Leibniz gives an account of knowledge as a product of using definitions, placing definitions on the side of signs. A definition is an "explanation of a word" (A VI, 2, 479; Dascal 147). In a note he says, "A definition is a signified idea" (A VI, 2, 479; Dascal 154). Speaking of necessary truths, he writes, "All these [necessary] propositions are such that they follow solely from a precise and distinct exposition, i.e. from definitions," thus remaining on the level of signs (A VI, 2, 479; Dascal 147). How can we learn anything new from definitions of words we already know? Leibniz's answer is that we learn things that we had thought, but thought unclearly or without reflection. We also learn how to clarify and manipulate signs. Thus he writes, "When I learn that two multiplied by two is four, do I learn more than a numeral name, whose use afterwards in speaking and calculation is more economical?" He then expands the scope of his example to include all lengthy chains of reasoning, and then to call this kind of thought "blind" (A VI, 2, P 481; Dascal 149). The important point of this example is that, because almost all of our thinking and reasoning is symbolic and conducted in words/notions, thinking well depends on using signs well. In this case, the signs concerned are words, and thus thinking well depends on giving and using definitions. Thus Leibniz concludes, "We can observe, therefore, that those who have developed the art of using adequate words constantly usually also reason, i.e. order their thoughts, with accuracy" (A VI, 2, P 481; Dascal 149). Such a conclusion naturally leads to the study of other languages, and Leibniz followed this lead. We began this section by noting that the challenge in establishing a connection between Leibniz's philosophy and his pluralism is to show how he avoids the position of Descartes and Spinoza, a position that allows for the sufficiency of self-reflection based on innate ideas. We can now begin to see that, although all knowledge is contained in each monad as a body of innate ideas, our access to these innate ideas is mediated by experience, in this case, by signs and language, and thus by culture.

The second way that our expression of the universe conditions our expression of innate ideas involves how we concretely come to have any particular thought. We have already seen that our finitude means we can only bring into apperception a limited amount of all the necessary truths that are in us confusedly. Our knowledge of necessary truths thus follows an order of discovery. What determines this order? Leibniz distinguishes the natural order of ideas from the order in which we discover them, which depends on effort and the circumstances in which we find our self, which depend on our bodily placement in the world (NE III, i, § 5; RB 276). This distinction between having an innate idea and concretely bringing the idea into apperception is crucial to Leibniz's defense of innate ideas, because it allows for the importance of experience. Thus Theophile says that, if by notion we mean an idea, then all people have a notion of God, "But if 'notion' signifies an idea which involves actual thinking, then it is a proposition of fact, belonging to the natural history of mankind" (NE IV, viii, § 4; RB 430). This dependence on "the natural history of mankind" could just as well be called a dependence on culture. Thus when Philalethe argues that the simplest people should have the greatest grasp of innate truths, because they are the freest of conditioning, Theophile responds that apperception of innate truths *requires* conditioning (NE I, i, § 27; RB 87–88). Leibniz's citation from the *Meno*, of Socrates prompting a boy through mathematical proofs, offers a good example (DM 26; AG 58; cf. NE I, i, § 5; RB 77). In the story, the boy's relationship to the necessary truths is not culturally conditioned, but his relationship to Socrates is. Someone expressing the universe from a position within a prominent geometry school would more likely reach necessary truths about triangles. The assistance revelation gives in finding the truths of natural theology offers another example of how concrete circumstances affect discovery of necessary truths. In a culture which holds books discussing monotheism, one would be much more likely to think of those necessary truths relating to the existence and nature of God. Given this effect, different cultures should have different bodies of necessary truths.

This conditioning has a deeper root in our dependence on experience for any thinking at all. Leibniz answers Philalethe's above objection – that innate ideas should be grasped best by the least educated – with a concession to empiricism: "The senses provide us with materials for reflection: we could not think even about thought if we did not think about something else, i.e. about the particular facts which the senses provide" (NE II, xxi, § 73; RB 212).[28] He concludes that created minds never lack bodies, because without bodies they would have no experience and would be unable to discover even necessary truths. Not only do we depend on experience in general to think necessary truths in general, but we depend somewhat – not completely – on particular experiences to think particular necessary truths. This dependence leads to the split between the order of truths themselves and the order in which we discover them, and thus the influence of culture on our access to necessary truths.

The third effect of our expression of the universe on our expression of innate ideas is related to the order of discovery. In this case, however, the effect of the body is negative. Our participation in the realm of existing things constantly distracts us from the contemplation of necessary truths.

---

[28] For other examples, see RB 74, RB 87, RB 128.

On the one hand, we are forced to concentrate on practical matters in order to maintain our bodies. On the other hand, we are bombarded by confused perceptions that limit our attention. In the *Theodicy*, Leibniz writes that the passage from head to heart is long and explains, "in addition to the judgment of the understanding, of which we have an express knowledge, there are mingled therewith confused perceptions of the senses, and these beget passions and even imperceptible inclinations, of which we are not always aware [*apercevons*]. These movements often thwart the judgment of the practical understanding" (T 310; H 314). The unconscious perceptions we have as reflections of the universe limit our ability to use necessary truths. Leibniz presents this conditioning in a different way when he writes of "children and savages". He writes, "Innate maxims make their appearance only through the attention one gives to them; but those people have almost no attention to give, or have it only for something quite different. They think about little except their bodily needs; and it is appropriate that pure and disinterested thoughts should be the reward for having nobler concerns" (NE I, i, § 27; RB 87). Once again, our concrete living circumstances affect our access to, and ability to follow, necessary truths. In particular, a practical freedom from the senses enhances our ability to know and focus on necessary truths. This shows the influence of our body on our access to necessary truths and Leibniz's example connects this influence to culture – savages and Europeans do not differ by nature but by culture, by their concrete placement in the universe. In other words, our chance of progressing in necessary truths is limited if we are born in a "savage" culture, where our attention must be directed toward sustaining our bodies. Any culture which encourages freedom from desires will tend to grasp necessary truths better, while a consumer culture that cultivates desire will grasp less. This point is not as trivial as it may seem, because one of Leibniz's central claims about China is that the Chinese exceed the Europeans in practical morality, so that in some ways the Europeans appear as "savages" in comparison with the Chinese. Leibniz's praise for Chinese morality would lead us to expect that they had clearer access to necessary truths.

As with everything else, this influence of embodiment on access to necessary truths has a deeper root in Leibniz's metaphysics. In discussing our dependence on experience, Leibniz says that all created minds need a body in order to have experience at all, so our body serves us in this way. More often, though, the body is a sign of imperfection. The body limits our access to necessary truths because of our bombardment with confused perceptions and our concern for practical matters. Leibniz often links imperfection, finitude, passivity, createdness, and embodiment, but it is difficult to locate them in a hierarchy of dependence. The problematic ontological status of space and body further complicates these relationships. At times, Leibniz claims that our access to necessary truths is necessarily connected to embodiment. For example, in the *Theodicy*, he writes, "What would an intelligent creature do if there were no unintelligent things? What would it think of, if there were neither movement, nor matter, nor sense? If it had only distinct thoughts it would be a God, its wisdom would be without bounds" (T 124; H 198; cf. M 60; AG 220–21). This passage suggests that both our dependence on experience and our distraction by experience result necessarily from our imperfection. In addition, it claims that without bodies our access to necessary truths would be unlimited and we would be godlike. If we would be godlike without our bodies, the role of embodiment is deeper than it at first seemed. It had seemed that, in itself, our expression of God is not limited qualitatively, but is limited quantitatively. That is, we can perceive necessary truths perfectly, but only in limited quantities. Which particular quantity we come to know is determined by our bodily placement in the universe, through a concrete order of discovery and the interference of our body on our access to necessary truths. Now it seems that this quantitative limitation is itself expressed in the fact that we have a body, that we are placed in the universe. Without bodies and our expression of the universe, we would no longer *express* the ideas in God's understanding; we would simply *have* them.

In conclusion, our expression of the ideas of God is not in itself culturally conditioned. The properties of a triangle are the same no matter where you come from, and where you live does not entirely determine what ideas you apperceive, since these ideas are not derived directly from experience. Unlike the idea of ice, we need no particular experience to come to the idea of a triangle. Thus our expression of the mind of God seems to undermine the importance of comparative philosophy. We have seen, however, that in its dependence on signs, its dependence on an order of discovery, and its competition with the demands of embodied existence, our expression of ideas is conditioned by our culturally limited expression of the universe. We can see now the complicated relationship between the human mind and God. The human mind is an image of God in that both hold ideas of possibles and that these ideas maintain set relationships among themselves in both. Nonetheless, the *experience* of reasoning is distinctively human, because we always express God's mind in a particular embodied experience of the universe. The human experience of reason is embodied, temporal, and cultural, unlike reason in the mind of God.[29] As we have seen, Leibniz maintains the distinction between innate ideas and experience of the world as least as strongly as any other early modern thinker, grounding them in radically different ontologies. While they thus come into a monad from radically separate sources, this section has shown that they come into our *apperception* through one process – conscious experience. Innate ideas come to our attention through a concrete order of discovery, guided by signs we have learned, competing with the daily needs of our body. Similarly, perceptions of the universe come to our attention as structured by necessary connections and an awareness of possibilities. This simultaneous, interdependent emergence of innate ideas and perceptions of the world seems obvious given the nature of experience, but it receives little attention from either Spinoza or Descartes. This process becomes more central for Leibniz partly because a mind contains both the universe and innate ideas within itself, making them more difficult to separate. Leibniz takes a middle ground between empiricism and a kind of rationalism. This middle position allows him to keep the necessity of some truths while also privileging exchange, which is the study of how this middle ground emerges in other perspectives. This privileging of exchange leads him to address more seriously the history of philosophy and to turn toward China.

KNOWLEDGE OF THE SENSES

We have seen that Leibniz distinguishes three kinds of knowledge of existing things: demonstrative knowledge of the existence of God; intuitive knowledge of our own existence; and sensitive knowledge of other things (NE IV, iii, § 21; RB 387). At first glance, it might seem that the first comes from our expression of God's understanding; the second comes from our expression of the universe; the third comes from a mix of the two. In fact, all three depend on a mix of both kinds of expression, as we have seen. Even the ontological proof of God depends on our use of signs and language. Moreover, how have we happened upon this proof? Some experience led us to it, and this experience depends on our expression of the universe.

---

[29] This difference between human and divine knowledge undermines some arguments that privilege an intuitive grasp of ideas modeled on God's intuitive grasp of ideas (cf. Martin Heidegger, *The Metaphysical Foundations of Logic*. Trans. by Michael Heim [Bloomington: Indiana University Press, 1984], pp. 57–68). It also complicates views of rationality as a good in the created universe, since what is "pleasing to reason" seems only to apply to the human experience of reason (cf. Rutherford, *Rational Order*).

We probably read it in a book somewhere, and this book might not have reached us if we were living in a different culture, or born among "savages." Intuitive knowledge of the self, which might seem to be based purely on experience, likewise depends on a mix of both kinds of expression, and Leibniz emphasizes in particular that self-consciousness depends on the fact that we express God as well as the universe. So all three kinds of knowledge mix both expressions, but the third kind, knowledge from the senses, most clearly relies on both. In knowledge from the senses, instances of experience are mixed with knowledge of possibles to give systematic knowledge of what exists. The perception of immediate particulars, which would be our condition if we only expressed the universe, is united with pure knowledge of possibilities, which we would have if we only expressed God, into a general knowledge grounded in particulars but extending to other possible situations. This mixture allows us to draw necessary connections between existing things.

We can consider this process as a fourth way our embodied experience of the universe conditions our use of necessary truths and innate ideas. The first three limitations affect our access to all necessary truths, even the purely theoretical use of innate ideas, as in mathematics, but the greatest way our expression of the universe conditions our innate ideas is in bringing necessary truths to bear on existing things. First, in dealing with existing things, we rarely have clear and distinct or causal knowledge; we depend on experience to teach us the connections between things. Leibniz writes, "propositions of fact, i.e. experiences, such as that opium is a narcotic, lead us further than do truths of reason, which can never make us go beyond what is in our distinct ideas" (NE IV, viii, § 4; RB 430). Even when we can draw necessary conclusions, however, these remain conditional on being rightly applied. For example, that a simple substance cannot be naturally destroyed is a necessary truth, because indestructibility is a necessary consequence of being a simple substance. In other words, the proposition, "a simple substance is indestructible" is an identity, or reducible to an identity. These kinds of truths, however, are distant from existing things, because whether or not there are simple substances is a radically different question. All necessary truths, when applied in experience, are conditional: "As for *eternal truths*, it must be understood that fundamentally they are all conditional; they say, in effect: given so and so, such and such is the case" (NE IV, xi, § 13; RB 446). He gives an example: the necessary truth, that every three-sided figure has three angles, says only, *if* there exists a figure with three sides, *then* that same figure also has three angles

(NE IV, xi, § 13; RB 446–47). In geometry, this condition does not matter – whether or not a perfect triangle exists is irrelevant – but in most situations this condition is crucial. The application of necessary and universal truths requires bridging between innate ideas and existing things. Only one existential truth can be established through our expression of God alone – the existence of God. All other existential truths are related to experience, and the strong universality of our access to necessary truths is weakened by our perspectival access to existing things. For example, if we know that B is necessarily contained in A, then we know that if something is A, B is also necessarily true of it. The obvious question is, how do we know that this thing before us is in fact A? That B is necessarily true of this thing depends on the existential truth that this thing is A. This truth can only be gained through perspectival, cultural experience of the universe.

Unlike knowledge of necessary truths and immediate knowledge of experience, truths about existing things are neither certain nor universal: "There is not even a rigorous demonstration to prove that the objects of our senses, and of the simple ideas which the senses present us with, are outside us" (NE III, iv, § 2; RB 296). This does not mean that truths about the existing world are arbitrary or have no truth, but they remain provisional. Leibniz emphasizes fallibilism but he also emphasizes – particularly against Locke – that the senses bring real knowledge (NE I, ii, § 9; RB 94). Any experience has some truth as an expression of the order of the universe. In the *New Essays*, Leibniz pushes this point regarding secondary qualities. We should not think that perceptions like pain or color are arbitrary and have no natural connection to their source, for "it is not God's way to act in such an unruly and unreasoned fashion" (NE II, viii, § 13; RB 131). As expressions, secondary qualities have a determinate relation to their cause, and thus the order or relationships among those qualities has a ground in the order or relationship in or among the existing things. This relationship holds in spite of the radical difference between blue and the immaterial monads blue expresses.

In establishing the existence of things outside us, Leibniz differs from Descartes, who uses God's existence as a guarantee, and from Locke, who relies on a certain immediacy or intensity of feeling (IV, ii, 1–7). For Leibniz, only the systematic connection or order of phenomena establishes the existence of external things. This method follows because the truth of phenomena as expressions is not in their qualities but in the relationships they express. He describes this process:

I believe that where objects of the senses are concerned the true *criterion* is the linking together of phenomena, i.e. the connectedness of what happens at different times and places and in the experience of different men – with men themselves being phenomena to one another, and very important ones so far as this present matter is concerned. And the linking of phenomena which warrants the *truths of fact* about sensible things outside us is itself verified by means of *truths of reason*, just as optical appearances are explained by geometry. (NE IV, ii, § 14; RB 374–75)

The connection of phenomena must be taken over time as a coherent whole. A dream might be internally coherent but what convinces us that we were dreaming is that, when we wake up, we realize a more broadly coherent story of how we came to fall asleep (A VI, 2, 276; L 114). When writing of knowledge from the senses, Leibniz repeats these three factors: the overall connection of phenomena; the testimony of other people; and the use of necessary truths. These factors apply not only to establishing the existence of a world in general but also to the determination of what in particular exists. They apply to any attempt to determine what really exists and what the real properties of things are. The way to increase our ability to determine what exists is to increase our knowledge of phenomena, and the easiest way to increase our knowledge of phenomena is second hand. The knowledge of existing things is a communal project and benefits greatly from exchange, as building communities of seekers of knowledge was one of the central aims of Leibniz's life and work.

What does Leibniz intend when he writes that the linking of phenomena must be verified by truths of reason? He has already described innate ideas as the mortar or muscles and tendons of thought. Any making sense of experience relies on innate ideas and truths of reason, but Leibniz intends something stronger here. He often contrasts empirical connections with causal knowledge. An animal can remember that one event usually follows another, as a cat comes to the sound of the can opener. According to Leibniz, human beings usually operate at this level of merely empirical knowledge. Scientific or causal knowledge, however, depends on knowing that one event *must* follow another (T 59). So an empiric might know that gold will not dissolve in a certain solution, but a scientist will know that, given the nature of gold and the nature of the solution, the gold cannot possibly dissolve. Because it requires necessary connections, causal knowledge can never be induced from instances of experience alone and relies on reason. One way that Leibniz describes this process is by describing reason as a formal method for connecting observed experiences. Leibniz gives this view of reason in the *Theodicy*, writing, "Reason, since it consists in the linking together of truths, is entitled to connect also those wherewith experience has furnished it, in order thence to draw mixed conclusions" (PD 1; H 73). Reason is a way of connecting truths, and these truths can come from the senses or from reflection. In the appendix, the move to knowledge from the senses is explained as the mixing of truths of reason with immediate or primitive truths of perception (TH 409–10, 404–05). Leibniz gives some examples of these mixed truths in the *New Essays*, such as the proposition "sweet is not bitter," which combines the principle of contradiction with immediate facts from the senses (NE I, i, § 18; RB 82–83). A more complex example is the proposition "we should pursue joy and avoid sorrow." This proposition is innate, but it is known by instinct, not reason. Leibniz writes, "Given this principle, though, one can derive scientific conclusions from it, and I warmly applaud what you said, sir, about morality as a demonstrative science" (NE I, ii, § 1; RB 89). Even though the principle comes from the senses, is known confusedly, and even its components, such as joy and sorrow, are known only confusedly, reason can use it to form a demonstrative science.

To describe reason as the linking between ideas, though, is misleading. A true proposition always translates into the containment of the predicate in the subject, so that propositions correlate to the implications of the ideas involved. Knowing necessary truths about events, then, requires that we grasp the ideas involved, which returns us to the difficulty of applying necessary truths about ideas to existing things. Leibniz marks this step in the *New Essays*: "the nature of truths depends upon the nature of ideas, before either are explicitly formed, and truths involving ideas which come from the senses are themselves at least partly dependent on the senses" (NE I, i, § 11; RB 81). How do we move from the senses to ideas? First, because the senses are grounded in the reality of things, qualities like color and warmth are grounded in nature. To move to ideas, we provisionally identify sensory phenomena with general ideas or ideas of species. Leibniz explains this use of species in the *New Essays*. Philalethe claims that species have little reality and no connection to the true internal constitution of things (NE III, vi, § 13; RB 308). Theophile begins with some concessions, by admitting that no two things are identical and thus part of the same ultimate species. For this reason, we have no rigorous standards for distinguishing physical species. In addition, even though all appearances are grounded in reality, it can happen that two things with different internal structures appear the same. Yet even their association would have some reality, because there would be some reason for the similarity of their appearances. He concludes, "It can be said, then, that whatever we truthfully distinguish or compare is also distinguished or made alike by nature, although nature has distinctions and comparisons which are unknown to us and which may be better than ours" (NE III, vi, § 13; RB 309). It may be, and in fact must be, that we do not distinguish species from one another as finely as we should, but the distinctions we make express the nature of things. We must simply be careful and willing to revise our categories. Leibniz summarizes this method:

If we regard them as only provisional with reference to actual bodies, and as subject to experiments which have been or will be made to discover more about them, and if we have recourse to the experts when fine points arise about whatever it is that the name is generally understood to stand for, then we shan't be doing anything wrong. Thus, although nature can furnish more perfect and more convenient ideas, it will not give the lie to any ideas we have which are sound and natural even if they are perhaps not the soundest and most natural. (NE III, vi, § 30; RB 322–23)

Since the information coming from our senses expresses the nature of things, we can tentatively match our ideas to our experience. In this way, we come to know necessary connections between events and we can predict the future. Leibniz uses the example of gold (NE IV, vi, § 4; RB 400). We can know many things about gold with certainty, for example, that the body with the greatest known ductility is also the heaviest known body, because all of these properties must have a ground in the essence of gold. A body with these characteristics could someday be found which would be differentiable from gold. If so, the criterion now used for gold would become a genus, rather than the lowest species, but it would remain a true expression of the essence of gold.

This account of Leibniz's method remains vague if only described on a general level. Let me give a concrete example to illustrate the process he has in mind. I walk past a tree and think of an idea of a tree that is a substance. As I examine my idea, I see that the idea of being a substance includes indivisibility, which in turn includes non-existence in space. On this reflection, I realize that my current idea of the tree contains a contradiction and thus is not an idea at all. At the same time, I might realize that, because the tree has a kind of unity and unity must be grounded in a substance, the tree must be an expression of an immaterial simple substance, a monad. Now let's say I study this tree and determine some of its properties, for example that it relies on photosynthesis and thus must have light in order to survive. Reliance on light is then a necessary part of this idea. From this idea I can conclude that if a tree is deprived of light, it will eventually die, necessarily. This kind of causal knowledge differs from mere empirical observation. Now imagine that I learn that some trees do indeed grow without any light.

What does this mean for the process so far? It would not necessarily mean that my current idea of the tree is not truly an idea, because, unlike my idea of the tree as itself a substance, my idea of a tree requiring light might not be contradictory. What this discovery would mean is that my idea of the tree, from which I drew necessary conclusions, did not in fact correspond to these things I had been experiencing, and calling trees. I would have to determine a new idea that better corresponded to the phenomenon. For example, I might think of an idea of a tree in which photosynthesis was not the only means of life. I could draw new causal connections from this idea, but those connections would always remain provisional, depending on how well this new idea matched the phenomenon.

Leibniz gives a more positive foundation to the physical sciences than Locke, but severe limitations remain.[30] We have seen two. The first is the difficulty of matching our ideas to existing things. A second limitation is the gap between our general ideas and the ideas of particular things. The idea of any particular thing contains the entire universe, is infinite, and lies beyond our grasp. Ideas from the senses can be infinitely analyzed, which means that our ideas of sensory things can always become clearer. Leibniz says that this kind of analysis has already been carried out regarding rainbows and prisms, and provides a fruitful starting point for natural science (NE IV, iii, § 16; RB 382–83). Nonetheless, analysis can never reach bottom: "if our eyes became better equipped or more penetrating, so that some colours or other qualities disappeared from our view, others would appear to arise out of them, and we should need a further increase in acuity to make them disappear too; and since matter is actually divided to infinity, this process could go on to infinity also" (NE II, xxiii, § 12; RB 219). When we apply our ideas to things, we substitute limited, abstract, one-sided ideas for the infinitely complex idea of the particular thing. We could say that our knowledge of the world is always rooted in possibles, while the world itself is made up of actuals.[31]

These limitations mean that our knowledge of the universe never captures the full order of the universe. The level of knowledge that we can reach Leibniz calls "natural." We can determine the general or natural laws of the universe, but we cannot determine the precise laws which determine the future. In the "Discourse on Metaphysics," Leibniz calls natural law God's "custom," in contrast to God's particular decisions (DM 7; AG 40).

---

[30] For an excellent view of both the power and limits of science for Leibniz, see Herbert Breger, "Maschine und Seele als Paradigmen der Naturphilosophie bei Leibniz." In *Zeit und Logik bei Leibniz*. Ed. by Carl Friedrich von Weizsäcker and Enno Rudolph (Stuttgart: Klett-Cotta, 1989).

[31] Cf. Breger, "Maschine und Seele," pp. 81–82.

Regarding the self, he writes, we can distinguish our essence, which expresses the whole universe, from our "nature," which is limited, belongs to us in a particularly close way, and "depends on the less general maxims that creatures can understand" (DM 16; AG 48–49). Everything which God creates is orderly, and in that sense nothing is miraculous, yet we can distinguish between the maxims that God usually follows and those that we cannot foresee and appear irregular. We call the former laws of nature and the latter miracles.

In order of certainty, necessity, or completeness, knowledge of natural existential events comes late, but it is the main body of our knowledge. Although knowledge of nature does not fully grasp the true order of the universe, Leibniz strongly criticizes attempts to explain things without following natural laws. If we do not stick with the order of nature, we strike against reason, lose philosophy, and injure the idea of God (RB 66). Part of this criticism is directed against Locke's claims that matter might be made to think or attract at a distance. He writes, "the modifications which can occur to a single subject naturally and without miracles must arise from limitations and variations of a real genus, i.e. of a constant and absolute inherent nature" (RB 65). As we have seen, we can grasp something of these inherent natures by connecting phenomena to complex ideas from which certain necessary consequences follow. Within the order of nature, God will not arbitrarily attach qualities to substances: "He will never give them any which are not natural to them, that is, which cannot arise from their nature as explicable modifications" (RB 66). Matter could not regularly attract things at a distance, because such a power does not follow from the nature of matter. This claim is not based on induction from experience but on the necessary implications of the idea of matter. In other words, given Leibniz's idea of matter, it is impossible for matter to attract at a distance. We should note that Leibniz's claim could err in two ways. He could mistakenly analyze his own idea, failing to see that attraction at a distance is compatible with the idea of matter. Alternatively, he could be right about his idea of matter but be wrong in applying it to the created world. In this case, he would need a new idea that better fit the phenomena. Exchange with people from different perspectives could help to avoid both errors.

In speaking of the two forms of expression, I have set up an opposition with our expression of innate ideas as universal, and our expression of the universe as perspectival. Since knowledge merges both expressions, the greater universality of our access to necessary truths is shaped by our expression of the universe. This opposition and reconciliation is more complex than it appears. We should remember that both expressions contain some limits, and that both contain something consistent. Science is possible only because our expression of the universe itself reveals consistent connections. Thus this opposition between one expression as universal and one as perspectival is misleading. We participate in two different orders, and, although our grasp of both orders is limited, neither is exactly perspectival. Perspective emerges because apperception emerges at the intersection of these two orders. This claim depends on showing that our expression of the universe in itself is limited but not perspectival. In other words, it makes no sense to speak of an animal as having a "perspective." The relationship between a monad and the universe clarifies this claim. Each monad is affected by every other, but the effects from each monad are not equal, so that closer monads affect a monad more strongly. Perception exactly parallels this arrangement, as the preestablished harmony between mind and body guarantees. In this sense, the way a monad expresses the universe in perception is completely adequate to that monad's place in the universe. The monad is simply a living mirror. While the monad does not grasp the entire universe equally, there is no reason that it should, since it is not in the whole universe equally. Leibniz suggests this point when he says, "And since God's view is always true, our perceptions are always true; it is our judgments, which come from ourselves, that deceive us" (DM 14; AG 47). This passage echoes Descartes' attribution of error to judgment; what Leibniz means is that, as mirrors of the universe, monads simply reflect what exists, and in this sense perception is true to position. Error comes when we step beyond that position, making judgments about things distant in time or space. Judgment is a mix of necessary truths and immediate perceptions, and can never be perfect or infallible. Through our expression of ideas, minds are not limited to any one place in the universe, and in a sense perceive the whole universe, in so far as they recognize truths that are universal. We can see here the contrast between Leibniz and Spinoza. Spinoza maintains the harmony between our mind and our placement in the universe – in his terms, the parallel modes of infinite thought and infinite extension – only by absolutely constraining the mind to the "place" of the body. We learn some things about the universe beyond our small portion only because some facts about our portion are true of the whole. For Leibniz, knowledge of possibles draws us out of our immediate placement in the universe. Our expression of the understanding of God allows us – forces us – to move from how things are to how they could be, and then to how they might be in other parts of the universe. Our ability to overstep our concrete place in the universe is crucial to Leibniz's view of perfection and contemplation. Leibniz expresses this progression beautifully in the essay "On the Ultimate Origination of Things," translated as a poem by Emily Grosholz:

> Thus already many substances
>   have arrived at great perfection,
> although, given the infinite divisibility
>   of the continuum,
> there are always other parts asleep
>   in the abyss of things,
> yet to be aroused, to be advanced
>   to better and greater things,
> as one might say to better cultivation.
> Thus progress never comes to a conclusion.[32]

This progression is not simply an increase of knowledge, because a monad *is* the universe in a certain perspectival way. The progression of knowledge actualizes into apperception the universe and the ideas which each monad already contains at a dim level of perception. In this progression of knowledge, we become more god-like.[33] This expansion depends on communication and the exchange of perspectives. It depends on cultural exchange.

At the same time, this expansion beyond our place in the universe opens us to error and to having what can properly be called a "perspective." This claim may seem insignificant, but is essential for the question of what we have in common. So far, it seemed that, because we express the universe, our view is perspectival and cultural and these limitations make our knowledge fallible and cultural exchange valuable. Now a different model appears. What makes our knowledge perspectival, fallible, and in need of cultural exchange is that consciousness emerges between the embodied world and our stock of innate ideas. If we could limit ourselves to one or the other, our knowledge could perhaps be perfected, but because we participate in both, our experience is perspectival. I believe that Leibniz's account of human knowledge as drawn between experience of the world and reason is his main contribution to intercultural understanding and underlies his success in interpreting Chinese philosophy. In placing knowledge between experience and reason, Leibniz unites narrow versions of empiricism and rationalism, just as he balances skepticism and dogmatism. In this way, as in many others,

---

[32] Emily Grosholz, "Plato and Leibniz against the Materialists," *Journal of the History of Ideas* (1996), p. 271.
[33] Cf. Grosholz, "Plato and Leibniz," pp. 274–76; Friedrich Kaulbach, "Subjektivität, Fundament der Erkenntnis und Lebendiger Spiegel bei Leibniz," *Zeitschrift für philosophische Forschung*, 20/3–4, pp. 471–95.

Leibniz can be seen as a forerunner of Kant, but Leibniz's position is crucially different, because he leaves no way to distinguish clearly between reason and experience. Even the narrowest necessary truths depend on language and signs learned through experience. From a Kantian perspective, my analysis would support the claim that Leibniz confuses some crucial distinctions, but this very "confusion" drives Leibniz's greater pluralism and openness to cultural exchange. In the following chapters, we will see how this basis functions in Leibniz's writings on China.

CHAPTER 3

Exchange with China

LEIBNIZ AND CHINA

Thus far we have examined Leibniz's philosophy as a basis for cultural exchange and comparative philosophy. On a metaphysical level, exchange is driven by the value of diversity in the best possible world and the derivation of diversity from variations in monadic perspectives. On an epistemological level, exchange is driven by the necessary limits of our own perspective and the fact that monads in distant places have different and complementary perspectives. This foundation grounds many forms of exchange, such as the reconciliation of church factions and the founding of learned societies, but it particularly drives exchange with distant monads. For Leibniz, this drive for exchange was directed almost exclusively toward China. In this chapter, we will see how Leibniz conceived that exchange and what he hoped to learn. Leibniz showed an interest in China and other cultures from an early age, and, of Europeans who never left Europe, he became one of the most knowledgeable about China, particularly in the breadth of his knowledge. His interpretation of Confucian thought has serious flaws, but stands well above those of his contemporaries, and even some of the missionaries. From his research into Leibniz's sources, David Mungello concluded that Leibniz had probably read or was familiar with every significant book that had been written on China.[1] Leibniz mentions almost all of them at some point in his correspondence.[2] Leibniz affirms his knowledge of the available sources in a letter to Simon de la Loubère from 1692. La Loubère had lived in Siam

---

[1] David Mungello, "Die Quellen für das Chinabild Leibnizens," *Studia Leibnitziana*, 14 (1982), pp. 233–43.

[2] In the early 1670s he mentions the first European translation of Confucius, by the Jesuit Intercetta (A I, 1, 187–89; A III, 1, 43). In 1675, and frequently thereafter, he refers to Martini's book on China (A IV, 1, 569–70). In 1687, he mentions the translation of the Confucian classics edited by the Jesuit Couplet (A I, 4, 622). Brosseau sent him a copy of Le Comte's *Mémoires de la Chine* in 1696, soon after its publication (A I, 13, 269). Leibniz's major work on Chinese philosophy is written in response to three major anti-Jesuit writings, by Nicholas Longobardi, Antoine de Sainte-Marie (Antonio Caballero a Santa Maria), and Nicholas Malebranche.

as a French ambassador from 1687 to 1688 and in 1691 he published an influential book entitled *Du royaume de Siam*, cited by Leibniz, Locke, and Bayle, among others. Leibniz praises La Loubère's book and laments that La Loubère never went to China, because most of the authors writing of China speak of superficial things, not serious research (A I, 7, 553). Apparently, Leibniz thought he knew the literature on China well enough to judge it, and he was hoping for better sources. His involvement in the Jesuit mission, begun a few years earlier, directly attempted to improve the flow of information from China.

Leibniz's first mention of China was in his *De Arte Combinatoria*, in 1666, when he was 20 years old. By the mid-1670s, Leibniz comfortably discussed China in his writings. His earliest correspondence concerning China was with the orientalist Gottlieb Spitzel. Most of this correspondence consists of discussions of Christianity and the threat of atheism, but Spitzel mentions the Jesuit Athanasius Kircher and recommends the Jesuit Prospero Intercetta's translation of Confucius, in which he has seen an "exact moral and political philosophy, or knowledge of natural things" (A I, 1, 187). Leibniz responds in 1672 that he has read Intercetta, as well as other books published in France, coming from the Jesuits in China. He suggests his later division, that in theoretical arts Europeans are superior, but in more immediate sciences the Chinese win (A I, 1, 192). Around that same time, Leibniz had an exchange with Henry Oldenburg concerning the Chinese language (e.g. A II, 1, 239–42). The most important early source for Leibniz's relationship to China, however, is his plan for the invasion of Egypt.[3] The plan was intended for Louis XIV and written under the patronage of Baron Johann Christian von Boineberg, the elector of Mainz. Leibniz claims to have come up with the idea on his own about four years earlier, in 1667 (A IV, 1, 268). The plan arose in response to French threats to invade Holland and the danger that Germany might be drawn into the war. Leibniz hoped to avoid this outcome by convincing Louis XIV to invade Egypt instead. The documents on the Egyptian expedition are difficult to interpret: Leibniz was young, possibly under the influence of Boineberg, and more concerned with avoiding war in Europe than encouraging war elsewhere. Thus the main document, the "Justa Dissertatio," begins with a

---

[3] The best sources on the Egyptian Expedition are Paul Ritter, *Leibniz Ägyptischer Plan* (Darmstadt: Otto Reichl Verlag, 1930); and Jean Baruzi, *Leibniz et L'organisation religieuse de la terre d'apres des documents inédits* (Paris: F. Alcan, 1907). A partial translation and summary was published anonymously in London in 1803, entitled *A Summary Account of Leibnitz's Memoir*. It was written as part of the propaganda effort against Napoleon's invasion of Egypt, which the translator believed was inspired by Leibniz's plan.

description of the advantages of peace, but then narrows to the advantages of peace *within Europe* (A IV, 1, 273–74). The documents are written as propaganda meant to encourage politicians to attack Egypt, so the rhetoric is more inspirational than objective. For all these reasons, the Egyptian expedition has been almost entirely ignored. Nonetheless, we should not miss the degree to which Leibniz relies on Euro-centric views, reinforcing many of the assumptions that would later characterize the discourse Edward Said described as "Orientalism." These writings illuminate Leibniz's relationship with China in direct and indirect ways.

Indirectly, although the plan is driven by European concerns, it shows that at an early age Leibniz looked to the world outside of Europe. The plan is astonishingly detailed. Leibniz describes the Egyptian populations, cities, political structures, and various Christian groups from whom help might be expected. For example, he concludes that only three passes lead from Asia into Egypt, he describes how to defend each pass, and he explains why previous defenses have failed (A IV, 1, 307). Although the goal is to invade – not learn from – Egypt, the plan could only be conceived, researched, and written by someone curious about other cultures, and someone who envisioned Europe on a world stage. In an ironic way, he already reflects his famous claim, made near the end of his life: "I am not one of those impassioned patriots of one country alone, but I work for the well-being of the whole of mankind, for I consider heaven as my country and cultivated men as my compatriots."[4] At this point, however, the "well-being of the whole of mankind" coincides with the imposition of European religion and culture on "barbarians." Beyond his detailed knowledge of Egypt, the plan for the Egyptian expedition reveals Leibniz's understanding of the developing politics and economics of colonization. Leibniz comments on details of intra-Asian trade, such as the tendency of India and China to accumulate gold and how this monetary policy relates to trade between the Philippines and China (A IV, 1, 246; cf. 252). He repeatedly argues that the invasion would most effectively strike against Holland by disrupting its trade links with the East Indies, the roots of its power and stability (A IV, 1, 246, 252). Egypt is described as the best option for French colonial expansion, given that the easiest pickings were already taken by other European powers. Egypt would provide an entry for further expansion, with France eventually controlling the Red Sea, the Persian Gulf, the island of Ormuz, which had been controlled on and off by the Portuguese since 1508, and

---

[4] *Leibniz Selections.* Trans. by Philip Wiener (New York: Charles Scribner's Sons, 1951), pp. 596–97; G. W. Leibniz, *Lettres et opurcules inédits de Leibniz.* Ed. by A. Foucher de Coreil (Paris: Ladrange, 1854), vol. VII, pp. 506–15.

the island of Madagascar, where the Dutch and English were already trading and the French were struggling to establish a presence (A IV, 1, 278). Leibniz had this knowledge when he was only in his mid-twenties. The Egyptian expedition is sometimes dismissed as the unrealistic imaginings of a young intellectual, but it must be read against the real background of colonial expansion. The Portuguese had already fought and defeated the Egyptians in the Indian Ocean, and, at the time Leibniz wrote, the French were establishing a presence in India, with a trading post at Surat in 1668 and Pondicherry in 1672. Based on the Egyptian expedition, Leibniz seems well on his way to becoming a colonial official, but he does not take this route. With all of his later plans to promote exchange with China, he never advocates colonies. This lack of interest might suggest that Leibniz was a bookish scholar with no understanding of the economic pressures of international trade, but the Egyptian expedition shows the contrary, that Leibniz was probably as knowledgeable as anyone not directly involved with trade. When he proposes a "commerce of light," he is by no means ignorant of the "commerce of goods" driving international relations.

Also of indirect relevance for Leibniz's approach to China are his views of Christianity, European culture, and war. Leibniz shows little reluctance to impose European religion and culture on others through violence.[5] He justifies the expedition as a "holy war," and compares it with earlier Crusades. Thus he writes:

> If the most rigid censor of inner conscience should pass judgment, he would not only approve but even order the war. That exceptional Bacon rightly shows in a fragment on holy war, that a war (having the greatest efficacy) for promoting culture and religion among barbarians is just; yet with that moderation which reason dictates, so that it could not be expected to be more damaging than advantageous, as it tends not to the extermination nor the servitude of a people but to wisdom and happiness and the emendation of human kind. . . . And wars should not be waged on men but on beasts (that is, barbarians), and not for killing but for taming. How much more right when this is undertaken not only to extend but also to serve piety, and a miserable people groaning under the yoke of barbarians, with the remnants of a soon to be lost faith, are rescued. The welfare of a great part of human kind depends on these deliberations: by this, an affair of God and the spirit is certainly put in motion. (A IV, 1, 379)

Supporting this argument for war, Leibniz declares that Asians are particularly soft and incompetent in war, emphasizing that a small group of

---

[5] The most disturbing writing in this regard is the "Modus Instituendi Militiam Novam Invictam," written at the same time as the Egyptian writings. The plan calls for the creation of an army capable of conquering the world by training a mixture of captured "barbarians" from places like Africa, Arabia, America, and New Guinea on an isolated island like Madagascar. (A IV, 1, 408–10).

Tartars captured all of China (A IV, 1, 279, 326). This softness contrasts "the cultivated, warlike and freedom loving peoples" of Europe (A IV, 1, 273). Leibniz's views may be typical for his time, but they contrast with his later views, where he does not advocate force and is more concerned with learning that spreading European culture. The change in approach is impossible to explain with certainty. Already in these writings, Leibniz has a more favorable view of China than of Egypt, and his contemporaries would generally have had harsher views of Muslims than of the Chinese. As Leibniz's later plans are directed to China, he might have thought an invasion would be less appropriate or necessary. Thus, in a plan for the Berlin Society of Sciences, he writes, "among missionaries going to civilized, not barbarian, lands, the real sciences are the best instrument after the help of God."[6] How one should deal with barbarian lands is conspicuously unaddressed. Other than the Egyptian expedition, Leibniz writes remarkably little about Islam, so it is difficult to know if his views evolved. Leibniz may have become convinced that violence would simply not work, so that more peaceful means had to be found. Perhaps, though, his views evolved in conjunction with the development and extension of his philosophy, so that his view of minds as different, complementary expressions of the same universe helped him to extend his "conciliatory eclecticism" beyond the reaches of Europe.

The Egyptian expedition contains several direct references to China. Some give factual reports about the Manchu invasion, Chinese monetary policy, and the closing of Chinese ports to foreign trade. Leibniz describes China as self-sufficient, leading him to call France the "China of the Occident," as he calls Egypt the "Holland of the Orient" (A IV, 1, 268). He emphasizes the weakness and incompetence of the Chinese in war, but more striking is his praise for China. His positive view of China is already implied in its comparison with France. He also compares China favorably with ancient Egypt: "Egypt has been most highly valued by all others. Whether the Chinese are from the Egyptians or the latter from the former, I dare not say; certainly the similarity of their institutions and hieroglyphics along with their kind of writing and philosophizing suggests that they are consanguineous peoples. Both are parents of the arts and sciences" (A IV, 1, 270–71). In another document, he says that either Egypt was a colony of China, or China was a colony of Egypt (A IV, 1, 384). In either case, his comparison connects China with the origins of European science. He would have taken this connection from sources like Kircher and Spitzel,

---

[6] Hans-Stephan Brather, *Leibniz und Seine Akademie* (Berlin: Akademie Verlag, 1993), p. 163.

both of whom praised Egypt and connected it to China. The height of Leibniz's praise for China is that it is the world's most cultivated land, if we set aside Europe's possession of the true faith. Similar praise, with the same exception, appears later in his preface to the *Novissima Sinica*.

Leibniz's initial approach to China is part of his interest in international politics and economics, as the Egyptian expedition shows. This practical focus continues but comes to be dominated by cultural interests: the "commerce of light" overtakes the "commerce of goods." This focus on the exchange of knowledge is present early as well. A parallel scholarly interest focused on the Chinese language and its use for his universal characteristic.[7] The most significant event in this regard was his encounter and correspondence with Andreas Müller, an orientalist in Berlin. Müller gained fame with his claim to have discovered a "*clavis sinica*," a "key" to the Chinese language. The key would be something like a decoder, allowing Chinese to be easily understood and translated. It also showed that the Chinese language had a rational structure. The possibilities of this structure for the creation of a universal characteristic intrigued Leibniz and others. What made Müller notorious was that he advertised the key but would only share it if someone would pay. No one would. In spite of pleas from poor scholars, he supposedly burned whatever he had discovered shortly before his death. No one knew if Müller ever really had such a key, although Leibniz believed he had discovered something.[8] From this point on, the correspondence between Müller and Leibniz consists of Leibniz pleading for information, and Müller refusing. Ultimately, Leibniz learned almost nothing from Müller, but Müller's key sustained Leibniz's hopes and interest in the Chinese language. Leibniz's letters to Müller reveal his knowledge and interests at that time, almost a decade before he met anyone who had visited China. A letter from June 24, 1679, is particularly revealing (A I, 2, 491–92). In this letter, Leibniz lists fourteen questions, which Müller subsequently refused to answer (A I, 2, 499). All of the questions are directed either toward the use of the key or the structure of the Chinese language. The questions are those one might ask about a philosophical language or universal characteristic: do the characters refer to words or things? are they reducible to a basic alphabet? are immaterial things expressed through material or visible things? is the language artificial or was it formed gradually by use? does it make the nature of things understood and make them rational? do the

---

[7] E.g. to Oldenburg, A II, 1, 239–42.

[8] For example, in the *Novissima Sinica*, he writes that in Müller "peevishness contended with learning," but that he had clearly discovered something (NS 18). In a letter to Paul Pellisson-Fontanier, he calls Müller the "man in Europe who knows the most of the Chinese language" (A I, 8, 180).

signs referring to natural things refer to things directly, or to characteristics which distinguish them from one another? (A I, 2, 491–92). Leibniz and Müller exchanged a few more letters, but the only one that draws any significant response from Müller is a request for him to translate a book from Chinese, translating each character, giving its pronunciation and meaning in Latin (A I, 2, 508). Surprisingly, Müller agreed to do the translation, but wanted to see the book first, at which point he declined and asked for another, claiming he had already treated this one (A I, 2, 517). I believe the book sent by Leibniz was of the classical Confucian philosopher *Mengzi*.[9] This exchange surely increased Leibniz's confidence in Müller, and it shows that as early as 1679 Leibniz was in possession of at least one Chinese book.

Leibniz's efforts toward China accelerated and broadened with his contact with the Jesuit Claudio Filippo Grimaldi in Rome in 1687. From that time on, Leibniz was actively involved in the Jesuit mission and corresponded with several Jesuits living in China. The philosophically most substantial of these correspondences are with Jesuits directly involved with the mission, notably with Grimaldi and Joachim Bouvet, both of whom were missionaries in Beijing; and Antoine Verjus, the procurator of the missions. The mission was a frequent topic in Leibniz's correspondence with other Jesuits such as Adam Kochanski, Bartholomaeus des Bosses, Ferdinand Orban, and René-Josephe Tournemine. In much of this correspondence, Leibniz discussed the "Rites Controversy" and his astonishment and disappointment at the Church's decisions. Contact with the mission gave Leibniz some control over his sources of information and allowed him to give advice for the mission. The most significant result of this interaction is the publication in 1697 of the *Novissima Sinica*, a collection of Jesuit documents relating to China, which Leibniz edited and introduced. The preface is a wonderful document, with its call for cultural exchange, the need to learn from China, and the complementary strengths of East and West. The goals surrounding the publication of the *Novissima Sinica* will be taken up in more detail later.

From the time of his contact with Grimaldi, Leibniz wrote almost constantly about China in his correspondence. Much of this exchange concerns the progress of the mission and the Rites Controversy, and Leibniz's most extensive discussions of Chinese philosophy support the Jesuit position of accommodation. Most interesting is the breadth of Leibniz's interest and

[9] A title page of *Mengzi* in Chinese is found in the folder of letters to Müller (LBr 666).

his role as a conduit for information. Leibniz writes something to someone about all of the main controversies in China – polygamy, the discovering of an ancient Nestorian monument, the conflicts between the Biblical chronology and the Chinese historical records, the rumors of a Jewish community in China. In 1697, Leibniz wrote to Sophie Charlotte:

> I will thus have a sign placed at my door, with these words: bureau of address for China, because everyone knows that one has only to address me in order to learn some news. And if you wish to know about the great philosopher Confucius, or about the ancient Chinese Kings quite close to the Deluge and consequently the first descendants of Noah, or about the drink of immortality which is the philosopher's stone of that country, or about some things which would be a little more sure, you have but to order it.[10] (A I, 14, 869)

Leibniz remained a "bureau d'adresse pour la Chine," answering questions and gathering information from his Jesuit sources. An interesting example is a long letter from John Toland, from February 22, 1710 (LBr 933, Bl 17–18). Toland complains that the Jesuits always write that Chinese is so difficult, yet he recently heard from an Augustinian monk that it is fairly easy.[11] The Jesuits, he suspects, exaggerate the difficulty of the language as a defense, so they can dismiss their opponents as unable to understand. He asks Leibniz's opinion. What makes this letter interesting is that Toland wrote it to Leibniz in the first place. He had confidence that Leibniz could answer his concerns, and Leibniz responded correctly – the Jesuits correctly say that the written characters are difficult, but the spoken language is not (LBr 933, Bl 33). Another interesting example is a letter to the duchess of Orléans, to be communicated to her son. Leibniz had been asked about the mental capabilities of a person born without the ability to speak or hear. He responds that it would depend on many factors, including education. He then offers Chinese as an example. Under favorable circumstances:

> They would be capable of inventing some new artifices and even sciences, without the help of words, in employing some equivalent characters, either in the fashion of the Chinese or by paintings. And the Chinese would not lose as much as we if they were born for all the future deaf and mute. For their language is poor and their characters abundant and independent of language, so that often in order to explain well in conversation they have recourse to the characters. (Klopp, I, 7, 3, p. 171)

---

[10] Leibniz sends the same motto to Thomas Burnett of Kemney in January, 1696 (A I, 12, 370).
[11] The Augustinian monk was Nicolas Agostino Cima, who had been to China and was critical of the Jesuits there. Leibniz met with him and he was one of Leibniz's only non-Jesuit sources.

These two examples illustrate some of the breadth of Leibniz's discussions of China. Often he served as a conduit for scientific information. He forwarded medical questions from the physician Lucas Schröck to China and Batavia (now Jakarta).[12] He sent geographical information from the Jesuits to Nicholas Witsen, who published a well-known world map. With the linguist Hiob Ludolf, he discussed Chinese and Tartar words.[13] The diagrams of the *Yi Jing* (Book of Changes), which Leibniz thought to be an ancient binary arithmetic, were discussed with several mathematicians and intellectuals, including Cesar Caze, Wilhelm Tentzel, and Louis Bourget.[14] Sun spot observations from the Jesuit missionary Jartoux in China were sent to Gottfried Kirch, the official astronomer for the Berlin Society of Sciences.[15] Leibniz even forwarded extracts of a letter from China to Peter the Great.[16]

Among these discussions of China, one significant event should be mentioned – the discovery of a connection between Leibniz's binary arithmetic and the hexagrams of the *Yi Jing*. When Leibniz developed his binary arithmetic, a system based only on zero and one, he realized that it provided an illustration of how God could create all things out of unity and nothingness. Thus he sent a medallion inscribed with numbers in his binary system to Duke Rudolph of Brunswick in 1697, writing:

> After all, one of the high points of the Christian faith, which agrees least with the philosophers and is not easy to impart to pagans, is the creation ex nihilo through God's almighty power. Now one can say that nothing in the world can better present and demonstrate [this power] than the origin of numbers, as it is represented here through the simple and unadorned presentation of One and Zero or Nothing.[17]

Thinking that this numeral system might serve the missionaries as an explanatory tool, he sent an explanation to Grimaldi in 1697 and to Bouvet in 1701 (W 33–43 and W 134–43, respectively). At that time, Bouvet was working on the *Yi Jing*, convinced that it held some secret knowledge because of

---

[12] LBr 838, Bl 2–3.

[13] Much of Leibniz's correspondence with Ludolf is published in John Waterman, *Leibniz and Ludolf on Things Linguistic* (Berkeley: University of California Press, 1978).

[14] These writings are collected in Hans Zacher, *Die Hauptschriften zur Dyadik von G. W. Leibniz* (Frankfurt am Main: V. Klostermann, 1973).

[15] Leibniz's letter is missing, but Kirch thanks him for the information in a letter from August 25, 1705 (LBr 472; Bl 4). Heuvel attributes the source to Jartoux. (Gerd van Heuvel, *Leibniz in Berlin* [Berlin, 1987], p. 45.)

[16] Woldemar Guerrier, *Leibniz in seinen Beziehungen zu Russland und Peter dem Grossen* (Hildesheim: Gerstenberg, 1975), pp. 205–08.

[17] Julia Ching and Willard Oxtoby, *Moral Enlightenment: Leibniz and Wolff on China* (Monumenta Serica Monograph Series, Vol. XXVI; Nettetal: Steyler Verlag, 1992), p. 72; original in A I, 13, 116–25.

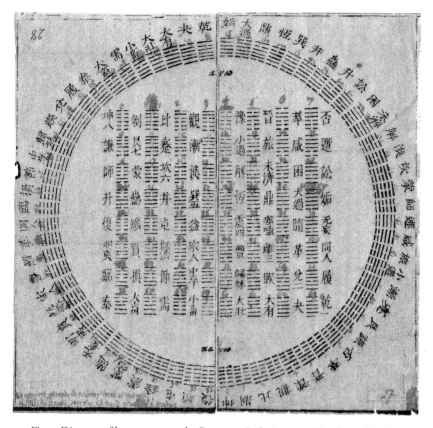

Fig. 1 Diagram of hexagrams sent by Bouvet to Leibniz, 1701. (Numbers added by Leibniz.) Image courtesy of Leibniz Archive, Miedersüchische Landesbibliothek.

its connection to Fuxi and the Biblical Patriarchs. Leibniz's description of his binary arithmetic came to Bouvet at just the right time, so that Bouvet was struck by the similarity – which he saw as identity – of the two binary systems. The similarity was particularly striking because one of the traditional orderings of the hexagrams, the *xiantian tu* ordering made by Shao Yong, was, with a few modifications, the same order found in Leibniz's binary arithmetic.[18] Bouvet was convinced that the hexagrams represented a binary arithmetic, and after he announced this to Leibniz in 1701, Leibniz was also convinced. In 1703, Leibniz sent the article, "Explication de

---

[18] For a good source on the similarities and differences between the hexagrams and Leibniz's binary arithmetic, see Zhonglian Shi, "Leibniz's Binary System and Shao Yong's Xiantian Tu," in Li and Poser (eds.), *Nueste über China*.

l'arithmétique Binaire," to the Paris Academy. The article included an explanation of binary arithmetic and its connection to the hexagrams. A succession of letters discussing this connection followed. As with Leibniz's faith in the existence of a *clavis sinica*, the main significance of the connection between the binary arithmetic and the hexagrams was its impact upon Leibniz's approach to China. The discovery reinforced Leibniz's belief that the wisdom of the ancient Chinese surpassed that of the modern Chinese, and his belief that Europeans could help to rediscover these truths. The connection also increased Leibniz's faith in a rational structure underlying the Chinese language.

The last stage of Leibniz's engagement with China was through his promotion of scientific societies. Leibniz's first plan for a German society was written in 1669, and in 1671 he referred to the value of Chinese medicine in a plan for an academy. Before his death, he would be involved with attempts to found the Berlin Society of Sciences, a Saxon academy in Dresden, an academy in Kassel, and an academy in Vienna, and he would advocate an academy and the promotion of arts and sciences in Russia. He even suggests to Bouvet and another Jesuit missionary, Jean de Fontaney, that a European-style academy be formed in China, including Tartars, Chinese, and Europeans (W 204, W 206). Each of these projects includes at least a mention of exchange with China as a goal.

A COMMERCE OF LIGHT

At the center of Leibniz's multi-directional efforts toward China is his desire to increase the exchange of knowledge between China and Europe. Every mind expresses the universe from a different perspective, and how different this perspective on the universe is depends on our spatial location. In China, Leibniz found a developed culture, almost completely unknown to Europe, located almost as far away as possible. A letter to Bouvet from December 12, 1697 reveals his expectations. Giving Bouvet a list of information he would like, he writes:

I come to *physique* and I understand presently under this name all the experimental notices of corporeal things for which one still cannot give the reason by geometrical principle or mechanics. Therefore these cannot at all be obtained by reason and *a priori*, but only by experience and tradition; and I do not at all doubt that the Chinese surpass us much on this point, because their experience is longer and their tradition less interrupted and more polished than ours. (W 62–63)

Earlier in the same letter, Leibniz writes that he expects the Chinese to have many inventions that Europeans lack, even though the latter use better principles, because such inventions depend not only on principles but also on chance occasions, from which thousands of consequences and inventions can be drawn (W 62). Given the perspectival nature of our experience, diversified by our embodied position in the world, we would expect any different culture to be a rich source of knowledge, but Leibniz considers China particularly excellent in that area most useful for cultural exchange: the accumulation of experiential truths. The Chinese have an exceptionally long history, relatively unbroken and well recorded. In a letter to Grimaldi, Leibniz notes that the Chinese have managed to preserve ancient traditions lost in Europe through the migrations of peoples (W 3). This excellence among the Chinese leads to a particular complementarity between Chinese and European cultures, which again reinforces the importance of cultural exchange. The most famous expression of this complementarity is in the preface to the *Novissima Sinica*. In the practices of everyday life, the two are roughly equal and both have much to learn from the other. In theoretical disciplines, including logic, geometry, metaphysics, and astronomy, Europe is the winner; while in observations of experiential truths, the Chinese are the victors. They also win in "practical philosophy, that is, in the precepts of ethics and politics adapted to the present life and use of mortals" (NS 2–3). Chinese excellence in practical philosophy leads to another complementary aspect of the two cultures: the natural theology of the Chinese complements the revealed theology of Europe (NS 10). Based on his comparison, Leibniz claims that an expert in the excellences of peoples would have to judge the Chinese as better, except for Europe's possession of Christianity (NS 17).

Upon hearing this claim, we must question Leibniz's seriousness. Is this merely rhetoric meant to criticize Europe and inspire exchange? The Chinese have practical precepts, but the Europeans have geometry and first philosophy. Does Leibniz really think this a fair division? One need not look far to find Leibniz praising geometry: in the preface itself he writes, "since virtue flows from wisdom, and the spirit of wisdom is truth, those who thoroughly investigate the demonstrations of geometers have perceived the nature of eternal truths and are able to tell the certain from the uncertain" (NS 9). It seems like the Europeans, armed with geometry, have all the advantages, but the earnestness of Leibniz's efforts to foster exchange with China testifies to the sincerity of his praise. We have seen in Leibniz's method the interdependence of necessary truths and existential truths. Without knowing that this thing is A, knowing the necessary truth that A is certainly B is of little help. We only know that this is A from experience, the kind of experience in which Leibniz thought Chinese culture was particularly rich. Excellence in necessary truths, without the experience to apply these truths, is fruitless, and Leibniz thought this fruitlessness was reflected in the moral poverty of Europe in his time. Of course, the Chinese have just as much to learn. The accumulation of experience, without the clarity and structure of logic, is confused and stunted, and Leibniz thought Chinese philosophy and science reflected this weakness. How this exchange of complementary strengths would work can be extrapolated from Leibniz's above comment about inventions. In that passage, he says that inventions depend on chance occasions, but really they depend on both observation and reason, because from these chance discoveries one can "draw forth a thousand beautiful consequences and find a thousand inventions" (W 62). Imagine the rewards, then, if these chance occasions, recorded so well by the Chinese, were submitted to European reasoning. Leibniz names the much-praised Emperor Kangxi as a concrete example of the combination of Chinese and European excellence. We have already seen in Kangxi's own words his willingness to learn from the missionaries. With this combination, Leibniz says, "his foresight and his grasp of affairs can only elevate him above all other Chinese and Tartars, exactly as if on a pyramid of Egypt a European steeple should be placed" (NS 7).

Leibniz writes that this exchange of knowledge should be reciprocal, but in practice he emphasizes learning from China. One reason is that Leibniz believes European knowledge is more easily learned, both because it is based more on reason, and because it is more public; while the Chinese knowledge is based more on experience, held by men of profession, and passed on by tradition (W 179).[19] The main reason for Leibniz's emphasis, however, is to counteract the bias of his sources. The missionaries went to China to teach Christian religion, not to learn Chinese culture. Learning came as a by-product of the main goal of teaching. As the missionaries used their scientific knowledge to gain acceptance in China, they were not only teaching European religion but also European science. Leibniz criticized Grimaldi for this imbalance, and constantly emphasized to his correspondents the need to bring knowledge of China to Europe.[20] This imbalance leads to Leibniz's persistent fear for the missionary effort, that the Chinese will take up what the Europeans know, while the Europeans will neglect what they should learn from the Chinese. The result will be that the two cultures will no longer be complementary – the Chinese will

---

[19] Nathan Sivin supports Leibniz's view: "In China there was no single structure of rational knowledge that incorporated all the sciences . . . The sciences developed a great deal more independently of each other than in the West. The practitioners of each science extended and revised the concepts and assumptions about physical reality with which that science began" (Nathan Sivin, *Science in Ancient China: Researches and Reflections* (Brookfield, VT: Variorum, 1995), VI, p. 169.

[20] For Leibniz's criticisms of Grimaldi, see letter to Simon de la Loubère, from October 5, 1691 (A I, 7, 398); also to Melchisedech Thevenot, August 24, 1691 (A I, 7, 357).

be superior to Europe in all fields. At that time, they may cut off the trade in knowledge, leaving Europe behind (NS 10). For the Chinese perspective, we can turn again to Kangxi, who assumed the Chinese were already superior but also gaining and improving on European knowledge:

In the late Ming Dynasty, when the Westerners first brought the gnomon, the Chinese thought it a rare treasure until they understood its use. And when the Emperor Shun-chih got a small chiming clock in 1653, he kept it always near him; but now we have learned to balance the springs and to adjust the chimes and finally to make the whole clock, so that my children can have ten chiming clocks each to play with, if they want them. Similarly, we learned in a short time to make glassware that is superior to that made in the West, and our lacquer would be better than theirs, too, were it not that their wet sea climate gives a better sheen than the dry and dusty Chinese climate ever could.[21]

Such learning would have greatly pleased Leibniz, if it were mutual.

Leibniz shows extreme confidence in the value of cultural exchange, or a "commerce of light." All knowledge expresses God, either directly through our ideas, or indirectly through our expression of a universe which in turn expresses its creator. Through knowledge, perspectives converge, so that learning never threatens either religion or harmony. Guided by the principle that two truths cannot contradict, Leibniz confidently embraces knowledge from China. The best example is the controversy surrounding the Chinese chronology. We have already seen some methods of accommodating this chronology, but often the Chinese chronology was taken as a threat, met with deliberate blindness or dismissal. Leibniz has no fear of the Chinese records. He writes to Bouvet, "And in all this it is necessary to go with all the good faith possible, without any disguise, which could be prejudicial to those who are authorities among us; for it is certain that one will always find that one truth is in accord with another, and that the holy Scripture never holds anything wrong" (W 61).[22] Leibniz had no fear of accommodating European thought to any truth.[23]

Leibniz is as confident in the ease of exchange as he is in its value. He speaks as if knowledge were a homogeneous mass – we can give ours to the Chinese, they can give theirs to us, and we will each have twice as much. His image of Kangxi combining European and Chinese knowledge shows his view of exchange – an Egyptian pyramid with a European steeple simply

---

[21] Spence, *Emperor of China*, pp. 67–68.
[22] Cf. letter to Hermann von der Hardt, December 21, 1697 (A I, 14, 881–83).
[23] For Leibniz's own verdict that the Chinese records must be accommodated, see his letter to Samuel Chappuzeau, September 12, 1692 (A I, 8, 429); and letters to Daniel Larroque from June 19, 1693 (A I, 9, 487) and September (2nd half), 1693 (A I, 9, 574).

set on top. Leibniz recognizes some of the practical problems in the actual exchange of knowledge. He suggests to the missionaries the value of his proposed universal characteristic for missionary work, writing to Verjus:

And the new philosophical Calculus of this universal Species, being independent of any language, would be a marvelous aid in order to make the most important and abstract truths of natural religion, on which the revealed is like a graft, favorable even to the most different peoples, in which the languages differ as much from ours as Chinese and those like it. (W 57)

In spite of his recognition of the linguistic challenges to the acquisition of new knowledge, Leibniz's fears of imbalanced exchange between Europe and China reveal his confidence in the ease of exchange. Leibniz believed that in a short time the Chinese could take up the whole of European knowledge, then cut off exchange. As Leibniz feared, the trade in knowledge between China and Europe did not last long, but, contrary to his prediction, neither Europe nor China learned much from the exchange. Both learned something, and perhaps China learned more, but Leibniz's expectation never materialized: "We could give them our knowledge almost at once and by a kind of infusion, and on our side, we could learn from them also at once a world of new instructions that, without them, we would not at all obtain in I know not how many centuries" (W 64). This over-confidence in the ease of exchange may be one of Leibniz's greatest errors regarding China.

In spite of his own focus on exchange, Leibniz says that the exchange of knowledge is the most important thing, *except* for the spread of Christianity (e.g. W 86 or W 266). Such statements, however, are addressed to the missionaries on which he depended for information, making them difficult to assess. I believe that the spread of Christianity in China was of importance to him, as his own efforts to help the missionary effort establish, but his immediate objective remains exchange. While Leibniz was confident in the value and ease of cultural exchange, he was skeptical of the prospects of Christianity in China. Implicit in his fears of an imbalanced exchange between China and Europe is the fear that ultimately Christianity might not take root. Through the time that Leibniz was involved with the missions, he had some moments of confidence, but more often expressed skepticism. Early, he wrote that, unless the pope allows polygamy for the Chinese, Christianity has little chance.[24] Even in the optimistic time around the *Novissima Sinica*, Leibniz writes to Johann Jacob Julius Chuno, a Berlin

---

[24] See letters to Landgraf Ernst von Hessen-Rheinfalls from July 14, 1690 (A I, 5, 617); and to Simon de la Loubére from October 5, 1691 (A I, 7, 398).

official and later member of the Berlin Society of Sciences, "France, the Pope, and the Jesuits are now sending missionaries upon missionaries. I am afraid that their ardor goes too far, and that finally a reverse like that in Japan will happen, if they give any suspicion" (A I, 13, 611–13).[25] These fears take on a more frantic tone later in his life, as the tide turned against accommodation. He writes to Charles le Gobien in 1707, "I have always feared that one day our missionaries and all the other foreigners will be chased out, when they [the Chinese] no longer think they need us" (W 64). A year earlier he wrote, "For it is very apparent that the Europeans will be chased out one day and that they will regret the lost occasion" (W 235, cf. W 196). The result of these fears is that, while Leibniz encourages the spread of Christianity, he constantly warns the missionaries to take on the more secure work of transmitting knowledge, before it is too late.

A more fundamental reason why Leibniz emphasizes the exchange of knowledge is the relationship between knowledge and religion. The way to establish Christianity in China, he thought, is through science and philosophy. Knowledge, including scientific knowledge of the world, leads to God by illuminating the wonder and order of the universe. On a more practical level, worldly knowledge gave the missionaries access to China and to the court. In the *Novissima Sinica*, Leibniz explains the edict of toleration for Christianity in China: "Then the strength of our geometry, as soon as it was tasted by the king, was so much to his liking that he easily came to believe that those who had learned thus to reason might teach correctly in other things" (NS 13). Leibniz repeatedly attributes the success of the Jesuits to their use of science and math in his attempts to call Protestants to the mission, with the claim that the Protestants excel the Jesuits in science.[26] For both practical and philosophical reasons, Leibniz focused on the exchange of knowledge as an indirect, but perhaps more certain, route leading to the conversion of the Chinese. The form of Christianity to be introduced follows from this relationship between knowledge and religion. Leibniz focuses on establishing a core of natural theology to precede the more difficult and supernatural truths of revealed religion. The missionaries should follow the method of the ancient Church, he says, not giving all mysteries at once, but at the same time not subverting any Christian doctrine (NS 12). Three elements in particular lead Leibniz to promote a stripped-down version of Christianity. The first was the belief that the missionaries should introduce Christianity through philosophy, a belief which Leibniz shared

---

[25] The Jesuit mission in Japan enjoyed extraordinary success in the beginning, but was violently suppressed from the beginning of the seventeenth century.

[26] E.g. to Morell, 1697, A I, 14, 203.

with many of the Jesuit missionaries. For this reason, Leibniz writes to the missionaries with philosophical ideas for their use. The second reason why Leibniz emphasizes natural theology is his belief that the ancient Chinese had their own natural theology that could form the foundation for the introduction of Christianity. This belief was also common among the Jesuit missionaries, with Bouvet as a particular advocate. So in the *Discourse*, Leibniz writes: "For me I find all this quite excellent and quite in accord with natural theology. . . . It is pure Christianity, in so far as it renews the natural law inscribed in our hearts – except for what revelation and grace add to it to improve our nature" (Discourse 31). This last part reveals Leibniz's own bias toward natural theology – some might see leaving out revelation and grace as a big exception. The third element comes from Leibniz's view of the conflicts within Christianity, believing that all Christians share a core of beliefs, and that this simplified core should form the basis of reunification and missionary work. In the preface to the *Novissima Sinica*, he wishes that the conflicts among Christians could be kept hidden from the Chinese: "For we all universally consent to those principles of the Christian faith which would ensure the salvation of any people who would embrace them, so long as nothing heretical, spurious, or false were daubed on besides" (NS 12). Such a unified core would not only facilitate the introduction of Christianity in China but would also unify Christians within Europe. Leibniz's wish did not turn out, and, in a spirit not so different from that of Leibniz, Kangxi remarked on the un-Christianlike conflicts between the missionaries:

Every country must have some spirits that it reveres. This is true for our dynasty, as for Mongols or Mohammedans, Miao or Lolo, or other foreigners. Just as everyone fears something, some snakes but not toads, some toads but not snakes; and as all countries have different pronunciations and different alphabets. But in this Catholic religion, the Society of Peter quarrels with the Jesuits, Bouvet quarrels with Mariani, and among the Jesuits the Portuguese want only their own nationals in their church while the French want only the French in theirs. This violates the principles of religion. Such dissension cannot be inspired by the Lord of Heaven but by the Devil, who, I have heard the Westerners say, leads men to do evil since he can't do otherwise.[27]

In sum, a core natural theology prepares the ground for revealed religion, harmonizes with ancient Chinese thought, and provides a harmonious basis for all Christians. Leibniz's focus on natural theology can easily be taken as an attempt to undermine Christianity, but his focus on natural theology

[27] Spence, *Emperor of China*, pp. 80–81.

is compatible with the goal of establishing Christianity. In other words, if Leibniz's primary goal were to spread Christianity, we would expect him to act as he did.

THE DIPLOMATIC FRONTS

Besides Leibniz's efforts to carry out an exchange of knowledge through his correspondence, he exerted considerable diplomatic effort toward increasing and easing exchange, reflecting his political interests and skills. From early on, Leibniz was an enthusiastic consumer of information from China, but his role changed in 1689, when he met the Jesuit Claudio Filippo Grimaldi. Grimaldi had been living in Beijing, and was soon to return as head of the imperial bureau of mathematics. Through Grimaldi, Leibniz struck up a correspondence with several other Jesuits involved with the mission, moving from an avid but passive recipient of knowledge, to an active participant in the missionary effort. On the one hand, through this correspondence, Leibniz could tailor the information he received to his own interests and questions. On the other hand, he could give his own advice and input into how the missionaries should proceed. This active connection to the Jesuit missionaries, and even its central themes, can be traced back to Leibniz's first correspondence with the Jesuit Daniel Papebroch, one of the editors of *Acta Sanctorum*. In January 1687, Papebroch wrote to Leibniz telling him of Couplet's translation of the Confucian classics (A I, 4, 612–13). Leibniz responded by suggesting that they publish it in an interlinear version with the Chinese characters. He also praises the value of a "key" to Chinese (A I, 4, 622). Papebroch replied by describing the overworked condition of the missionaries, claiming that they had more important things to do than gather knowledge for Europeans (A I, 4, 630–31). Leibniz responded in turn by describing the work the missionaries have done so far, without damaging their success as missionaries, and that the search for knowledge could even aid the mission (A I, 4, 655–56). Leibniz's first contact with someone who had lived in China was with Grimaldi. Two letters, one to Grimaldi and one to Giovanni Laureati, another Jesuit departing for China, reveal Leibniz's vision of the missions and China at that time. The most significant aspect of these letters is how he characterizes the missions, giving high praise for the missionaries, but as agents of exchange not as missionaries. He writes to Laureati: "[I hope] you will remember the great business that has been given to you, promoting commerce between two such widely separated spheres. A commerce, I say, of doctrine and mutual light" (A I, 5, 484; cf. W 11). The missionaries have been chosen to fill

great and weighty roles, not as spreaders of European truth but as conduits
for knowledge. In both letters, Leibniz expresses confidence that the Chinese have much of value to teach. In the letter to Grimaldi, he describes
the complementarity of Chinese and European knowledge (W 3). In the
letter to Laureati, Leibniz writes of his fears of the current imbalance in
exchange: "And it would be unfair to Europe if China alone should stand
in possession of all the light" (A I, 5, 484; cf. W 12).

Leibniz used his contact with the Jesuit missionaries as a source of information but also to contribute to the mission. He writes to Verjus in
1698: "This Mission seems to me so important for the good of the faith
and of humankind, that it interests me extremely, and I often think on
that which could serve it" (W 87). He tried to help and influence the
mission in three primary ways, which follow from what we have already
seen. First, Leibniz tried to convince the missionaries to learn as much as
possible from the Chinese. He did this partly by arguing that it was their
duty to Europe, praising how they were selected to help both China and
Europe through exchange. At the same time, he raised suspicions that giving
the Chinese knowledge without learning in return might leave the missionaries in a vulnerable position. Mostly, though, Leibniz argued positively
that knowledge of China, and even the transmission of that knowledge
to Europe, would benefit the missionary efforts. Only by understanding
Chinese culture could the missionaries know how best to convert them.

The second way Leibniz tries to help and guide the mission is by sending
specific information. We have seen that Leibniz thought the best way to
convert the Chinese was through knowledge and philosophy. In his correspondence with the Jesuits he tries to supply some of this knowledge and
philosophy, and, more importantly, he tries to convince the missionaries
that this is the proper method. He explains his intentions in a letter to
Verjus, where he writes that he would like to contribute to the mission but
all he can really do is contribute through his work in general. Regarding
the progress of science and the arts, he can contribute

[P]rincipally in two things which are, in the first place, the advancement of an art of
invention (which is the art of arts), both by new methods and by selections of some
consequence, and in the second place, the establishment of a solid philosophy, in
which piety and truth are equally accounted. (W 55–56)

Often he sends scientific news in his letters. He begins a letter to Bouvet
from February 15, 1701, by describing his new analysis of infinitesimals, a
newly discovered "spiritum igneum" that ignited when mixed with oil, and
the use of a barometer to forecast weather (W 134–35). Sometimes, he sends

his own discoveries, as he does with his binary arithmetic, which he sent first to Grimaldi in 1697, and then to Bouvet in 1701 (W 33–43, and W 134–43, respectively). After explaining the arithmetic, he says he hopes it may carry great weight with the Chinese philosophers, and even the emperor himself, as an illustration and confirmation of creation *ex nihilo*. He adds that they may benefit from the emperor's good will if he learns that the inventor is a friend of Bouvet, who has sent it from Europe expressly for the emperor (W 138–39).

The third way Leibniz tries to contribute to the missions is through advice for increasing the flow of information from China to Europe. He often urges the missionaries to publish more, and Leibniz himself published some of their writings in the *Novissima Sinica*. Sometimes he gives brief suggestions, such as the recommendation that some Chinese come to Europe as "nomenclateurs vivans" (W 57). Other times he offers more developed plans, as with his plan for a dictionary or encyclopedia of Chinese knowledge. He had heard that a great Manchurian–Chinese dictionary was being compiled, as the imperial court of the newly founded Qing Dynasty still used Manchu as its mother tongue. Leibniz proposed having this dictionary simultaneously translated into a European language, and expanding it to include figures, illustrations, and knowledge of specialized professions. The latter would appeal to the Manchus, he thought, as they might still feel excluded from these professions. "This dictionary would be the key to everything," he writes to Bouvet (W 218). Leibniz – ever a diplomat – even suggests how the emperor might be convinced to fund the translation. Bouvet could propose to him the advantages of such a dictionary and explain that the best way to make it would be with European expertise. They would be glad to help. Of course, the whole thing would have to be translated into a European language (W 217–18).

The publication of the *Novissima Sinica*, in 1697, marks another transition in Leibniz's relationship with China. While the meeting with Grimaldi gave Leibniz an active role within the Jesuit missionary effort, the *Novissima Sinica* shows Leibniz stepping into European politics. As the title, *The Latest from China*, indicates, the book is a source of news on China. Leibniz includes various reports written mostly by Jesuit missionaries, and within his preface he remarks on the most significant recent events in China: Grimaldi's failed attempt to reach China by land; the issuance of an edict of toleration for Christianity; how the missionaries helped to negotiate the treaty of Nipchou [Nerchinsk] between China and Russia; and the confirmation that a monument found in Xian had been left by Nestorian Christians in China. The real hopes behind the book, however, go beyond spreading information about China. Leibniz concludes the preface: "Certainly the size of the Chinese Empire is so great, the reputation of this wisest nation in the Orient so impressive, and its authority so influential an example to the rest that scarcely since apostolic times has any greater work appeared for the Christian faith to accomplish" (NS 22). If this is the message of the preface, the goal is "to rouse European courts and churches, so they may send laborers to the waiting harvest" (NS 16). In trying to inspire enthusiasm for missions to China, Leibniz gives even greater praise for the Chinese, commenting on their civility, politeness, and order. He praises the emperors in general, noting that they avoid shameful acts for fear of the judgment of posterity (NS 6), and then turns to Kangxi specifically:

I remember the Reverend Father Claude Philip Grimaldi, an eminent man of the same society, telling me in Rome how much he admired the virtue and wisdom of this prince. Indeed (passing by, if I may, the comment on his love of justice, his charity to the populace, his moderate manner of living, and his other merits), Grimaldi asserted that the monarch's marvelous desire for knowledge almost amounted to a faith. (NS 8)

Leibniz attributes the emperor's greatness partly to his combination of Chinese and European learning, and partly to his knowledge and appreciation of geometry. The second edition of the *Novissima Sinica* included an essay by Bouvet describing and praising Kangxi, translated from French into Latin by Leibniz.

Beyond the general goal of encouraging exchange, in the preface we find a complex political document displaying Leibniz's diplomatic skills. In spite of its brevity, Leibniz raises three specific political goals, all of which afterwards continue to draw his attention and interest. The first is his position of accommodation in the Rites Controversy. He says directly that Arnauld's criticism of the Jesuits is too harsh, and that the rites to Confucius seem to be free of religion (NS 11). He then criticizes the attempt "to force on far-off Christians all the formulae of the West" (NS 12). His frequent praise for the Jesuits and for the Chinese make an even stronger case for accommodation. Leibniz's position in the Rites Controversy will be discussed in the next chapter. The second political goal of the preface is the creation of a Protestant missionary effort, although Leibniz nowhere in the preface directly expresses this.[28] His reticence is understandable, given his dependence on the Jesuits: "I did not wish to criticize the Jesuits in a work for

---

[28] Merkel covers this aspect of Leibniz's writings in Franz Rudolf Merkel, *G. W. Leibniz und die China-Mission* (Leipzig: JC Hinrichs'sche Buchhandlung, 1920). Lach discusses Leibniz's missionary efforts as they relate to the German political scene (Lach, *Novissima Sinica*, pp. 39–55).

which they furnished the information," he writes to an unidentified British correspondent (Grua, p. 205). Instead, he calls all to the mission, careful to speak as a European rather than a German, and as a Christian rather than a Protestant, calling his book an attempt to rouse *European* courts (NS 16), and exchange with China the greatest task facing *Christianity* (NS 22). As a Protestant editing a book of Jesuit writings, he does not hesitate to speak of "we Christians" (NS 12). His very lack of partisanship opens the door to participation by all groups. Leibniz's vision that a streamlined Christianity, acceptable to all Christians, be introduced in China also indicates his wish to attract and accommodate Protestants. His attempt to speak as a Christian not only indicates his desire to attract Protestants to the missionary effort but also another motive underlying the preface: that the missionary effort could unite different Christian factions in one common effort. In his writing on the Berlin Society of Sciences, Leibniz narrows his goal at least to bring together Protestant factions.[29]

The call for a Protestant mission in the *Novissima Sinica* was subtle enough that Leibniz felt he should point it out in a flurry of letters written immediately after the book was published. In a period of less than a month, between April and May, Leibniz wrote to seven prominent Protestants in several countries.[30] Each letter contains a similar message – the real goal of the preface is to stimulate Protestants to the missions, and this message was cloaked in order not to offend the Jesuits. We can take the letter to Chuno as an example. Leibniz begins, "I hinted in my preface the end that I had in publishing these pieces, but I did not wish to touch this line too overtly, so as not to set up my own opinion or to offend the Jesuits" (A I, 14, 145). He then praises the purity of Protestant doctrine, and emphasizes the historic importance of the missions in China, comparing the task to the conversion of Rome. Next, Leibniz describes the benefits Protestants have over Catholics:

I consider still that the Monarch of this great Empire [Kangxi] has honored strictly in his edict in favor of the missionaries only the science of Europe, and as the Protestants surpass or at least equal the Roman Catholics in the sciences, they will do at least as much as them. The Muscovites would rather give passage by land to the Protestants than to the Jesuits. And as the Protestants are the principle masters of the navigation of the East Indies, they have all the advantages on their side. (A I, 14, 146)

[29] Merkel, *Die China-Mission*, pp. 65–66, 145–48.
[30] On April 26, 1697, to Johann Chuno (A I, 14, 145–46) and to Jakob Wilhelm Imhof (A I, 14, 147–48); on April 27, to Etienne Chauvin (A I, 14, 154) and to Jacob Hop (A I, 14, 158); on May 11, to Andreas Morell (A I, 14, 203); on May 18, to Gilbert Burnet (A I, 14, 217) and to Thomas Burnett of Kemney (A I, 14, 223).

The other letters repeat these points. In later writings Leibniz goes further, to claim that Protestants would have an advantage in the sciences because they are less constrained by dogma.[31] To some correspondents, he adds material motives, such as the benefits for trade or nation.[32] Although Merkel says that Leibniz's call was well received in Protestant circles, it never met with the success he wished for.[33] The most enthusiastic respondent was Augustus Hermannus Francke, who became an advisor to a Danish mission to India. Konrad Mel was inspired by the *Novissima Sinica* to write a book promoting missions as a means of cultural exchange, published in 1701, but this work itself had little impact.[34] Leibniz claimed that his efforts provided the stimulus for the founding of the "English Society for the Propagation of the Gospel in Foreign Parts."[35]

We should not assume that Leibniz is duplicitous with his Jesuit correspondents and open with his Protestant ones. In spite of his criticisms, he holds a favorable view of the Jesuits in China. The publishing of a volume of papers by Jesuit authors itself implies approbation, and in the preface he directly says that most of the missionary efforts have been carried out by the Society of Jesus, "whose virtue in this enterprise deserves praise even from those who consider themselves its enemies" (NS 10). Any attempt by Leibniz to dismiss these comments as flattery seems disingenuous, and Leibniz later became a prominent defender of the Jesuit mission in the Rites Controversy. In spite of the implicit call for Protestant missions, Leibniz writes to Kurfürstin Sophie that the preface is written in favor of the Jesuits (Klopp I, 7, 2, p. 144). His opinion in a letter to Etienne Chauvin, editor of the *Nouveau Journal des Savants* and later member of the Berlin Society, seems most true: "I spoke favorably of the designs of the Jesuits in everything which merits our approbation and imitation, without touching that little which should be blamed" (A I, 14, 154). Leibniz's goal is what he says it is in the preface: to draw people to the opportunity that China presents.

---

[31] Merkel, *Die China-Mission*, pp. 142–43.   [32] E.g. to Burnet, 1697, A I, 14, 217.

[33] Merkel, *Die China-Mission*, p. 53. Lach says that the preface stimulated significant response for about a decade following its publication, mentioning Francke and Mel in particular, but adds that none of these responses led to a mission focused on cultural exchange (Lach, *Novissima Sinica*, pp. 59–63). For some responses to Leibniz's call, see the correspondence with Augustus Hermannus Francke, printed in Merkel, pp. 214–24; and with Vincent Placcius, printed in Dutens, IV, P 1, 77–81.

[34] Lach, *Novissima Sinica*, pp. 60–61.

[35] Adolf Harnack, *Geschichte der Königlich Preussian Akademie der Wissenschaften zu Berlin* (Hildesheim: Georg Olms Verlag, 1970 [repr. from 1900], p. 143). Leibniz discussed this with John Wallis, esp. GM IV, 75–80, and with Eduard Gee, esp. LBr 301, Bl 11. Lach claims that Leibniz played little role in the founding of that society, which was not focused on exchange. Leibniz sent the *Novissima Sinica* and several letters promoting a Protestant mission to Gilbert Burnet, the bishop of Salisbury and founder of the society. For examples of Leibniz's letters to Burnet, see A I, 14, 217 and A I, 16, 435.

He encourages anyone to do so, Protestant or Jesuit. If part of encouraging them is playing them against one another, he is not above doing so.

The third political goal is the opening of a land route to China through Russia.[36] Leibniz became acutely aware of the difficulties of reaching China through his relationship with Grimaldi. Soon after the two met in Rome, Grimaldi set out to return to China through Russia. Leibniz became an information center on Grimaldi's trip, sending letters of inquiry, and spreading whatever news he had acquired.[37] Grimaldi first failed to cross through Russia, then failed to cross through Persia, and was eventually forced to travel to China by the standard sea route, controlled by the Portuguese. Leibniz's correspondence with the Jesuits in China also emphasized the difficulties of communication, since there was sometimes a year lag between letters, and delivery was always uncertain.[38] The usual route to China was from Lisbon through the Portuguese colonies of Goa and Macau and then into China. Beyond the inherent dangers of the trip, access to China was controlled by the Portuguese, or by the Spanish coming the long way across the Pacific from the Americas, and was often threatened by Dutch ships. Leibniz's hopes of a Protestant mission depended on establishing a different route of access. In a letter to Chauvin, Leibniz mentions two hopes for such a route. One would be through the seafaring powers of Holland and England. The other would be through Germany's improved relationship with Russia (AI, 14, 154). He writes to Chuno in the same year that, as English and Dutch lack adequate access to China from the sea, the land route is critical (A I, 14, 806–07).

As with Leibniz's call for Protestant missionaries, the call for a land route through Russia is only implicit in the preface. The two paragraphs dedicated to Grimaldi's failed journey carry an implicit appeal to make this route easier, but the most important step toward Russia is in the first paragraph. The "singular plan of the fates" to bring Europe and China together includes Russia. He writes, "I do not think it an accident that

---

[36] For a more detailed discussion of the relationship between Russia and Leibniz's missionary plans for China, see Merkel, *China-Mission*, pp. 151–56. Lach also gives an excellent overview of the need for a land route through Russia (Lach, *Novissima Sinica*, pp. 5–20). For a broader discussion of Leibniz's plans for Russia, see Baruzi, *L'Organisation religieuse.*

[37] For example, from Daniel Papebroch, August 7,1690 (A I, 5, 644), from Antonio Magliabechi, June 30 (?), 1691 (A I, 6, 536–39), to Paul Pellisson – Fontanier, March 18, 1692 (A I, 7, 291–92), to Wilhelm Ernst Tentzel, March 16, 1692 (A I, 7, 628–29). NS 17 and 19 also discuss the trip.

[38] According to Lach, in 1695 the Jesuits sent some letters and a report from China to Europe through Russian intermediaries. In transit, copies of the materials "fell into other hands" and eventually made their way to Leibniz, who used them in the *Novissima Sinica* (Lach, *Novissima Sinica*, pp. 15–16). Leibniz mentions these materials in letters to Verjus from May 27 and October 4, 1695 (W 30 and 32, respectively).

the Muscovites whose vast realm connects Europe with China and who hold sway over the deep barbarian lands of the North by the shore of the frozen ocean, should be led to the emulation of our ways through the strenuous efforts of their present ruler and their Patriarch, as I understand it, in agreement with him" (NS 1). Including Russia in the divine plan shows that the intention of the book – to increase support for exchange – is directed not only at Europe but at Russia as well. Donald Lach adds that the publication of the *Novissima Sinica* was timed to coincide with Peter the Great's tour of Europe in 1697 and 1698.[39] Like his efforts for a Protestant mission, the implicit call in the *Novissima Sinica* for a Russian land route is expanded in Leibniz's correspondence.[40] A letter to Heinrich Wilhelm Ludolf, a Danish official who had just returned from a trip to Moscow, can be taken as an example. In this letter, Leibniz again describes the circumstances with China as being so favorable as to be the work of providence. He writes, "Two of the greatest Monarchs of the world show an extraordinary ardor to draw into their states that which is good among us. These are the Czar and the Monarch of China. And what is more important is that the state of the Czar joins Europe to China" (A I, 14, 555). Again, Leibniz laments that the great opportunity has been left solely to the Jesuits. He then describes concretely how to put his plans into action, asking what benefits the Czar has granted to the Dutch, and how the latter might combine trade in merchandise with trade in virtue and piety (A I, 14, 555). The rest of the letter gives specific suggestions on how to interest the Czar. For example, since the Czar loves the sea, he might be convinced to do a series of experiments on magnetic declination. In the later part of his life, Leibniz wrote many plans for the promotion of arts and sciences in Russia, sending some to Peter the Great and others to his ministers. Almost all of these emphasize the role Russia could play as mediator between China and Europe.[41] In 1716, near the end of his life, Leibniz sent such a plan to Peter the Great, in which he says, "I consider heaven as my country and cultivated men as my compatriots," lays out his plans for the development

---

[39] Lach, *Novissima Sinica*, p. 16.

[40] See, for example, to Chauvin, April 27, 1697 (A I, 14, 154), to François Lefort, August 4 (?) (A I, 14, N 225), to Augustus Hermannus Francke, September 30 (A I, 14, 545–46), to Andreas Morell, October 1 (A I, 14, 550), to Heinrich Wilhelm Ludolf, October 2 (A I, 14, 555–57), to Chuno, November 28 (A I, 14, 806–07).

[41] For examples, see "Denkschrift für Peter" from December 1708 (Guerrier, *Beziehungen zu Russland*, pp. 95–99), Leibniz to Herzog Anton Ulrich from 1711 (Guerrier, p. 170–171), or "Specimen einiger Puncte, darinn Moscau . . ." (FC VII, 395–403).

of Russia, and offers his own services.[42] Russia's special position between Europe and China, and the need for a land route, still form a significant part of this plan. Such letters reveal the intersection of two of Leibniz's great political schemes: exchange with China; and the promotion of arts and sciences in Russia.

Although Leibniz's main concern was cultural exchange, his practical focus was always on the missions. We have seen two stages of involvement: the first with the Jesuits; and the second in his call for a Protestant mission with the assistance of Russia. A third stage develops out of the latter. As noted, Leibniz promoted learned societies in Kassel, Dresden, Vienna, Russia, and Berlin, and he mentions China and missionary activity in relation to each of those, continually raising his motto: *propagatio fidei per scientias*. In 1700, Leibniz founded the Berlin Society of Science, and placed exchange with China at the center of its concerns.[43] Almost every document concerned with founding the society contains some discussion of China. In a list of projects, Leibniz writes, "The most important intention of the Society would be the mission for the propagation of faith through science."[44] In another plan, he adds that "the *propagatio fidei per scientias* was one of the main intentions in founding this Royal Society."[45] The most complete statement of Leibniz's plans bears the long title "Thoughts on how the *propagatio fidei per scientias* can be most beneficially instituted by the new Royal Society of Science according to its instruction."[46] Leibniz begins by noting his correspondence with missionaries in China, his promotion of a Protestant mission in the *Novissima Sinica*, and the role of the *Novissima Sinica* in the recent founding of an English society for the propagation of faith. He then begins a section on the training of missionaries with the statement that next to God's direct help the sciences are the best means for promoting Christianity. To that end, missionaries would be trained by the society in mathematics, astronomy, medicine, and requisite languages, preferably by native speakers. He lists some of the advantages of Protestants that we have already seen, adding that papal authority arouses suspicion with national leaders, which is why the Jesuits were driven out of Japan and why they are now in trouble in China. Leibniz continues in this manner, discussing how the missionaries should be equipped, how the Czar can be

---

[42] Partially translated in Wiener, *Leibniz Selections*, pp. 597–98; original in Leibniz, *Lettres et opuscules inédits . . .* Ed. by A. Foucher de Coreil, VII, 506–15.

[43] For an excellent study of Leibniz and the Berlin Society, see Brather, *Leibniz und Seine Akademie*. The works relating to the Berlin Society are collected in Harnack, *Königlich Preussian Akademie*.

[44] Ibid., p. 112.   [45] Ibid., p. 142.   [46] Ibid., pp. 141–45.

convinced to help, how the project could be funded, and how it might
increase unity among Protestants. He notes that a further goal might be to
send missionaries to Turkey, Persia, and India, but that for now a mission
through Russia to China seems most promising.

The tone of these writings differs from the *Novissima Sinica* and Leibniz's
other correspondence, in that it seems far from his "commerce of light,"
focusing instead on spreading the evangelical church to China. As he puts
the goal: "to think on means and ways to determine how the truths of
Christianity and purity of the Evangelicals can be more and more brought
through prepared missions to distant peoples still sitting in darkness."[47]
Such comments echo the more Euro-centric views of the Egyptian expedition, and they complicate an argument for Leibniz's pluralism, but I do
not believe this promotion of Christianity reflects Leibniz's main intention
or a change in his views of China. The writings surrounding the founding
of academies show Leibniz using all of his skills as a diplomat. He writes
for powerful people and tends to tell them whatever he thinks will be
most effective. He appeals to patriotism (emphasizing it will be a *Teütsch-
gesinnete Societät*[48]), financial gain (through trade), military strength (war
is the rule of force, that is, mathematics and mechanics[49]), and religion.
Even so, he slips in some elements meant to encourage the exchange of
knowledge. Leibniz's proposed school for training missionaries – as with
most of the plans involving the Berlin Society – never materialized. The
society took some steps toward exchange, for example, corresponding with
Brochhausen, who was traveling across Russia with a caravan heading to
Siberia. Brochhausen sent back some samples and information on mining
in Siberia.[50] In September 1705, Leibniz received a brief but encouraging report of this from Daniel Ernst Jablonski, the secretary of the society.[51] Pierre
Jartoux, another Jesuit missionary in China, offered to form some connections with the society, but his suggestion was never taken up (W 198–99).
In the first proceedings of the Berlin Society, published in 1710 as *Miscellanea
Berolinensia*, Leibniz included an essay on the origins of peoples, which
included information from Grimaldi and Bouvet, but focused more on
European and West Asian languages.[52] Two of Leibniz's numerous schemes
for financing the society may have derived from his enthusiasm for China.

---

[47] Ibid., pp. 97–98.   [48] Ibid., p. 112.
[49] Leibniz makes that comment in a letter to Empress Amelie, promoting an academy in Vienna
(Klopp, XI, 44).
[50] Mentioned in *Bericht des Secretars der Brandenburgischen Societaet der Wissenschaften*. Ed. by Adolf
Harnack (Berlin, 1897), pp. 34, 39.
[51] The letter from Jablonski to Leibniz is in *Bericht des Secretars*, p. 34.   [52] Dutens, IV, ii, 186–98.

One, which was attempted with much guidance from Leibniz, was a monopoly on silk production. The other was a plan for a state monopoly on calendar sales, a practice common in China and described by Ricci.[53]

What Leibniz seeks to learn from the Chinese is directed both by his epistemology and by his evaluation of the complementary strengths of European and Chinese knowledge. Leibniz sets up an opposition between the simple recording of experiential data and the use of necessary truths, putting China on one side and Europe on the other. We can get a survey of his goals by looking at a list of questions he wrote to Grimaldi in 1689 (W 3–4). These were answered by Grimaldi in conversation, although Leibniz recorded some responses (W 7–10). The questions cover a wide range of topics, but the majority relate to useful tools or processes, such as the making of porcelain, glass, paper, and a kind of fire. Others ask about natural resources, such as useful plants that could be transported to Europe. Leibniz's focus is practical – several of the questions relate to mining, as he had been advising the mining operations in the Harz Mountains through 1686.[54] This practical focus contrasts the list of questions Leibniz sent to Müller in 1679 and is reminiscent of his earlier interest in trade. Leibniz shows a thoughtful knowledge of the information then available on China and many of his questions fill in gaps or verify information found in other published works.[55] Strikingly, Leibniz not only seeks no necessary truths from the Chinese – he never asks, for example, if their geometry has developed anything unknown in Europe – he also asks little about systematic knowledge that we might call science. The closest he comes is to ask if there are vestiges of demonstrative geometry or metaphysical things in ancient China, and to inquire about a key (W 5–6). His focus is raw data, as in two of his main concerns – astronomical observations and historical records.

Primary truths of experience, such as "I see x," seem close to what Leibniz seeks in China, as, "in this certain year, I saw the sun and the moon in these positions." These simple truths of phenomenal observation represent one pole of human thought, closest to our expression of the universe. On Leibniz's division, Europeans would hold the other pole, which is the

---

[53] Silk had been produced in Europe for centuries, so the monopoly on silk production was not necessarily connected to China. Lach connects the calendar proposal to China (Lach, *Novissima Sinica*, pp. 51–52).

[54] E. J. Aiton, *Leibniz: A Biography* (Boston: Adam Hilfer Ltd., 1985), pp. 107–14.

[55] Widmaier gives the sources for many of these questions (W 6–7).

connection of necessary truths or the expression of innate ideas. As we have seen, however, although the roots of all consciousness lie in these two poles, apperception always blends the two. All conscious experience involves necessary truths, and all necessary truths involve embodied experience. Consequently, Leibniz's division of Chinese and European knowledge cannot be as clear cut as it first appears. We can look again at how Leibniz describes this division. In the letter to Bouvet, he writes, "I come to physics and I understand presently under this name all the experimental notices of corporeal things for which one still cannot give the reason by geometrical principle or mechanics. Therefore these cannot at all be obtained by reason and *a priori*, but only by experience and tradition" (W 62–63). This passage seems to separate empirical knowledge or the recording of observations from deductive *a priori* knowledge, but between these two lies the systematic but merely probable body of knowledge that is science. This middle ground gains structure from necessary connections between ideas but remains provisional as these ideas map onto existing things. Where is Chinese knowledge placed? Leibniz treats this question in a letter to Jean Baptiste Colbert, the powerful minister of Louis XIV, from 1679 (A III, 2, 918–19). He begins by saying that the Chinese reign in knowledge of experiments, but, since Europeans excel in knowledge of necessary truths, they can give a better description of the earth and the movement of the sky, and devise more miraculous machines. This division carries through to a division between Chinese strength in the practice of life and in observation and European strength in military power and geometry. He notes, "on both sides a certain severe rigor is demanded." This last sentence suggests that Chinese knowledge goes beyond recording of observations, as is clear in the "practice of life," which could not be accomplished by recorded experiences alone. Leibniz's previous sentence implies first that the Chinese not only have a mass of data, but also have a description of the earth and of celestial movement; these descriptions are just not as good as those of the Europeans. Second, Europe surpasses China in disciplines that depend most on necessary truths, such as astronomy. This superiority should not be taken to mean that in all sciences, even though the Chinese have more data, the Europeans have a better understanding. The division between the knowledge of China and Europe is better understood as a division *within* science. Both have a kind of science and both use observation and reason in developing it. This must be the case, as all thought occurs at this intersection of perception and innate ideas. Within these sciences, the Chinese excel on the observation side, and the Europeans excel on the reasoning side. This might mean that, in the sciences in which principles dominate, such as astronomy, Europeans rule, and in the sciences in which data dominate, such as pharmacology, the Chinese rule, but the two need not divide so neatly. In any case, in learning science from one another, both would learn some mix of data and reasoning, even if what each side most gained differed. It must be admitted, however, that Leibniz focuses on collecting data from the Chinese, not principles of science. One exception may be Leibniz's interest in Chinese technology. Although he considers Europe technologically superior, he is still concerned with importing Chinese technology. Of course, Europeans had already been transformed by Chinese technology – printing, gunpowder, and the compass.[56] Even with technology, though, Leibniz does not seek mechanical principles by which the Chinese make machines, and in this sense he seeks data, i.e. descriptions of useful machines.

Some remarks should be made at this point regarding Leibniz's evaluation of Chinese science. Leibniz's view seems to be that Chinese science is inferior to that of Europe, but that it was highly developed and had probably discovered some things not yet known in Europe. Leibniz would have drawn this evaluation from his Jesuit sources, who praised Chinese philosophy but not Chinese science and mathematics. The Jesuits gained their power in the court through math and science: Schall and Verbiest both took their posts as heads of the Bureau of Astronomy after open challenges to the court's Chinese and Muslim astronomers. In a sense, Leibniz and the Jesuits rightly asserted the superiority of European science. Defining science by the methods and goals of modern Europe, Chinese science was inferior. By the same definition, Chinese science had been superior until the Renaissance, particularly in mathematics and astronomy.[57] Chinese astronomical observations were more accurate than those in Europe until the sixteenth century, and their observations were remarkably well recorded. Yoke gives several examples of twentieth-century astronomers using these records in just the way Leibniz hoped.[58] If we consider science, though, not as an objective, culture-neutral mirror of nature but rather as a social phenomenon constructed around cultural institutions and particular goals, we can see the absurdity of trying to rank the "sciences" of various cultures.[59] In Leibniz's time, the goal of science was emerging as the observation and manipulation

---

[56] Sivin discusses the origins of these three technologies in China, with reference to a passage from Francis Bacon, who says "For these three have changed the whole face and state of things throughout the world": Sivin, *Science in Ancient China*, VI, pp. 165–66.

[57] Ho Peng Yoke, *Li, Qi and Shu: An Introduction to Science and Civilization in China* (Seattle: University of Washington Press, 1985) makes this case and gives a good introduction to Chinese science and mathematics. The most thorough study of Chinese science is Needham (1954–). Sivin, *Science in Ancient China* and Nathan Sivin, *Medicine, Philosophy and Religion in Ancient China: Researches and Reflections* (Brookfield, VT: Variorum, 1995), contain essays on a variety of themes in Chinese science.

[58] Yoke, *Li, Qi and Shu*. pp. 150–52.

[59] As obvious as this point may be, it did not occur to me until Henry Rosemont directed me to read Nathan Sivin. My account here is based on Sivin, *Science in Ancient China*, VII, pp. 45–66.

of nature, which soon merged into European institutions of industrialization and colonialization. From within this framework, European science became superior to that of any other culture, but it makes little sense to judge Chinese "science" by this European framework. In other words, the success of European science, with its nuclear weapons and environmental destruction, would appear as a failure from within the framework of Chinese science, which focused on harmony with natural processes and tended toward a contempt for both war and the commerce of goods. Ironically, Leibniz himself did not separate the goals of modern science from the goal of greater reverence for the created natural world, a reverence leading to God. The worldwide dominance of European science leaves us no examples of what a contemporary science in a traditional Chinese framework would look like. One possible exception is Chinese medicine and in particular recent attempts to integrate contemporary medical discoveries into a more holistic approach to health.

Chinese medicine is the one exception to Leibniz's general disinterest in Chinese science. Leibniz's praise must be coupled with his disdain for the study of medicine in Europe, as he suggests in 1671: "As foolish and paradoxical as the Chinese rules in medicine appear, they are however much better than ours" (A IV, 1, 552). A year later, Leibniz wrote to the orientalist Gottlieb Spitzel that the most promising thing to come from China is its medicine (A I, 1, 192). As Leibniz developed his knowledge of China, his concern for Chinese medicine also developed, and he sometimes says that, besides the conversion of the Chinese, the most important task for the missionaries is to learn Chinese medicine (W 86). Partly, Leibniz wants observations – what drugs have what effect – but he suggests that he also desires a science of medicine from the Chinese. He asks Bouvet for notices "with regard to some extraordinary experiences of physics or specific proofs of medicine" (W 139). This phrase suggests that Leibniz seeks more than just extraordinary observations, and that what he wants involves proofs, the use of necessary truths. This conception of medicine is reinforced in another letter to Bouvet, in which Leibniz writes:

I do not at all doubt that there are still with them some very considerable things to be learned above all in medicine, which is the most necessary of the natural sciences. . . . But all the physical sciences and even medicine have as final end the glory of God, and the supreme good of men; for in preserving it they give the means of working for the glory of God. (W 63)

Medicine appears as a natural science and part of the overall projection of science toward God. Leibniz's view of Chinese medicine is sometimes inconsistent, as in a letter to Kurfürstin Sophie from August 1697 (A I, 14, 12), in which he writes that the Chinese do not know of the circulation of the blood, and that Grimaldi said their medicine does not seem to be anything great, but, facing contradictory statements, we should look at Leibniz's actions, which show that he continued to seek knowledge of Chinese medicine well after his meeting with Grimaldi in Rome. As far as I know, Leibniz did not attempt to study Chinese medicine himself, but he did encourage the doctor Lucas Schröck to do so, forwarding a set of twelve questions from Schröck to Bouvet and to Andreas Cleyer, a doctor living in Batavia, the capital of the Dutch East Indies, now Jakarta.[60]

LANGUAGE AND THE UNIVERSAL CHARACTERISTIC

Another significant exception to Leibniz's interest in collecting data from China is his interest in the Chinese language. We have seen that our embodied expression of the universe conditions our expression of innate ideas through the dependence of thought on signs. This conditioning elevates the importance of adequate signs for reasoning. As signs are a consequence both of the structure of our innate ideas and our position expressing the universe, the concern for signs leads to cultural exchange. Simply put, although innate ideas are not in themselves culturally conditioned, our apperception of these ideas depends on culturally conditioned language. One way to ease the limits on our innate ideas is to refine our language and systems of signs, and perhaps the greatest resource for this task is other languages. In Leibniz's own attempt to foster cultural exchange, he projects a field of comparative linguistics. In the *New Essays* he writes, "And when there are no more ancient books to examine, their place will be taken by mankind's most ancient monument – languages. Eventually every language in the universe will be recorded, and contained in dictionaries and grammars; and comparisons will be made amongst them" (NE III, ix, § 10; RB 336). Leibniz himself lays the foundations for such comparisons through his wide contacts. His main interest is the progression of languages from Central Asia into Europe. He explains his desires in a letter to Bouvet, in which he requests copies of the "Lord's Prayer" in Chinese and neighboring languages (W 60–61). The same request recurs elsewhere in Leibniz's correspondence. With time, he writes, we will need them from Korea, Japan, Siam, Burma,

---

[60] Widmaier gives a brief description of these questions (W 71). The questions themselves are in LBr 838, Bl 2–3. Leibniz briefly discusses Cleyer in his correspondence with another physician, Conrad Barthold Behrens (e.g. A I, 15, 154; LBr 46, Bl 94 v°).

and the rest of the Indies, but most of all from the Tartar languages of the peoples to the north of China, India, and Persia. Bouvet sent an interlinear Manchurian–Latin version to Leibniz in 1698 (W 75–77). In the following two years, Nicholas Witsen sent a number of interlinear translations to Leibniz, which remain with Witsen's correspondence in the Leibniz archive.[61] Relative to his time, Leibniz shows a significant knowledge of Central Asian languages, asking specific questions about the progression of languages from east to west and about the relationship between Tibet and the Tartars. Through this correspondence he managed to find some connections between these different languages, most notably in the word for horse, drawing on information from Grimaldi and Bouvet.[62] Throughout his writings on China, language is one of Leibniz's main concerns, and in the time before his meeting with Grimaldi it is almost his sole concern.

As with most of Leibniz's serious interests, comparative linguistics fulfills several functions, such as opening up the wealth of texts in other languages (W 63), and aiding the conversion of the speakers of the language, a point Leibniz emphasized to his missionary correspondents (W 60–61). For our purposes, the most important reason for comparative linguistics is mentioned in the *New Essays*, where Leibniz writes that it "will be extremely useful for the knowledge of things, since their properties are often reflected in their names (as can be seen from the names of plants among different nations), as well as for the knowledge of our mind and of the marvelous variety of its operations" (NE III, ix, § 10; RB 336–37). As the intersection of our expressions of innate ideas and the universe, signs and languages express both the universe and the structure of our mind. Thus the study of languages allows us to learn about existing things, to clarify and broaden our expression of the universe, and to learn about minds, to clarify and broaden our expression of innate ideas. Different languages may have some commonalities, but their variety should give different insights into our common stock of innate ideas. One final reason for comparative linguistics is the light it sheds on the origin and migrations of peoples. Leibniz's insistence on this point may seem odd, but we must remember that, with his contemporaries, Leibniz saw changes in languages as a degeneration

---

[61] These are labeled as: Samojet (two different versions), Czexemise Turk, Permien, Progolitz, and Moegalo (LBr 1007).

[62] Leibniz mentions Celtic *Mar*, ancient German *Mare* or *Märe*, Manchurian *morah* or *morin* and Chinese *ma*. Leibniz first mentions this connection in a letter to Hiob Ludolf from April 18, 1692 (A I, 8, 127). In a letter to Edward Bernard from May 7, 1693, he writes that he learned the Tartar word for horse from Grimaldi (A I, 9, 330). Bouvet sends the word for horse in Manchurian (as *morin*) and in Chinese (as *ma*) (W 77).

beginning with the Tower of Babel.[63] Leibniz was skeptical of the possibility of retrieving an original "Adamic" language, but he hoped to clarify the origins of language as much as possible. The older a language, the more likely its connection to the original, and Chinese was thought particularly old and well preserved. Leibniz provides an excellent example of his plan in "De Originibus Gentium Ductis Potissimum ex Indicio Linguarum," published in the proceedings of the Berlin Society of Sciences. The essay traces in detail the relationships among European languages and their origins in Eastern Europe and West Asia, making some connections further east, citing Bouvet and Grimaldi. Leibniz notes the similar words for horse across Europe and Asia, and notes the connection between the "Oriental-Tartar" *kan* and the European words *können*, *King*, and *König*.[64] He takes these similarities as either traces of an ancient common language or as evidence that Europe and Asia were once united within a great empire.

Because of the connection between language and knowledge, knowing any languages through cultural exchange may increase our access to necessary truths, but Chinese was not just another language for Leibniz. Along with comparisons of languages, the study of languages can increase our access to necessary truths by helping us to create new languages and sign systems. Given the connection between language and culture, such a project leads naturally to cultural exchange, and, in Leibniz's attempt to create his "universal characteristic," he turned to Chinese. The reasons Leibniz sought help for his characteristic from other languages center around the need for an alphabet of human thought, a set of simple ideas with which the characteristic would calculate. Leibniz's unsuccessful struggle to generate these elements himself led him to look elsewhere. Unlike most contemporaneous attempts to create artificial languages, Leibniz did not believe the signs should arbitrarily connect to ideas. The characters should have a natural connection to what they represent, which made them difficult to create from scratch. As each character had to contain its relationships to all the others, they were difficult to create one by one.[65] These difficulties led Leibniz to look for existing characters he might modify. Since the point of the characteristic is to enable us better to use necessary truths, we see Leibniz turning to cultural exchange in order to improve Europe's access to innate ideas.

A series of coincidences and connections inspired Leibniz's belief that Chinese might be particularly useful for his characteristic. These

---

[63] NE III, ii, § 1; RB 281–82; also to Larroque, A I, 10, 249–50.
[64] Dutens IV, part II, pp. 187–88.   [65] AG 9; GP VII 189.

connections have been well treated in Rita Widmaier's *Die Rolle Der Chinesischen Schrift in Leibniz's Zeichentheorie*. For Leibniz, the universal characteristic would serve several purposes, but the most relevant is that it would enable us to think better; that is, it gives us better access to the innate ideas we contain but do not apperceive. As Marcelo Dascal argues, the universal characteristic is not just a "psychotechnique" to aid reason but rather a constitutive element of reasoning itself.[66] In a letter to Bouvet, Leibniz writes of the characteristic, "it gives a *filum Ariadnes* to reason, that is to say, a palpable manner to form some calculus in order to conduct itself both in acts of judgment and of invention" (W 184). Without going into too much detail, Leibniz wanted to combine a semantic function and a syntactical function into one system of signs.[67] The characteristic would have a set of basic elements signifying different ideas, and a formal system allowing calculation with these elements (AG 10; C 84). The former gave Leibniz the greatest difficulty, but he hoped for help on both from China. Thus he writes to Antoine Verjus in 1698 that his characteristic would not only signify, as Chinese characters do, but also allow calculations. Then he adds, "I thought that, if one were well informed, one could perhaps one day adapt these [Chinese] characters not only to represent as the ordinary characters do, but also to calculate and aid imagination and meditation" (W 88).

Leibniz required three qualities for the characters: that they have a non-arbitrary connection to what they represented; that they represent ideas directly rather than through spoken language; and that they be read by peoples speaking different languages.[68] On the first point, Leibniz believed that the Chinese characters were ideographic. He writes to Bouvet that he doubted any connection between Egyptian hieroglyphics and Chinese characters, because the former are pictographic and material, while the latter "are perhaps more philosophical and seem based on more intellectual considerations, such as giving numbers, orders, and relations; thus there are some detached traits which do not support any resemblance with some kind of body" (W 188). That is, both Egyptian hieroglyphs and Chinese characters represent ideas in visual signs, but Chinese signs are based on abstract philosophical concerns rather than images. This leads to the second point, that the characters represented ideas directly, rather than representing sounds which represented ideas. On the third point, Leibniz knew that the Chinese characters were read in Japan and Korea, so that they were

---

[66] Dascal, *Sémiologie de Leibniz*, p. 174.
[67] Widmaier, *Rolle der Chinesischen Schrift*, p. 17.   [68] Dascal, *Sémiologie de Leibniz*, p. 148.

already a universal script.[69] As we have already seen, Leibniz even suggests that Chinese might aid the deaf. One final point that led Leibniz to look to China for his characteristic was its projected connection to the more perfect pre-Babel language. The antiquity and preservation of the Chinese language gave Leibniz good reason to believe this original language left more traces in Chinese than in other more recent, changeable languages.[70]

These qualities of Chinese characters naturally drew Leibniz in his search for an alphabet for his characteristic. In fact, Chinese characters could plausibly reduce to an alphabet of a few hundred simple ideas, whose iconic nature would make them easy to remember, and which would be understandable in separation from any particular spoken language.[71] The difficulty is how one could use these characters to calculate. Leibniz's belief in a *clavis sinica*, though, gave him hope for finding a combinatory system. As we have seen, he was led to this belief by Andreas Müller, who advertised such a key. Other correspondents, including Bouvet, affirmed its possibility (e.g. W 73). In 1699, Leibniz received a supposed key from Christian Mentzel, the successor of Andreas Müller in Berlin (LBr 641, Bl 10 v°). Later, in 1707, Maturin Veyssière La Croze wrote to Leibniz, ". . . I flatter myself to have found the true key of the Chinese language; that is to say, a necessary supplement to that which Mr. Mentzel has written, an aide with which one can learn without too much pain to read, pronounce, and understand all the Chinese books" (LBr 517, Bl 7; cf. LBr 517, Bl 5 r°, Bl 6 v°). La Croze was a librarian in Berlin, a member of the Berlin Society of Sciences, and a gifted linguist. He studied some Chinese, and was one of Leibniz's later sources on Chinese language. These opinions reinforced Leibniz's belief in a key, but he continues in this belief primarily because of the very complexity of the Chinese characters. He doubts the language could really be as difficult as it seems, concluding that it must at least have rules of derivation and composition (W 143). Leibniz projected what such a system would be like, speaking of Müller: "Thus I suspect that he glimpsed some relationship of the ordinary numerical characters of the Chinese to the radical characters of things, and perhaps also some observations on the small additions which vary the radical characters in order to make derivatives, or perhaps even of composition" (W 187). If Chinese could supply a basic alphabet of characters, and if it had a system of derivation and composition, Leibniz would be well on his way to the characteristic of his dreams.

---

[69] GP VII, 11; quoted in Widmaier, *Rolle der Chinesischen Schrift*, p. 35.
[70] Widmaier, *Rolle der Chinesischen Schrift*, p. 35.   [71] Ibid., p. 188.

At this point, it is helpful to explain a little about the structure of the Chinese language. In a sense, Leibniz's belief that there must be a system was correct. Although there is nothing like a "key," the characters are not utterly diverse and unsystematic. Characters are generally composed of a large set of frequently recurring elements, some of which associate with a particular meaning (a semantic element), while others associate with a particular sound (a phonetic element). These recurring elements, however, are nothing like the neat system Leibniz envisioned. First, there are too many of them. Attempts to isolate semantic elements have yielded from 186 to 540 elements, while the number of phonetic elements ranges from 838 to 1348.[72] Second, the meaning or sound of an element often connects only obscurely to the meaning or sound of the character itself. For example, characters meaning star, early or morning, time or season, to understand and to be, all contain the basic semantic element *ri*, meaning sun. The connections between the element and the meaning of the character are obscure at best. DeFrancis estimates that, in 46 percent of characters with semantic elements, the meaning of the semantic element has no relationship to the meaning of the character itself. The system for organizing characters is based on a selection of common elements, called "radicals." The dictionary compiled by Kangxi used 214 radicals, which has remained the traditional number. The characters were not composed according to this organizational system; the system was imposed long after the development of the characters, making it rough and imprecise. An exemplar in the Leibniz archive suggests that the "key" discovered by Mentzel is in fact a discovery of this system of radicals.[73] La Croze is probably referring to something similar.

Everyone agreed that the Chinese themselves did not know of a key, but this fact did not dim Leibniz's expectations. He describes in detail how this key could be lost and confused over time. Fuxi began by assigning numbers to each of the radical characters, but, through popular use and capricious connections, the characters gradually changed, and the changes became solidified through incorrect reformations (W 184–84). Leibniz could expect that he and Bouvet might find the lost key, because they had already done something similar with the hexagrams of the *Yi Jing*, discovering their "true meaning" as a binary calculus. The connection between the hexagrams and Leibniz's binary arithmetic adds another reason why Leibniz hoped for help from Chinese for the system of his characteristic. It not only reinforced the

---

[72] John DeFrancis, *The Chinese Language, Fact and Fantasy* (Honolulu: University of Hawaii Press, 1984), pp. 93–94.
[73] An exemplar of Mentzel's key is found in the Leibniz archive, LBr 641, Bl 7–9.

idea that the Europeans could find things in the Chinese classics that modern Chinese had lost but also suggested that the *Yi Jing* contained a formal mathematical system that could be used in a characteristic. On one side, then, the Chinese language contained an alphabet of human thought; on the other side, the *Yi Jing* contained a set of 64 symbols linked in a formal mathematical system. If these symbols connect with the characters of the Chinese language, one would have the universal characteristic. This anticipated connection is implied in Leibniz's above account of the degeneration of the Chinese language. He posits Fuxi as the one who assigned the numbers to the root characters, and the number he gives is 64. The same Fuxi was the legendary creator of the hexagrams, and the number of hexagrams is 64. Such a connection is natural given Leibniz's sources. Spitzel believed that the original referents of the Chinese characters were the hexagrams of the *Yi Jing*, and that, if the characters have a system, it derives from the *Yi Jing*.[74] Bouvet presents the *Yi Jing* as much more than a formal mathematical system. He writes to Leibniz, "they represent in a very simple and very natural manner the principles of all the sciences, or to speak more correctly, this is the achieved system of a perfect metaphysics, in which the Chinese have preserved, it seems, the knowledge from a long time before Confucius" (W 74). This statement implies that the hexagrams not only were a formal system but also had a material content. In fact, the hexagrams do have a semantic content, in that each hexagram represents a certain kind of situation or balance of energies, and the hexagrams are part of a syntactical system, since certain hexagrams follow from others systematically. If Leibniz had known more, he would have been even more enthusiastic, because the *Yi Jing* is meant as a system of everything, and it was one of the explanatory frameworks used in Chinese science.[75] The system, however, does not allow for calculation. The hexagrams are a system for representing natural situations and the natural laws that direct these situations, rather than a formal system of calculation. Thus one determines the relevant hexagram through seemingly random methods, such as throwing and counting sticks or tossing coins. This hexagram leads to others according to laws handed down by tradition and observation, not according to mathematical formulae.

In spite of the fascinating connections, Leibniz never made significant use of the Chinese language for his characteristic. He lamented that he needed help, in assistants in Europe and in more information from China. Neither of these materialized. Throughout Leibniz's interest in China, he

---

[74] Widmaier, *Rolle der Chinesischen Schrift*, p. 93.   [75] Yoke, *Li, Qi and Shu*, pp. 42–45.

expressed both hopes and doubts about the usefulness of Chinese for his project. In his last letter to Bouvet in 1707, he writes, "I do not care much for the metaphysical usage of the characters of Fohi [Fuxi] and other similar ones, because I have a completely different idea of the true characteristic, which will serve equally to express thoughts and to direct, and will be like a living Logic" (W 267). Around the same time, however, he writes to La Croze, "You have made me rejoice in telling me your application to investigating Chinese characters, and I hope you have made some progress. This research moreover seems to me more important than I thought, for if we could discover the key of Chinese characters, we would find something which would serve the analysis of thoughts."[76] In spite of the fluctuations of Leibniz's hopes for the Chinese language, knowledge of the Chinese language was central to what he hoped could be learned through cultural exchange. This knowledge was meant to aid reason and necessary truths.

NATURAL RELIGION AND ETHICS

Another great exception to Leibniz's search for data is his praise for the morality and politics of the Chinese, and his conclusion that Europe needs to learn these from China. He makes this claim most clearly in the *Novissima Sinica*. We believe ourselves to be so cultivated, he begins, but now we find that we are surpassed by the Chinese in comprehending the practical precepts of life. He explains, "certainly they surpass us (though it is almost shameful to confess this) in practical philosophy, that is, in the precepts of ethics and politics adapted to the present life and use of mortals" (NS 3). Among the Chinese, laws are beautifully directed toward the greatest tranquillity and order. People treat their elders and superiors with such reverence that to speak against one's parents is treated as parricide would be treated in Europe. Between equals, there is remarkable respect and mutual duty. Peasants and servants treat each other so lovingly and respectfully that they go beyond the politest Europeans. The Chinese rarely show any hatred, anger, or excitement. Leibniz ends by cautioning that the Chinese do not attain to full and complete virtue, because that would require grace and Christian teaching, but he concludes that, in the competition between Europe and China, China would win, if it were not for Europe's divine gift of Christianity. Leibniz concludes in favor of exchange:

---

[76] Kortholt I, pp. 177–78; Widmaier, *Rolle der Chinesischen Schrift*, p. 132.

But it is desirable that they in turn teach us those things which are especially in our interest: the greatest use of practical philosophy and a more perfect manner of living, to say nothing now of their arts. Certainly the condition of our affairs, slipping as we are into ever greater corruption, seems to be such that we need missionaries from the Chinese who might teach us the use and practice of natural religion. (NS 10)

Leibniz's praise for Chinese ethics is not in itself strange. The politics and ethics of the Chinese had been a common theme in writings on China, in particular in Jesuit writings.[77] We have seen a brief sketch of Confucian ethics, but what most impressed the Europeans was that the Chinese took that ethics so seriously. Ricci describes China as administered by "The Order of the Learned," and he translates *ru*, the class of Confucian scholar–officials, simply as "The Philosophers."[78] In Ricci's description, China appears as a kingdom run by philosopher–bureaucrats, dedicating their lives to moral philosophy. He emphasizes in particular how the *ru* provide ethical constraints on the emperor and on the military. In a striking passage, Ricci writes:

[N]either the King nor his people ever think of waging a war of aggression. They are quite content with what they have and are not ambitious of conquest. In this respect they are much different from the people of Europe, who are frequently discontent with their own governments and covetous of what others enjoy. While the nations of the West seem to be entirely consumed with the idea of supreme domination, they cannot even preserve what their ancestors have bequeathed them, as the Chinese have done through a period of some thousands of years.[79]

As Leibniz read such descriptions, he lamented the faults of Europe. In a letter to Bouvet that troubles any account of Leibniz as a naïve optimist, he suggests that he may be unable to discover the universal characteristic, because God might reserve such a wondrous discovery for a more deserving time (W 186). Kangxi's Toleration Edict allowing free practice of Christianity stood in striking contrast to the intolerance visible in Europe, and the wise monarch of China easily contrasted with the monarch of France, who revoked the Edict of Nantes tolerating Protestantism in 1685. In short, given Leibniz's sources and experience, he had reason to concede Chinese ethical superiority.

The recognition that the Chinese have better practical philosophy or ethics, however, raises grave problems, indicating that, even though the

---

[77] Pinot writes, "Each proposed his hypothesis for the interpretation of the facts, but on the facts themselves, everyone agreed: the Chinese people were a fortunate and prosperous people, due to their excellent morals and their excellent politics" (Pinot, *Chine et la Formation*, pp. 352–52).

[78] Ricci, *China in the Sixteenth Century*, p. 55.   [79] Ibid., p. 55.

Europeans have a clear, well-articulated belief in God, their morals are inferior to those of the Chinese. Similarly, in spite of Europeans' superior knowledge of necessary truths and science, their morals are inferior. Both of these contradict Leibniz's usual emphasis on the importance of God and reason for virtue. Along with these tensions within his own system, Leibniz's praise of Chinese virtue poses a broader danger to Christianity. Leibniz raises this problem powerfully, if not explicitly: "In a vast multitude of men they have virtually accomplished more than the founders of religious orders among us have achieved within their own narrow ranks" (NS 4). Of what use is Christianity if the Chinese, in complete ignorance of Christ, maintain better morals among their common people than those Europeans who have dedicated their entire life to Christ maintain among themselves? This question remains unanswered – even unasked – by Leibniz. Nonetheless, others would push this very point to great effect in elevating a minimal natural theology at the expense of revelation. Leibniz's philosophy and writings on China can be seen as one step toward the triumph of natural theology and deism, but I do not think this was Leibniz's intention. I have already shown how Leibniz's focus on the introduction of natural theology in China is compatible with a desire to spread Christianity. Leibniz's theory of natural theology will be examined further in the following chapter, but we must now examine more carefully what Leibniz could have meant in praising the practical philosophy of the Chinese, in order to understand what he thought Europe should learn.

Leibniz himself does not explain why the Chinese have superior morals, and his few comments point in different directions. What initially appears most likely follows Leibniz's division between the Europeans and the Chinese, based on their respective excellences in necessary truths and in observation. The letter to Colbert from 1679 supports this approach, in which Leibniz groups together Chinese strength in experiments, observation, and the practice of life (A III, 2, 918–19). We might hypothesize that, while Europeans have better ethical theories, the Chinese have better practice, and this practice is what the Europeans must learn. Leibniz suggests this interpretation in a letter to Bouvet, where he begins by praising the excellent rules the Chinese have for the good order of civil affairs. He then explains: "For the true practical philosophy (true, not simulated philosophy as they say of our *Juresconsultes Romains*) consists rather in these good orders for education, and for the *conversation and sociability* of men, than in the general precepts on the virtues and rights" (W 61–62). Here Leibniz says that the true practical philosophy consists in specific rules, and these are what the Chinese have. Similarly, in a letter to Simon de la Loubère, he praises the "orientals" for being *façionners*, making so many laws that they keep people from the edge of sin (A I, 7, N 312). When Leibniz seeks information on Chinese morals, he usually asks for these kinds of practical rules. In contrast, the Europeans would excel in general rules about the virtues and rights, that is, in theory.

While Leibniz does think Europe can learn practical precepts from China, Chinese excellence in ethics does not easily fall into the division Leibniz projected between the knowledge of China and Europe. The division in excellence does translate into a division between theory and practice. Rather, it is a difference between a greater skill in drawing the necessary consequences of ideas, and a greater skill in making and recording observations of experience. Practice, however, is a mix of observation and necessary truths, which is why even in astronomy the Europeans can learn from China, and even in *physique* the Chinese can learn from Europe. If this division were carried into the field of morals, we would expect the Chinese to have many recorded observations about how people act, and perhaps how they should act, in particular situations, while the Europeans would have theories about what different virtues and rules entail, and how these connect to a necessary, just God. Practice would fall somewhere in between, giving Europe just as much claim to it as China. In fact, in the intersection of reason and observation, Leibniz usually gives favor to reason, so that, even though science and technology are intersections of the excellences of Europe and China, Europe is superior. Leibniz's praise of the practical philosophy of the Chinese thus does not fit with his previous division of knowledge.

Moreover, Leibniz does not see ethics and morals as a probabilistic science like *physique*. His view of ethics contrasts with some of his contemporaries. For example, in the "Passions of the Soul," Descartes presents ethics as a kind of management of the bodily machine. So Descartes concludes that essay, "But the chief use of wisdom lies in its teaching us to be masters of our passions and to control them with such skill that the evils which they cause are quite bearable, and even become a source of joy" (CSM v I, p. 404). This use of wisdom resembles a psychological science, with ethics connecting observation and theory like any other science. The Chinese could just as likely contribute to this study as they could contribute to the study of medicine. Locke presents ethics similarly (Essay, III, xx). Leibniz, in contrast, is concerned less with ethics as a science of controlling the body or of managing psychological laws and more with the direct connection between reason and virtue. With some complications, Leibniz sees everyone as motivated by the apparent good, writing that the difference between

God's will and human will is that God's will tends to what is good, while human will tends to what appears good. This distinction suggests that bad actions result only from misunderstanding; reason and knowledge allow us to discern what is truly good and thus to become more virtuous. In the appendix to the *Theodicy*, "Causa Dei," Leibniz claims that we have freedom from the passions because we can combat them with reason, and sometimes simply with a thought about our freedom (CD 105). This interaction between reason and virtue acts both ways, with reason leading to virtue, but lack of virtue clouding reason. In discussing final causes, we have seen that a moral person seeks to act as God would wish, much as we might follow the wishes of an absent boss. Another practical way that reason helps us, then, is in discerning what would increase the perfection of the world. The important factor on these different levels is a kind of practical wisdom and perceptiveness, which would require both innate ideas and astute observation.

Besides this dependence on practical wisdom, Leibniz connects reason and virtue more fundamentally. One of the central ideas in Leibniz's view of cultural exchange with China is that knowledge of the universe leads to knowledge of God. Leibniz takes a further step, however, claiming that knowledge of God leads to virtuous action as well. He indicates this connection directly in the *Novissima Sinica*: geometry is important as a study of truths, "since virtue flows from wisdom, and the spirit of wisdom is truth" (NS 9). Geometry makes us more virtuous. One bridge between knowledge and virtue is prudence. While love of God should lead us to virtue, most people are led by hopes of reward and punishment. Since in this life wickedness sometimes seems rewarded, occasional wickedness might seem prudent if there were no afterlife. The only way to guarantee the unconditional conjunction of virtue and prudence, then, is to show that the soul is immortal and that perfect justice will rule in an afterlife (NE IV, viii, § 9). Revelation shows this, but reason can establish it more forcefully and securely. The more fundamental bridge between knowledge and virtuous action is love. To love God, we must know his perfections. Knowledge of the perfection of God and the universe leads to the love of God, love of God leads to pleasure in harmony and good, and pleasure in harmony leads toward actions promoting harmony. Leibniz describes this connection in the *Theodicy*: "One cannot know how to love God without knowing his perfections, and this knowledge contains the *principles* of true piety" (T 52; GP VI 28). He continues, "the triumph of true reason illumined by divine grace is at the same time the triumph of faith and love" (PD 45; H 99). He concludes the final appendix with an explanation of this progression: "the more we recognize not only the power and wisdom but also the goodness of the Supreme Mind, the more we are excited to love God and are inflamed even to the imitation of divine goodness and justice" (CD 144; cf. CD 278, T 438, GP VI 432). Because of this connection, Leibniz sees the *Theodicy*, which attempts to solve a philosophical problem, as a moral task:

Our end is to banish from men the false ideas that represent God to them as an absolute prince employing a despotic power, unfitted to be loved and unworthy of being loved. These notions are the more evil in relation to God inasmuch as the essence of piety is not only to fear him but also to love him above all things: and that cannot come about unless there be knowledge of his perfections capable of arousing the love which he deserves, and which makes the felicity of those that love him. (T 6; H 127)

The connection of goodness and knowledge goes to the heart of Leibniz's system, as the sufficient reason by which God creates the universe comes from his goodness, making the order that we know in the universe, that is, the object of our sciences, a moral order. In any case, morality develops by way of reason and God. Recording instances of experience seems of secondary relevance at best.

If, in his writings on China, Leibniz seems to praise a morality developed without knowledge of God and with limited use of reason, we must examine if he intends something else. In fact, Leibniz praises not only the moral practice of the Chinese but also their natural theology. In the above passage from the *Novissima Sinica*, Leibniz supports learning moral precepts from the Chinese, but frames this exchange as one between Chinese "natural religion" and Europe's "revealed theology" (NS 10). Now it is possible that, by "natural religion," Leibniz means something other than "natural theology," but its very opposition to revealed theology suggests not. In fact, Leibniz uses the two phrases interchangeably and, as far as I know, he never makes a distinction between natural religion and natural theology.[80] In the *Discourse*, Leibniz makes the connection more clear: "there is in China a public morality admirable in certain regards, conjoined to a philosophical doctrine, or rather a natural theology . . ." (Discourse 3). If we take this last statement seriously, then what Leibniz desires from China is a natural theology resulting in better morals. If so, then in this case, Leibniz does seek necessary truths from China. This interpretation preserves the connection of knowledge of God and necessary truths with good action, but could Leibniz seriously mean that the Chinese have a better natural theology than the Europeans? We have already seen that Leibniz believed the Chinese had

---

[80] For the use of the phrase "natural religion," see *Discourse* 11, T 294; or RB 59.

a poor grasp of necessary truths, yet necessary truths are crucial to natural theology. In the *Novissima Sinica*, Leibniz says that the Europeans have impressed the Chinese with their geometry, but they still have another gift – first philosophy, through which they attain knowledge of incorporeal things (NS 9). The implication of this statement is that the Chinese do not have such knowledge, or at least that the Europeans have it better. By Leibniz's time countless works of natural theology, proofs of the existence of God, and so on had been written, and Leibniz's own philosophy is part of the complex of European natural theology. In the *Discourse*, Leibniz attributes a developed natural theology to the Chinese but, given the development and articulation of natural theology in Europe, Leibniz could not seriously believe the Chinese had either a more extensive or more articulate natural theology to teach Europe.

The problem thus far is that both Europe and China have a natural theology – that of Europe is more developed and articulate, while that of China is more effective in producing good behavior. One way to deal with this problem is to turn from natural theology itself to the relationship between natural theology and virtue. The reason why Europe's morals are in a worse state might not be the extent of their natural theology but their relationship to it. While Leibniz never breaks the bond between knowledge and virtue, he occasionally addresses the fact that people do things they "know" are bad. These references are scattered through his writings, and are based on a distinction between different ways of knowing. In the *Theodicy* he explains our failure to do what our mind knows we should, because "the understanding to a great extent proceeds only by faint thoughts, which have only slight power to affect" (T 311; H 314). We fail to do what we know we should because we know it only vaguely. In a dialogue against skepticism, he explains that most people treat matters of religion and reason as a manner of diversion or show, "as the students in philosophy dispute of virtues, vices, and passions, without these touching them in any fashion" (A VI, 4, 2251). In another essay, "On the True Theologica Mystica," he writes, "Most men have no earnestness. They have never tasted truth and are bogged down in a secret unbelief," and he makes the statement that, if someone does not act according to his faith, he does not really have faith (L 369). Taking these statements together, Leibniz does not believe that we do what we know we should not, but we may *think* we know something when we really do not, or we may know it in a superficial way, which is not real knowledge. If both Europe and China have a natural theology, yet China has better morals, one reason could be that the Chinese take their natural theology more seriously. Though their natural theology might be less developed and articulate, it might have more effect on their actions. Chinese missionaries would come to Europe not to introduce new truths but to help Europeans take these common truths more seriously.

In chapter 2, we noted that one way in which existential factors condition necessary truths is through morality, as our grasp of innate ideas competes with our desires and immediate self-interest. Now we see another version of this influence, where a kind of morality, which might be called attentiveness or reverence, serves not to introduce new necessary truths, but to know them more clearly. Why are the Chinese better able to know these truths of natural theology, even though they lack Europe's skill with necessary truths? Many answers could be given: their education, their practical precepts, their reverence for elders and the past, even just luck or chance or grace. In any case, this grasp of necessary truths comes not from a difference in their expression of the necessary truths contained in the mind of God, but from the concrete conditions of their expression of the universe. This practical context should not distract from the fact that Chinese excellence in ethics is also an excellence in knowledge. Leibniz's distinction between two kinds of knowing connects back to the distinctions we have already seen between ideas and mere notions and between intuitive and symbolic knowledge. Leibniz seems to mean that, when our grasp of innate ideas is improperly mediated by signs, those ideas do not motivate action. On this account, the Chinese express the innate ideas about God more clearly than the Europeans, and this explains their ethical superiority. We thus see again the complex ways our culturally conditioned expression of the universe conditions our more universal expression of the mind of God.

A few letters reinforce this interpretation and clarify the reasons for Europe's moral problems. We can begin with the reason why Leibniz so laments the moral poverty of Europe: conflicts and wars between religious factions. In a letter to Bouvet, he writes, "As for the affairs of Europe, they are in a condition to make us envy the Chinese"; he then goes on to describe the various wars involving almost all of Europe: the recently ended war of Austria, Poland, and Russia against Turkey (1683–99), the newly begun Great Northern War of Sweden against Russia, Poland, Denmark, and Saxony, involving all of the Baltic region (1700–21), and the newly erupted War of Spanish Succession, with France fighting against Britain, Austria, and the Dutch Republic (1701–14) (W 180). Germans were involved with all these conflicts. He often attributed the lack of success in exchange with China to the interference of European wars (e.g. W 206; cf. to Orban, LBr 157, Bl 51). Leibniz's intention to reunite the Church is too complex to deal with here, but Leibniz felt the conflicts resulted from a lack of focus on the fundamental commonalities to which all Christians agree and which ensure salvation.[81] Religious conflicts allow what is unessential to strike against what is essential. Two letters to the Electress Sophie – written more than a decade apart – strengthen the connection between European conflicts and Leibniz's praise for Chinese ethics. The first letter, from September 10, 1697, is directed against the sectarian spirit reigning in Europe. The electress had written a letter to the Catholic Marie de Brinon, and Leibniz responds with a wish that the letter will make Brinon more equitable and less quick to condemn. He then criticizes the conflicts between Luther, Calvin, and the pope, writing, "I wish to speak at present only of some essential truths of religion and piety, disfigured in a frightful manner by the sectarian spirit of condemners, even so far as to pervert the idea of God, to whom they give qualities unworthy of him, and worthy rather of his enemy" (A I, 14, 72). These sects consider God to be a petty, quibbling sectarian like themselves. This passage presents a conflict between the essential truths of religion and piety and the disfiguration of these among Leibniz's religious contemporaries: "Thus for the sake of religion they destroy the more fundamental religion, which is to honor and love God" (A I, 14, 72).

At this point, Leibniz turns to China:

I have said and I still say: we send Missionaries to the Indies in order to preach revealed religion. This is good, but it seems we need the Chinese to send us Missionaries in turn, for us to learn the natural religion that we have almost lost. For in effect, the government of the Chinese would be incomparably better than that of God, if God were like the scuffles of the Sectarian Doctors, who attach salvation to the chimeras of their party. (A I, 14, 72)

This is shockingly strong praise for Chinese morality. The letter sets up a conflict between natural theology and the current state of revealed theology in Europe, and Leibniz gives his preference: he would prefer the natural theology of the Chinese to the corrupted revealed theology of Europe. This statement emphasizes the importance attached to the core of religion as opposed to fine points of doctrine, and it shows the sufficiency of reason for religion and virtue. The implication is that the Chinese govern themselves better than the Europeans and that their success is grounded in their use of reason. A puzzling point is Leibniz's claim that natural religion has been almost lost in Europe. He surely cannot mean that Europeans have lost the

---

[81] A good source on Leibniz's efforts for reunification is Paul Eisenkopf, *Leibniz und die Einigung der Christenheit* (Munich, 1975). Merkel briefly addresses the role of reunification in Leibniz's missionary writings (Merkel, *Die China-Mission*, pp. 65–66, 145–48).

ability to prove that God exists or that the soul is immortal; he believed he had himself given these a stronger footing than ever. In saying that natural religion is almost lost, Leibniz must mean something else, that natural theology has lost the attention of the Europeans, who concentrate instead on the distractions of sectarian debate. These conflicts and distractions keep our innate ideas out of our apperception. So Leibniz does not expect the Chinese to teach Europeans how to reason better or to give them new proofs for the existence of God; rather, the Chinese would help to purify religious discourse in Europe by emphasizing its essential core. This interpretation is reinforced by a letter to René-Henri de Crux de Monceaux written a month later. René-Henri had written an enthusiastic letter to Leibniz referring to his call for missionaries from China in the *Novissima Sinica* (A I, 14, 563). Leibniz quickly replies that he spoke against the various sects in Europe, not against religion in general. It is only because of the sects that a natural theology must be brought from the Chinese. He then goes on to describe the wars and problems caused by religious division in Europe (A I, 14, 608–09).

Leibniz gives a slightly different interpretation in another letter to Electress Sophie, written ten years later in April 1709. In this letter Leibniz argues, "I am persuaded that Religion should have nothing which is contrary to Reason, and that one should always give to Revelation a sense which exempts it from all absurdity" (K I, ix, 3, p. 300). Leibniz begins by appealing to China:

One sends some Missionaries all the way to China to preach the Christian religion, and it does good, but (as I have already said publicly a few years ago) we need some Missionaries of Reason in Europe, to preach the natural Religion, on which Revelation itself is founded, and without which Revelation would always be taken poorly. The Religion of Reason is eternal, and God has engraved it in our hearts, our corruptions have obscured it, and the end of Jesus-Christ has been to render its luster, to restore men to the true knowledge of God and of the soul, and to make them practice the virtue which makes the true good. (K I, ix, 3, p. 301)

This passage holds several remarkable points. The first is the domination of natural theology over revealed theology. Natural religion here becomes the foundation of revealed religion. Jesus, in so far as he is mentioned, introduces nothing that we could not get on our own from reason – he simply reinforces what is already in our hearts. Leibniz's next statement continues, saying that revelation is necessary because of our weakness, not because it adds something new. Later in the letter, Leibniz says that both reason and revelation teach us to believe in God and to do whatever we can to promote the good. With this moral imperative, we have "the reunion of natural religion and revealed religion, at least in practice. For the mysteries regard rather knowledge [than practice]" (K I, ix, 3, p. 302).

This passage also clarifies that, in praising Chinese morality, Leibniz is not just praising practical rules and observations – he is praising a rational system, moving between "natural religion" and "religion of reason" as synonyms. While praising the Chinese, the letter offers some explanation for the loss of natural religion in Europe. In the passage quoted, Leibniz says simply that their corruptions have obscured it. Later he gives three motives why people turn against or fail to grasp natural religion: ignorance; bitterness about their intellectual limitations; and maliciousness (K I, ix, 3, pp. 302–03). These motives have a complex relationship to the direct ability to use logic and necessary truths. On the one hand, these moral failings serve as distractions that keep one from properly apperceiving the innate ideas each mind contains. Apperception is dominated instead by minute perceptions. On the other hand, these feelings themselves follow from an insufficient grasp of the truth. For whatever reason, the Chinese seemed less prone to these weaknesses, so that their corruptions obscured natural religion less and their grasp of innate ideas kept these corruptions from appearing. Leibniz does not explicitly say so, but the fact that Europeans have revealed truth naturally raises the conflict between revelation and reason, which Leibniz here disputes. The Chinese, lacking revealed perplexities like the trinity, might be less tempted to turn against reason and natural religion. This explanation connects with the previous letter, because reason establishes the common ground that Leibniz thought Christians and Chinese shared.

In conclusion, in both letters, Leibniz contrasts a core of natural religion with the corrupt state of revealed religion in Europe. In both, Leibniz believes the Church in Europe has been distracted from the essential truths of religion by conflicts about revelation and between sects. They need a reminder of the natural religion they vaguely know, and missionaries from China were to be that reminder. One final point to consider is the connection between Leibniz's writings on China and the anti-Christian tendency of the Enlightenment. Earlier, we raised the question of what use is Christianity if the Chinese maintain better morals among their common people than European monks maintain among themselves? Leibniz did not address the question, but the praise of Chinese virtue was used against Christianity soon after Leibniz, particularly by Wolff and Voltaire, and in Leibniz's own time by Bayle, in his typically ambiguous way. Leibniz appears doubly responsible for this movement, as a "father of the Enlightenment" in general, and as elevating praise of Chinese morality. In these letters, Leibniz elevates natural theology at the expense of revealed theology. In the letters to Sophie in particular, Leibniz undermines revelation, grace, and the Mysteries. We should not, however, jump to the conclusion that Leibniz wants to undermine Christianity. The problem with such an interpretation is that Leibniz's natural theology is profoundly Christian. Patrick Riley argues this point, emphasizing that Leibniz extends natural theology to include charity, making his "religion of reason" particularly Christian. For Leibniz, natural theology coincides with Christianity, when Christianity is properly understood. Since there is no conflict between reason and faith, one never chooses reason over faith. Thus, natural theology is not obscured at all by Christianity, but it is obscured by the pettiness and bickering of the Christians in Europe. In so far as Christians are sectarian, however, they not only go against natural theology but also against Christianity. The situation is not unlike the one Leibniz describes, of philosophy students who wrangle about virtue, truth, and so forth without letting these things touch them. If someone really knew the essential core of Christianity, they would not allow differences to strike against it. Leibniz says that we should bear anything rather than harm the unity of the Church (A VI, 4, 2441–42). Those who perpetuate divisions and sects either do not really know or do not really believe the basic truths of Christianity – or natural theology. These people might become better Christians by learning to appreciate a streamlined natural theology taught by Chinese missionaries.

CHAPTER 4

Interpreting China

HERMENEUTICS

Thus far the application of Leibniz's philosophy to his engagement with China has focused on his views about exchange rather than his attempts to carry out a "commerce of light." In spite of the limitations of his knowledge, Leibniz was engaged with Chinese culture and thought and with issues of interpretation. Even the vision of exchange presented in the last chapter depends on certain interpretations of China. One reason to consider how Leibniz engages China is his relative success as an interpreter. My claim is that Leibniz's philosophy provides a rich foundation not only for promoting cultural exchange but also for understanding how exchange works. Leibniz makes many mistakes, but his interpretations of the complexities of Chinese thought far surpass those of his contemporaries in Europe, and even many of the missionaries in China. This very success prompts us to ask if some basis in Leibniz's philosophy enables him to make the interpretations he does. A second reason for considering Leibniz's hermeneutics is the centrality of interpretation to his own philosophical practice. He presents himself as finding the best in diverse texts and synthesizing them, not only with China but also with the history of philosophy and with various Christian factions. While Leibniz does not reflect explicitly on intercultural hermeneutics, the foundation for understanding and interpreting other cultures has already been established in chapter 2. So far, the focus has been on the relationship between minds and the world and between minds and innate ideas, but the process of cultural exchange requires a shift to consider directly the relationships between minds. The question of what different monads share has been answered in terms of expression. In expressing both a realm of ideas and the created universe, monads share two common grounds, as both experience and reason reveal common traits. The diversity of world-views comes from the emergence of human consciousness as a particular integration of these two common realms, creating a "perspective." If each mind *expresses* the same universe and same ideas, the same patterns or relationships should appear in each, while minds differ by which patterns they express clearly and apperceive, and which patterns they express less clearly, remain below the level of consciousness. Experience determines the form this diversity of minds takes. Given some consistencies in human experience, such as the need to eat, some patterns will be clear in all minds. Others, however, will be clear in only some minds, depending on experience. Monads with considerable shared experience, expressing the universe from similar places, will recognize more of the same patterns and will share a culture. When a mind from one culture meets a mind from another, it could expect to share some patterns already, such as those around the needs of the body. They could also expect a relative ease in teaching new patterns to each other, as these patterns are already known unclearly and unconsciously. This process of communication, however, must go through experience. Our sharing patterns has no relevance unless we can discover that we share the same experiences, or that we are "talking about the same thing." More specifically, once I recognize that the chicken foot you are offering me is "food," I can conclude certain things, such as that I should pretend I like it or you might be disappointed. This example is simple and common, but the same process applies to discussing the "soul." This process of understanding is roughly the same as the process of coming to know the natural world, but, instead of provisionally matching our ideas to natural events and then drawing conclusions, I match my ideas to your words, behavior, or writings, then draw conclusions. This chapter will examine specifically how this epistemological situation is expressed in Leibniz's interpretation of, and engagement with, China.

As a commentary on a commentary, an interpretation of an interpretation, the *Discourse on the Natural Theology of the Chinese* provides a particularly good view of Leibniz's approach to understanding a text. Leibniz had a number of sources for knowledge of China, and as early as 1687 he commented that Couplet's translation of the Confucian classics contained many excellent thoughts (A I, 5, 26), but the *Discourse* itself explicitly uses only two sources: one by the Jesuit Nicholas Longobardi; and the other by a Spanish Franciscan, Antonio Caballero a Santa Maria, known to Leibniz as Antoine de Sainte-Marie.[1] Both were well known supporters

---

[1] By Longobardi: *Traité sur quelques points de la religion de Chinois* (Paris, 1701). By Sainte-Marie: *Traité sur quelques points importants de la mission de la Chine* (Paris, 1701). Mungello identifies Caballero as the author of that text, but I continue to follow Leibniz in using Sainte-Marie. See Cook and Rosemont, *Writings on China*, pp. 39–40. For a study of Leibniz's sources for the *Discourse*, see Mungello, "Die Quellen."

of the anti-accomodation position, and Longobardi succeeded Ricci as head of the China mission. Leibniz remarks that, by using sources opposed to his own views, he can avoid the appearance of bias (Discourse 3). The *Discourse* was intended for Nicholas de Remond, who sent the two texts to Leibniz along with Malebranche's *Dialogue between a Christian Philosopher and a Chinese Philosopher.*[2] Remond asks for Leibniz's judgment on the issue. Although Leibniz sent some remarks and a summary of the *Discourse*, he never quite finished the essay itself.

The *Discourse* illuminates Leibniz as an interpreter, because we see not only how he interprets the citations from the Chinese but also what principles of interpretation he criticizes in Longobardi and Sainte-Marie. The latter are even clearer in Leibniz's marginal notes on those texts.[3] Leibniz's most basic hermeneutic principle is the assumption of a shared rationality. We have seen that, in the *New Essays*, Leibniz distinguishes between the explicit grasp of truths of reason or logic, and an instinct for logic that everyone possesses (e.g. NE I, 1, § 20–21; RB 83–84; NE I, 2, § 1; RB 88–89). This instinct appears primarily in the avoidance of obvious contradictions. Leibniz naturally assumes that the Chinese have this instinct. The capacity for reason depends not only on this instinctive use of the principle of non-contradiction but also on innate ideas. Given a particular idea, we can derive certain, necessary conclusions and this capacity is shared by all human beings. Although our ideas are also shared, which ideas we recognize and reason from varies. Thus Leibniz does not assume that Chinese and Europeans share all necessary truths, but, in spite of this variety of apperceived ideas, if we are talking about the same idea, we should be able to reach the same conclusions, even if we come from different cultures. This belief in the universality of rationality founds Leibniz's interest in China and his belief in accommodation. It also serves as an interpretive principle: if an interpretation of a text makes it look stupid or irrational or in obvious self-contradiction, that interpretation is probably wrong.

Sainte-Marie explicitly disagrees with Leibniz on this principle. Sainte-Marie recognizes the obvious contradictions and absurdities of the Chinese doctrines as he portrays them, but explains that this should not be surprising, since pagans often contradict themselves. Leibniz replies: "I believe that

---

[2] Leibniz acknowledges receiving the works by Longobardi and Malebranche in a letter from June 22, 1715 (GP III, 644–47).

[3] The texts and marginalia of Longobardi and Sainte-Marie are published in Kortholt. Longobardi's text is also published in Dutens, IV, i, 89–144. The marginalia on Malebranche's text are published in André Robinet, *Malebranche et Leibniz: relations personnelles, présentées avec les textes complets des auteurs et de leurs correspondants revus, corrigés et inédits* (Paris: Librairie Philosophique J. Vrin, 1955), pp. 483–90.

the contradictions are indeed expressed in the language they use, in *terminis terminantibus*. One may, however, attribute them to different sects, not the same sect. But if they are in the same sect, one should seek a conciliation and do so in the most equitable fashion" (Discourse 11). Leibniz applies this principle in the next section, where Sainte-Marie argues that the Chinese attribute contradictory properties to *li*. Leibniz responds: "I do not at all see how it could be possible for the Chinese to elicit from prime matter – as our philosophers teach it in their schools, as purely passive, without order or form – the origin of activity, of order and of all forms. I do not believe them to be so stupid or absurd" (Discourse 12). On the contrary, Sainte-Marie and many others were quite ready to believe the Chinese were that "stupid and absurd." This belief in the rationality of the Chinese guides Leibniz's interpretations of the texts throughout the *Discourse*, as he dismisses several of Longobardi's and Sainte-Marie's interpretations because they render the texts too absurd (Discourse 63). In one passage, he writes that the Chinese could believe in a world soul like Manicheans or Averroists, but this interpretation would contradict the texts, and would be contrary to reason and the nature of the individual (Discourse 64). Leibniz does not further explain his meaning, but if someone understands what it means to be an individual, then they should see that a world soul is incompatible with the existence of true individuals. In noting that the idea of a world soul contradicts reason and experience, Leibniz does not argue against this view, as he assumes his audience already agrees that the world-soul theory is wrong. Rather, Leibniz makes a hermeneutic argument – the fact that this interpretation makes the Chinese go against reason and experience suggests it is a bad interpretation. Leibniz states this principle more positively in another passage: "To be able to speak clearly of their dogmas, it is safest to consider the reason and the harmony of their doctrines, rather than superficial utterances" (Discourse 34a).

This assumption of rationality risks erasing cultural diversity by projecting a fundamental, trans-cultural agreement on the truths of reason. How does Leibniz account for the differences between cultures and the ways in which cultural others sometimes seem irrational? The assumption of reason is part of a two-sided principle, taking reason as relatively universal and experience as relatively limited or perspectival. Leibniz's method combines flexibility regarding facts and rigidity regarding logic. We can generally reason together from certain ideas, but whether or not we have the same idea is difficult to determine and depends on experience. His confidence in the universality of reason is clear in his estimation of Chinese philosophy, but his flexibility is more difficult to see. One example of how Leibniz allows for the perspectival experience of the Chinese, though, is in their lack of knowledge of revelation, a fact of culture. In some cases, even with the best use of reason, they cannot come to the truth, because their "perspective" lacks revelation. For example, Leibniz excuses the belief that *qi*, material force, is coeternal with *li*, because the dogma of creation is only knowable through revelation. In fact, natural theology for Leibniz is the attempt to apply correct and universal reasoning to a perspective limited by the lack of revealed theology. Because of the perspectival nature of this experience, such natural theology cannot avoid being incomplete, even though it can be rationally consistent.

This two-sided principle appears more clearly in Leibniz's understanding of his own activity of interpretation, and his warnings about how to interpret Chinese thought. Leibniz is extremely sensitive to his limited experience of the facts. He warns Europeans to be skeptical of their conclusions about China, writing, "I only wish that we had more complete accounts and greater quantity of extracts of the Chinese classics accurately translated which talk about first principles. Indeed, it would even be desirable that all the classics be translated together. But this not yet being done, one can only make provisional judgments" (Discourse 3). This skepticism about Europe's knowledge comes from the perspectival nature of experience – from Europe's perspective, China is a vague and distant place. This perspectivalism, however, is only one side of the principle. Leibniz remains confident in his ability to judge the reasoning of the Chinese. If they believe God is a world soul, then they are wrong. There is no chance that, from their perspective, God is a world soul, because God's separation from the world is a universal, necessary truth of reason. Where perspective enters is the initial "if" – whether or not they believe God to be a world soul depends on experience and can only be known provisionally. As a consequence of this two-sided principle, Leibniz sees errors and differences not in faulty deductions but in questions of experience, attributed either to limitations in what the Chinese have come to know from experience or to the limitations of Leibniz's own knowledge of Chinese thought. Leibniz's confidence in reason and skepticism of experience should be taken to weaken neither the fact that reasoning must remain fallible and that experience always has some truth, nor my claim that "perspective" is only a result of both together. In Leibniz's interpretive practice, we see an application of the same process by which we tentatively match truths about ideas to existing things. Rather than match these ideas to things in experience, as one would in science, interpretation matches these ideas to the words of the other. This process is no more secure than that of science, although Leibniz sometimes displays more confidence than his system seems to justify.

A second hermeneutic principle follows from this assumption of rationality, which might be called a principle of "generosity." Leibniz's generosity means interpreting a text as saying something reasonable and consistent. Such generosity is, of course, a mixed blessing, as it keeps open an interest and respect for the other, but tends to make the other seem more like one's self. Not surprisingly, Leibniz finds many other thinkers quite Leibnizian when interpreted correctly. This principle of generosity is not particular to Leibniz's writings on China, but underlies his view of interpreting anyone. He expresses this approach in the *New Essays*:

> Having diligently considered both the old and the new, I have found that most accepted doctrines can bear a sound sense. So I wish that men of intellect would seek to gratify their ambition by building up and moving forward, rather than by retreating and destroying. I would rather they emulated the Romans who built fine public works than the Vandal king whose mother advised him that since he could not hope for renown by rivaling those magnificent structures he should seek to destroy them. (NE I, ii, § 22; RB 100–01)

We can distinguish three particular applications of hermeneutic generosity. If a text is ambiguous or inconclusive, or if we lack sufficient knowledge to judge adequately, then we should take the most favorable interpretation. When a text is contradictory, with things that are good and things that are bad, we should preserve the good and leave the bad. Finally, an error in interpreting a text favorably is better than an error in the other direction, because the first error advances the cause of cultural exchange, while the latter hinders it. This generosity reinforces Leibniz's position of accommodation, and is itself an aspect of accommodation.

A third principle in Leibniz's interpretation of Chinese thought is more specific: that precedence should be given to the ancient texts rather than the moderns and their interpretations of the classics. The "moderns" would have included both the orthodox *li xue* Neo-Confucians like Zhu Xi as well as the *ru* with whom the Jesuit missionaries associated. The Jesuits considered these Neo-Confucians with their system based on *li* and *qi* to be atheists and materialists. The standard commentaries on the classical texts, which formed the basis for the examination system, were written from this perspective and edited by Zhu Xi. The "ancients" would have been Confucius and the early Confucian canon, but read in the context of the more ancient classics, as we have seen. Leibniz's Jesuit sources followed the same approach of privileging the ancients, and the main conflict between Longobardi and the Jesuits who favored accommodation was over which texts should take precedence. Leibniz does not simply take the principle over from his sources, however. His approach coincides with his belief that one

should return to classical Christian texts rather than accept Scholastic interpretations. Leibniz's main rhetoric against the acceptance of modern commentators in China is by analogy with Scholastics in Europe (Discourse 1),
and he criticizes Longobardi and Sainte-Marie as locked in Scholastic prejudices (Discourse 10, cf. Discourse 26).[4] The modern commentators have
no greater authority than medieval commentators on Roman law, or Arab
and Scholastic commentators on Aristotle. Longobardi and Sainte-Marie
"have judged the later Chinese school as the medieval European school
(with which they are preoccupied) would have us judge them, namely to
judge the texts of the divine and human Laws and of ancient authors by
their own interpretations and commentaries" (Discourse 39). This error is
common among philosophers, lawyers, moralists, and theologians, Leibniz says, dedicating particular criticism to medical doctors. He turns this
argument forcefully against the European opponents of accommodation,
who were largely Augustinian, writing that such Scholastic prejudices could
be expected from people like Longobardi and Sainte-Marie, but not the
"very clever theologians of our time, who prefer the doctrine of the ancient
Fathers of the Church to modern sentiments in speculative theory as well
as in morality" (Discourse 39a).

Longobardi's preference for the modern commentators has a persuasive
basis and cannot in fairness be dismissed as Scholastic prejudice. In his view,
the ancient texts are themselves ambiguous, so the question is not which
texts to follow but who can best interpret these texts. He answers that living Chinese scholars can interpret the classics better than those Europeans
who have only recently arrived and struggle even to understand the language.[5] Leibniz disagrees with this seemingly reasonable principle for several
reasons. His direct response was that the "official" view – Kangxi's affirmation of accommodation – should prevail over that of some interpreters.[6]
In addition, Leibniz's hermeneutic generosity meant that ambiguous texts
should get the most favorable reading, not the most probable reading, nor
that based on the moderns. Finally, Leibniz believes that the Europeans
might have more insight into the Chinese classics than the Chinese themselves. He writes, "It is indeed apparent that if we Europeans were well
enough informed concerning Chinese Literature, then, with the aid of logic,
critical thinking, mathematics and our manner of expressing thought –
more exacting than theirs – we could uncover in the Chinese writings of the

---

[4] See also Discourse 38 and 39. Similar comments are found in Leibniz's remarks on Longobardi's text,
particularly the series of notes on pp. 98–102 and 121–22 (Dutens V, i).

[5] Longobardi makes this argument throughout his text, but especially at pp. 100–01 (Dutens, V, i).

[6] Dutens V, i, 99, nn. 18 and 20.

remotest antiquity many things unknown to modern Chinese" (Discourse 68). That is, because Europeans have greater skill in analyzing ideas, they could gain some new insights into the Chinese texts, just as they could draw new knowledge from Chinese science and technology. He gives as an example the discovery by Bouvet of the correspondence between Leibniz's binary arithmetic and the hexagrams of the *Yi Jing* (Discourse 68). Leibniz adds that Christian scholars similarly interpret the ancient books of the Hebrews better than the Jews themselves (Cult 11).

The last reason that Leibniz chooses to follow the classic texts instead of the moderns is that he finds more truth in them. Finding a suitable natural theology in Chinese thought supported his method of introducing philosophy to the Chinese before the details of Christianity, and it grounded his praise for Chinese morality, allowing him to avoid portraying the Chinese as "virtuous atheists." The ancient texts provided the best chance for such a theology, with their use of theistic terms like *Shang Di* and *tian*. The very ambiguity of the classical texts allowed greater interpretive space, so that Leibniz's principle of finding the best meaning for ambiguous texts allowed him to draw forth a favorable natural theology. The correspondence between his binary arithmetic and the hexagrams of the *Yi Jing* added evidence for the greater wisdom of the ancients, as he says explicitly in the *Discourse*: "Now this shows that the ancient Chinese have surpassed the modern ones in the extreme, not only in piety (which is the basis of the most perfect morality) but in science as well" (Discourse 68a). The encounter with Müller also supported this bias toward the ancients, since they supposedly had the key now lost to the moderns. Lastly, the very antiquity of the classical books supported their claim to truth, closely connecting them to Noah and the Biblical Patriarchs. Leibniz's exact view on the relationship between the ancient Chinese and the Patriarchs is unclear, but several times in the *Discourse* he suggests that the unusual degree of truth in classical Chinese books may be due to their connection with the Patriarchs (Discourse 24a, 32, 37).

In comparative philosophy, or any cross-cultural understanding, we begin by shifting foreign thought into more familiar terms or forms. It may not be right, then, to designate a universal principle of interpretation as the fourth of Leibniz's hermeneutic principles. Now, however, we resist this shift into our own terms. Even if inevitable, we recognize that equating Bishop Butler with Mengzi is most likely a distortion.[7] In contrast, Leibniz

---

[7] This equation is given in James Legge's 1895 translation of Mencius, in which he writes that Bishop Butler's "views and those of Mencius are, as nearly as possible, identical" (Mengzi, *Works of Mencius*, p. 56).

and his contemporaries embrace this method of interpretation by identification with more familiar forms of thought. The main difference between Leibniz and his anti-accommodation opponents is with whom they identify Chinese thought. Those against accommodation identify Chinese thought with Western ideas of a God who is part of the world, either as a world soul following the Stoics or Averroes, or more often as a form of Spinozism. This identification is most apparent in Malebranche's *Dialogue Between a Christian Philosopher and a Chinese Philosopher on the Existence and Nature of God*, which Leibniz does not cite but also used as a source for the *Discourse*.[8] Malebranche knew little about Chinese philosophy, and bases his interpretation largely on an identification of Chinese philosophy with Spinoza. His arguments against Chinese philosophy follow his arguments against Spinoza.[9] Malebranche makes his approach clear in responding to a criticism that he unfairly portrayed the Chinese as an atheist. Malebranche responds, somewhat mockingly:

So, since there is not a single Chinese who subscribes to atheism and who, without harming the truth, could serve me as interlocutor in order to refute impiety, there is no satisfying the delicacy of the author but to change the Chinese to Japanese or Siamese, or rather, to French; for it happens that the system of the impious Spinoza wreaks great havoc here; and it seems to me that there are many correspondences between the impieties of Spinoza and those of the Chinese philosopher.[10]

Bayle similarly groups Spinoza and Confucianism together, discussing Confucianism and Buddhism in his entry on Spinoza, and discussing Spinoza in his entry on Japan.[11]

In the *Discourse*, Leibniz mentions this identification several times (Discourse 13, 23, 33). He concludes that some modern Chinese writers may fall into the errors of Spinozism, but without support from the classical texts (Discourse 23). Again he writes that without conclusive evidence that they

---

[8] Nicholas Malebranche, *Dialogue Between a Christian Philosopher and a Chinese Philosopher on the Existence and Nature of God*. Trans. by A. Dominick Iorio (Washington DC: University Press of America, 1980).

[9] Mungello identifies Malebranche's direct source on China as Artus de Lionne, an anti-accommodationist who had been a missionary in China and who persuaded Malebranche to write the *Conversation*. For the connection to Spinoza, see Pinot, *Chine et la Formation*, pp. 329–33; and David Mungello, "Malebranche and Chinese Philosophy," *Journal of the History of Ideas*, 41 (1980), pp. 551–78.

[10] Malebranche, *Dialogue*, p. 47.

[11] Pierre Bayle, *Mr. Bayle's Historical and Critical Dictionary*. Trans. by P. des Mazeaux (London: Routledge/Thoemmes Press, 1997; repr. from 1736), Vol. V, p. 199, and Vol. III, p. 550, respectively. For a discussion of Bayle and Malebranche on this issue, see Y. Lai, "The Linking of Spinoza to Chinese Thought by Bayle and Malebranche," *Journal of the History of Ideas*, 2 (1985), pp. 151–178.

hold these opinions, we should give the texts the benefit of the doubt and read them figuratively (Discourse 33). Instead of identifying Chinese views with those of the Stoics or Spinoza, Leibniz identifies them with more favorable writers, preferably from the Christian tradition. We can accept that Confucius does not explicitly mention spirits, he says, because Moses himself never mentions them (Remarks 5). The belief that God created spirits to control natural phenomena is wrong, but it is not anti-Christian because many Christians have thought the same thing. As an example, Leibniz gives the Scholastic belief that certain angels look after the celestial spheres (Discourse 2). When the Chinese say that *li* – which Leibniz connects to God as a prime mover – does not possess life, power, or knowledge, they could mean that *li* does not have these in a *human* form, just as Dionysius denies similar properties to God (Discourse 16b). That is, some denials about *li* should be taken in the spirit of negative theology. At other times, Leibniz favorably compares Chinese philosophy with that of the Greeks. He writes that, like Plato, Confucius believed in the unity of God but accommodated himself to the prejudices of the common people in some of his expressions (Discourse 34; cf. Discourse 24a, 42, 55). Leibniz even occasionally identifies Chinese philosophy with this own. Like himself, the Chinese may believe that all spiritual beings under God have some kind of body (Discourse 2). In his marginal notes on Longobardi, Leibniz makes comparisons to Plato, negative theology, Tertullian, Descartes, and a variety of Christian doctrines.

These identifications show how seriously Leibniz takes Chinese philosophy. While Sainte-Marie considers pagans as one group, all wrong and all superstitious, at best reducible to a kind of Stoicism, Leibniz places Chinese philosophers on the same level as Plato or Aristotle, or even some Christian writers. As a general principle of interpretation, the meaning of the willingness to identify foreign thought with more familiar thought is difficult to evaluate. Leibniz would have had little first-hand experience in confronting a foreign culture, with little way of knowing how far the variety of world philosophies outstripped the variety with which he was familiar. At the same time, this willingness to see similarities has a basis in his philosophy. Since, in knowledge, we approach God either directly through reason or indirectly through the created universe, as civilizations develop, they tend to come together or become more similar. Thus Leibniz would expect that ancient Greeks, ancient Chinese, and modern Europeans would have some similar explanations for experience. This expectation follows from his philosophy in the same way as his expectations for the ease of cultural exchange.

ARGUMENT

So far, Leibniz's method has been examined in relation to texts, although Leibniz applies the same principles to Chinese rituals as well. Leibniz's main concern, however, is in cross-cultural interaction and understanding. The central issue could be called cultural or philosophical synthesis: how can we understand the thought of another culture and appropriate elements of that foreign thought into our own thinking? A Leibnizian answer to this question can be extrapolated from the foundation so far elaborated, but it would be nice to turn now to some cases in which Leibniz actually carries out such a synthesis with Chinese thought. Clearly Leibniz is a thinker of philosophical synthesis in general. In the *New Essays*, Theophilus bears witness to this: "This system appears to unite Plato with Democritus, Aristotle with Descartes, the Scholastics with the moderns, theology and morality with reason. Apparently it takes the best from all systems and then advances further than anyone has yet done" (RB 71). Other than some of the hermeneutic principles just described, Leibniz gives no method for how to carry out this synthesis. We have seen what Leibniz hoped to learn and "synthesize" into his own knowledge from China. His interests extended beyond collecting data, but did not extend to philosophy. One reason would be his low estimation of Chinese philosophy, which he thought lacked rigor and strict reasoning. Joseph Needham suggested otherwise in an exciting, if controversial, claim:

I propose for further examination the view that Europe owes to Chinese organic naturalism, based originally on a system of "correlative thinking," brought already to brilliant statement in the Taoist philosophers of the – 3rd century, and systematized in the Neo-Confucian thinkers of the + 12th, a deeply important stimulus, if it was not more, in the synthetic efforts which began in the 17th century to overcome the European antinomy between theological vitalism and mechanical materialism.[12]

"Organic naturalism," a vision of a complexly interrelated, self-organizing world which reconciled "theological vitalist idealism" and "mechanical materialism," would run from Daoism to *li xue* Confucianism, and then through Leibniz to Hegel, Engels, and Whitehead. Needham bases his evidence on similarities between Leibniz's system and the philosophy of Neo-Confucianism, particularly regarding preestablished harmony. Some of these similarities are striking, as we have seen, and if Leibniz had realized them he could have learned much from China, but a close study of Leibniz's

---

[12] Needham, *Science and Civilization*, Vol. II, pp. 497–505.

writings and sources shows that his philosophy had matured long before he developed much understanding of Chinese thought.[13] In any case, we can rely on no example of Leibniz "synthesizing" anything from Chinese philosophy into his own. We can, however, take an angle on such synthesis by reversing our perspective. Instead of examining how Leibniz carries out this synthesis, we can examine how he projects the Chinese could carry it out. This projection takes place on two levels: in specific arguments; and in his overall vision of how to convert the Chinese.

Even finding arguments meant to influence the Chinese is difficult. Leibniz wrote nothing like Malebranche's *Dialogue Between a Christian Philosopher and a Chinese Philosopher*. Wherever Leibniz addresses Chinese philosophy, he means to defend it, not dispute it. Nonetheless, Leibniz makes some implicit arguments against Chinese philosophy, some of which have already appeared under the hermeneutic principle I have called the assumption of reason. Leibniz's argument that the Chinese do not mean that prime matter is the origin of activity converts easily into an argument against matter as the origin of activity, if the Chinese did in fact believe it was. Besides these implicit arguments, Leibniz projects a few arguments directly against some elements of Chinese thought. We can begin with an argument within the discussion of Chinese belief in souls and immortality. Longobardi reported that the modern Confucians did not believe in Paradise or Hell, and that they ridiculed Buddhists for such beliefs. Leibniz replies:

But perhaps they will not always ridicule it if they consider that this supreme substance – which on their own grounds is the source of wisdom and justice – could not act less perfectly on the spirits and the souls which it creates, than a wise king in his realm acts upon his subjects whom he did not create of his own will, and whom it is more difficult for him to govern since they do not depend on him absolutely. Thus this Kingdom of the Spirits under this great Master cannot be less orderly than a Kingdom of men, and consequently it follows that virtue should be rewarded and vice punished under this governance, justice being insufficiently done in this life. (Discourse 65)

The premise of the argument is that there is a supreme being that is the source of wisdom and justice, an existential truth here presupposed. Along with the claim that such a being exists is the presupposition that the Confucians share this particular idea of a supreme being. All minds as expressions of God have this innate idea; what Leibniz assumes is that both he and

[13] The best refutation of Needham's claim is in Daniel J. Cook and Henry Rosemont, Jr., "The Pre-established Harmony between Leibniz and Chinese Thought," *Journal of the History of Ideas*, 42 (1981), pp. 253–67.

the modern Chinese have brought this same idea into their apperception. Leibniz argues that, if these Confucians examine or analyze this idea, they will see with Leibniz that the idea of a supreme being who is the source of wisdom and justice contains the idea that this being would act more perfectly than a king. Presumably, the idea of a supreme being includes the idea that this being would act more perfectly than a lesser being, as an identity – to be a supreme being is to act more perfectly than a lesser being. Secondly, if these Confucians examine their idea of justice, which is itself contained in their idea of a supreme being, they will see that this idea contains the idea that virtue must be rewarded and vice punished. Again, Leibniz assumes not only that everyone shares this innate idea of justice but also that he and the Confucians have both brought the same idea into their awareness. From experience we know that justice is not realized in this life, and Leibniz takes it for granted that the Chinese have this same experience. Thus we could all conclude that justice must be done in the next life, and we must have souls.

Excluding the last premise, that perfect justice is not carried out here on earth, the argument proceeds by necessary truths and depends on our all having certain innate ideas and on these ideas being linked in the same necessary way. For Leibniz, each step reduces to an identity, as the idea of justice contains the idea that virtue and vice receive fitting reward. Why do the modern Chinese not see that the existence of Heaven is implied necessarily in their own belief in a supreme being? Leibniz would have to explain that, although they express the necessary ideas from God, they do not apperceive them clearly enough. We have seen possible reasons for this in the ways experience conditions the apperception of innate ideas. Since our innate ideas emerge in a finite order of discovery, perhaps experience has led the Chinese to other truths. Or perhaps their language and sign systems have kept them from clearly analyzing these ideas. Nonetheless, because both Leibniz and the Chinese share the same ideas, Leibniz believes the Chinese will be easily convinced. The ease with which necessary ideas convince is an important characteristic of Leibniz's view of cultural synthesis, and the fact that the modern Chinese were not easily convinced suggests a weakness in Leibniz's approach. An essential characteristic of Leibniz's argument, though, is that, in so far as it proceeds by necessary truths, it is hypothetical. *If* someone believes in a supreme being who is the source of wisdom and justice, then they can easily be convinced of reward and punishment in the afterlife. The goal of the argument is not a mere speculative truth about how certain ideas necessarily relate to others but rather an existential truth – Heaven really exists. Leibniz's argument depends entirely on the "bite" it gets into existential reality, with the shared belief that a supreme being exists. This form of argument, producing an existential truth through a chain of necessary truths beginning with a shared existential truth, is repeated in the *Discourse*, as in Leibniz's discussion of souls. The premise is that the ancient Chinese believed that intelligences controlled certain natural processes. From this belief, Leibniz claims he could easily convince them that these intelligences are themselves created by one supreme intelligence. Leibniz does not say how this argument would work, but again Leibniz emphasizes how easy it will be to teach this, and again this ease depends on the shared existential premise. Without this shared belief in controlling spirits, it would not be so easy to convince them (Discourse 74). Immediately following this claim, Leibniz adds that it will be more difficult to convince them of "the true philosophy of our time," that is, his own philosophy.

This same structure founds part of Leibniz's response to the Rites Controversy. Unlike other participants in the controversy, Leibniz asks not only what the Chinese think but if what they think can be redirected or clarified. Thus he writes that the Chinese do believe souls exist, and "this allows enough of an opening for knowledgeable missionaries to enlighten them and to clear up their confusion" (Discourse 58). In another passage, Leibniz writes that it may be that some Chinese believe God is the soul of the world and is joined to matter, but, given that they believe that *li*, principle, created *qi*, material force, "one need not reprimand them, but simply explain to them" (Discourse 2). Given that the Chinese have these existential beliefs, they can easily be convinced of the truth by showing what these very ideas entail. They can be shown this because the connection between ideas is shared in a more universal way than our experience of existing things. If they did not hold this initial existential truth, convincing them would be much more difficult.

Leibniz's form of argument leads to two conclusions about what monads have in common and what they do not. All human monads express the ideas in the mind of God, and all can express a number of these clearly and distinctly, making them easy to learn. Nonetheless, in the above cases, although the Chinese monads express these ideas, they do not express them clearly. They do not draw the conclusion necessitated by the very ideas they hold as true. Why? Leibniz does not say, but the reason must lie in their different position in the universe. They can come to express these ideas clearly, according to Leibniz, through interaction with the Europeans. Interaction with Europeans, of course, is a product of the perspectival expression of the universe. Thus we can see how knowledge of necessary truths again depends on experience, and benefits from cultural exchange. Because of our finitude, we can never draw all of the consequences of our ideas: we can always learn more necessary truths, and other cultures are one source of this knowledge. We have seen some of the limited ways in which Leibniz hopes to gain necessary truths through his engagement with Chinese culture, but he unfortunately never uses China as a source of philosophical thought. He had too high an opinion of his own philosophy and too low an opinion of Chinese philosophy.

Leibniz's engagement with Chinese thought shows that communication or argument depends on the intersection of *two* common grounds: one the shared realm of necessary truths; the other some common ground of existential or experiential truth. To prove the immortality of the soul to the Chinese, one would have to establish two things. The first would be that all substances are immortal: if you really understand the idea "substance" you will also understand it to contain the idea "immortal." According to Leibniz, this step would be relatively easy, because all human beings already have the concept "substance," and have it in a way that contains "immortality." The second step, however, would be to convince someone that each person is in fact that thing which Leibniz calls a "substance." In the next section, I will examine how the second step is explained or carried out, but Leibniz does not usually support it by appealing to nature directly. In the arguments in the *Discourse*, Leibniz presupposes that this step has already been carried out. This approach underscores one of Leibniz's main imperatives regarding China – to reveal the presence of a natural theology in their own texts. Thus if a modern Chinese did not believe in the existence of souls or God, one could convince him not only by appealing to experience but by appealing to texts which the Chinese recognized as authoritative. Given the perspectival limits of experience, the latter might be easier.

THE COMMON GROUND – NATURAL THEOLOGY

If this two-fold commonality is needed, then Leibniz's project of cultural exchange with China requires some common ground of existential truths. All of the arguments just seen depend on shared knowledge of God and the soul, the rudiments of natural theology. Leibniz's main thesis about Chinese philosophy is that it contains a doctrine of natural theology, as the very title of the *Discourse on the Natural Theology of the Chinese* indicates. The framework for Leibniz's theory of natural theology has been seen in chapter 2, through a survey of what we can know about God from our experience of the created world. Given the existence of the universe, we know it must have a sufficient reason, and that only God can supply this reason. This knowledge seems open to anyone, from any part of the universe. More broadly, as every effect expresses its cause, the universe which we each express from different perspectives also expresses God, so that knowledge of the universe tends toward knowledge of God. Again, this progression from knowledge of the universe to knowledge of God seems open to anyone. These general principles show the possibility of natural theology, but we have also seen the complexity of the question of what different monads have in common. Given the framework established so far, based on the fact that monads express both the universe and the realm of ideas, we must examine what accounts for the cross-cultural appearance of natural theology.

One possible explanation for natural theology in China should be mentioned immediately – that the rudiments of theology in ancient Chinese thought derive from the same revelation as the Judeo-Christian tradition. On this account, the theology of the ancient Chinese would not be "natural" at all. This view seems bizarre now, but we have seen it as a common early approach to China, held primarily by the "Figurists," whose most prominent member was Joachim Bouvet. The impetus for this view was the problem of ancient Chinese chronology, which placed the early Chinese emperors at the same time as the Biblical Patriarchs. A second support for this explanation was the early tendency to see the Chinese script as a degenerate form of Egyptian hieroglyphics. This was the view put forth in Athanasius Kircher's *China Monumentis Illustrata*, published in 1667, based on what he saw as the similarities between the languages and the religious ceremonies and customs of Egypt and China.[14] The connection between Egypt and China remained a popular view, so that La Croze as late as 1713 wrote to Leibniz: "For I already have some good conjectures on the origin of the [Chinese] hieroglyphics, and good enough proof of the resemblance of the ancient Chinese characters to those of Egypt" (LBr 517, Bl 69 r°). Bouvet reveals his Figurist views to Leibniz throughout his correspondence. For example, he writes that the better inventions and science of the ancient Chinese came in fact from "the ancient Patriarchs of all the nations" (W 104), and that, if a key for the Chinese language could be found, it would have to be developed through an account of Egyptian hieroglyphics (W 73). Leibniz's view of these Figurist interpretations is not entirely clear. In his earliest writings on China he claims that either Egypt was a colony of China, or vice versa (A IV, 1, 384), but later

---

[14] Mungello, *Curious Land*, p. 163.

he expresses skepticism of a connection between China and Egypt, even in his letters to Bouvet (W 188). Elsewhere he criticizes this syncretic tendency more harshly, complaining, for example, that people are too liberal in connecting ancient fables to the Bible, as if the ancients could not invent their own superstitions.[15] Nonetheless, Leibniz suggests several times in his writings on China the possibility of a connection with the Biblical Patriarchs. He puts this connection most strongly in a passage of the *Discourse* describing the Chinese doctrine of spirits, which, according to Leibniz, resembles the doctrine of angels. He writes, "There is a great likelihood that these expressions, so close to the great truths of our tradition, have come to the Chinese through the tradition of the ancient Patriarchs" (Discourse 110). He makes a similar comment regarding the Chinese claim that *li* creates *qi*, which he equated with the claim that God created the universe. Leibniz notes that the creation of the universe was unknown even to the Greeks, and traditionally exceeded the range of natural theology (Discourse 24a, cf. Discourse 32). Given Leibniz's ambiguous remarks, we must at least say that he considered some transmission of knowledge from the Biblical Patriarchs to the ancient Chinese possible. His overall verdict, however, is best revealed in his lack of interest in pursuing this connection. In spite of Bouvet's obvious enthusiasm in his letters, Leibniz expresses no interest and makes no effort to investigate these connections or their implications. This lack of interest contrasts his repeated focus on natural theology.

Leibniz writes on natural theology in many places and contexts, most prominently in the *Theodicy*. The focus in the *Theodicy* is on the relationship between faith and reason, and Leibniz characterizes it as a defense of natural theology, for "there is only too much tendency to overthrow natural religion to its very foundations" (PD 11).[16] Although the *Theodicy* begins by discussing Jesus, his role is limited: "I will show only how Jesus Christ brought about the conversion of natural religion into law, and gained for it the authority of a public dogma" (H 6). Jesus adds nothing new to what reason shows, but only converts this knowledge to a surer footing, overcoming the inconstancy of human reason.[17] Taking the broader context of

---

[15] To Ezechiel Spanheim, April 27, 1697 (A I, 14, 160–61). Mercer shows that Leibniz's early influences, like Thomasius, and Leibniz himself, at least early in his life, were hostile to the methods of ancient theology, while sharing tendencies toward "conciliatory eclecticism" (Mercer, *Leibniz's Metaphysics*, pp. 27–39).

[16] Riley emphasizes the *Theodicy* as a work of natural theology, pointing out that its original subtitle claimed its demonstrations were carried out with mathematical certainty from "natural theology and jurisprudence" (Grua I, 370; Riley, *Universal Jurisprudence*, p. 90).

[17] Cf. Riley, *Universal Jurisprudence*, p. 107.

Leibniz's work, as well as what he says specifically in his writings on China, the explanation for the common ground between China and Europe lies in his theory of natural theology. As described in the *Theodicy*, the scope of natural theology for Leibniz is fairly traditional. Excluded from natural theology are the mysteries of the trinity, incarnation, and holy communion, as well as such things as the creation of this world by God and the reasons why God chose to create this particular world (PD 16, 23). The keystones of natural theology are the existence of God and the immortality of the soul. Leibniz sets these as his goals in the early essay "Confessio Naturae Contra Atheistas" (A 1, 1, 489–93), as they are also the goal of Descartes' *Meditations*. Leibniz's philosophy as a whole can be taken as a natural theology, based on reason and experience rather than faith, but Leibniz rarely speaks of his philosophy in these terms, I suppose because it requires a level of development which would not make it common and in that sense "natural" (i.e. discoverable in a state of nature).

How do the truths of natural theology emerge? How can isolated peoples such as the Chinese and the Europeans discover the same truths about God and the soul? We can consider the proof of the existence of God first. Leibniz recognizes many such proofs, in the *New Essays* writing, "I believe indeed that almost all the methods which have been used to prove the existence of God are sound and could serve the purpose if they were rendered complete" (NE IV, x, § 7; RB 438). In the "Monadology," he distinguishes three specifically. The first proof is that the existence of eternal truths requires a God whose eternal understanding grounds them (M 43; AG 218). The second proof is Leibniz's revision of the ontological proof. The third is from the existence of contingent beings, who require a necessary sufficient reason. In terms of natural theology, it seems like the ontological proof would be dominant, because it is *a priori* and thus less relative to our spatially determined perspective on the universe. Leibniz rarely uses it in this context, however, probably because of the extreme subtlety of reasoning required by the proof. According to Leibniz, from Anselm through Descartes, no one clearly understood it but himself. If the reasoning involved was too subtle for Descartes and Anselm, Leibniz would hardly expect the Chinese or anyone else to manage it. Moreover, the proof depends on possessing a clear idea of God, but the question of natural theology is how one comes to that idea in the first place. Leibniz takes for granted that, from this clear and distinct idea of God, reason will convince you of other things, such as God's justice and necessary existence. The proof of God by the existence of necessary truths is also not commonly used by Leibniz, probably for the same reasons. To use this proof, one would first have to establish the existence of eternal necessary truths, a claim even some Europeans doubted.

The proof on which Leibniz relies to explain natural theology and the fact that other cultures have come to the idea of God is the *a posteriori* proof from the existence of a created, contingent universe. Leibniz relies on this proof not only in his explicit discussions of natural theology, but also in his arguments against atheism (e.g. "Confessio Naturae Contra Atheistas"; A I, 1, 489–93), and against skepticism (e.g. A VI, 4, 2265–71). When discussing natural theology, however, Leibniz emphasizes the need for a sufficient reason not just for something to exist but rather for the order and perfection of this particular universe to exist. In the *New Essays*, while discussing other cultures and arguments based on universal consent, Leibniz suggests that the widespread recognition of some idea of God could have come from an ancient widespread revelation, but adds:

> It appears that nature has helped to bring men to it without doctrine: the wonders of the universe have made them think of a higher power [. . .]. You must admit [. . .] that the inclination we have to recognize the idea of God is part of our human nature. Even if the first teaching of it were attributed to revelation, still men's receptiveness to this doctrine comes from the nature of their souls. (NE I, i, § 4)

We can note several points from this passage. First, this movement toward God depends on both reason and experience. The experience could be the experience of revelation, most likely second hand through a missionary or a Bible, but it could simply be an experience of the marvels of nature. At the same time, containing an idea of God and other necessary truths, the mind is predisposed to belief in God, based on our common expression of ideas. In broader terms, Leibniz here refers to the ability to reason about the origins of the marvels we witness in nature. Again, then, we see the appearance of two grounds: one of experience, resulting from our expression of the universe; and one of necessary truths, resulting from our expression of innate ideas. The two levels together issue a vague notion of an existing God. The second point to note is that Leibniz is not presenting a version of the cosmological argument. That is, we do not reason that because something contingent or causally dependent exists, then there must be a first, uncaused, cause. Rather, Leibniz gives a teleological argument: because we find nature so wonderful, we are led to think of God. This movement need not take the form of an explicit argument. In the *New Essays*, it is more of an unconscious response: "it is natural feeling that has brought about the tradition that there is a God" (NE I, ii, § 9; cf. NE I, i, § 4). This feeling resembles the feeling or instinct which leads us to avoid contradictions. Both feelings are the effects of ideas lying outside our conscious awareness; because we tend toward greater perfection and knowledge, we have a disposition to recognize this innate idea of God, just as we have a disposition to recognize the principle of non-contradiction. Even so, it would be consistent with Leibniz's account if the sense of a Creator remained below the level of apperception, manifesting itself only in a vague reverence for nature.

These intimations of God have two weaknesses for the spread of theism. First, the progression is only highly probable. In a dialogue between a skeptic and a religious hermit (representing Leibniz), the skeptic argues that, in spite of its apparent order, this world could result from chance, for example, if there were an infinite number of worlds and we just happened to end up in an orderly one. The hermit responds: "I remain agreed that this fiction is not impossible, absolutely speaking; that is to say, that it does not imply a contradiction when one considers but the reasoning presently taken from the order of things" (A VI, 4, 2268). He then gives his own fiction. If one were transported into another world or part of the universe, and there stood among clocks, books, furniture, and so on, no one would doubt these were the product of a conscious Creator. Of course, they might be chance atomic configurations, but, he concludes, "the appearance of the one is as little in regard to the other as a grain of sand in regard to the world. Since the appearance of this supposition is so infinitely small, it is morally null. And consequently there is a moral certainty that it is providence which governs things" (A VI, 4, 2268). This lack of complete certainty manifests the origin of the proof. We have seen only two sources of certainty: necessary truths; and primitive truths of experience. Neither of these grounds this demonstration of the existence of God. Rather, this demonstration follows the route of our third source of existential truths, based on observed consistencies in our experience and on probability. The demonstration depends on science, taken in a broad sense. The most naturally compelling proof is thus not the most certain proof. The second weakness of this progression to God is that the argument does not indicate an absolutely perfect Creator, since, as Leibniz admits, this world does not seem perfect from our limited perspective. In spite of these weaknesses, Leibniz believed the experience of nature's wonder along with the ability to reason makes natural theology fairly widespread. Leibniz represents the analogy between a worker and the work produced and God and the universe as extremely natural and even obvious. When we imagine ourselves transplanted into this new part of the universe, we think that we would have to be insane seriously to believe the books were a product of chance. The "naturalness" of the analogy suggests that natural theology would arise in different, isolated cultures. From any perspective on the universe, the marvels and order of things would suggest a Creator, at least as a felt reverence for something beyond.

The weaknesses of these intimations of God lead the development or promotion of natural theology in two directions, through reason or through experience. The first takes these vague suggestions and refines them through reflection, leading to the standard proofs of God and clarifying what the innate idea of God entails. We have already seen some examples of Leibniz engaging in this process, as when he argues that the idea of God entails justice and that justice entails an afterlife. The other direction for development emphasizes the perfection of nature, through science. We see the latter in the dialogue between the skeptic and holy hermit. The hermit begins by claiming that, because of the admirable order of things, all appearances favor providence. The skeptic objects that, although some things taken in isolation appear well made, the universe itself, taken as a whole, is not: "the strongest oppress the weak, the just and the powerful hardly meet, and there rules everywhere a certain hazard which plays with wisdom and equity" (A VI, 4, 2265). We would expect the hermit to respond by emphasizing the perspectival nature of the skeptic's experience. Leibniz makes this move in other places: we cannot judge the perfection of the universe as a whole, because we exist here for only a limited time; we cannot judge the perfection of the universe because there might be beings on other planets or spiritual beings of greater perfection living better than we do. Rather than taking this skeptical approach, the hermit answers by describing the omnipresence of wonders in nature, suggesting everywhere the existence of a Creator. He turns to science, to the microscope: "These people deceive themselves obviously, for in the end we see nothing done halfway; how do those ill-made things disappear so soon, how do they escape our eyes armed with microscopes? On the contrary, we find enough to be delighted with wonder, to the degree that we penetrate more and more into the interior of nature" (A VI, 4, 2267). In the essay "The Common Concept of Justice," the microscope appears again, to show that we can only know the perfection of a thing when we simultaneously grasp both the parts and the whole. We cannot do this for the universe itself, but we can see nature's perfection with the help of technology: "We find order and marvels in the smallest whole things, when we are capable of distinguishing the parts and of seeing the whole at the same time, as it appears in looking at insects and other small things in the microscope."[18]

Natural theology begins, then, in the feeling of wonder that comes with experience of the world. Science lets us penetrate further and further into the order and richness of nature, so seeming imperfections turn out to be misperceptions. The primitive intimation of God flowing from wonder becomes more determinate. This connection between science and knowledge of God is clearest in some notes Leibniz made on William Penn, cited by Patrick Riley, in which Leibniz remarkably connects knowledge of God not only with reason, as he often does, but with science in particular. He writes, "Now that providence has enriched our century through so many new lights which result from the marvelous discoveries which have been made in nature, and which more and more show us its beauty, we should profit from them by applying them to the ideas which Jesus Christ gives us of God" (Grua I, 91; Riley, *Leibniz's Universal Jurisprudence*, pp. 176–77). He continues: "True love is based upon a knowledge of the beauty of the loved object. Thus the beauty of God is apparent in the wonders of the effects of this supreme cause. Therefore, the better one understands nature and knows the solid truths of the natural sciences – which are like so many rays of divine perfection – the greater is one's capacity truly to love God" (Grua I, 91; Riley, *Leibniz's Universal Jurisprudence*, p. 177). And, as we have seen, love of God founds ethics. On Leibniz's account, it seems positively sinful not to promote science. In the previously mentioned dialogue, the hermit advises the now converted skeptic to combine practice and prayer. Prayer, however, sounds a lot like science: "a perpetual search for solid reasons for that which makes God appear to you great and lovable . . . for there is nothing in nature which does not furnish you to make a hymn" (A VI, 4, 2273).

The power of science to lead to God guides Leibniz's efforts to encourage cultural exchange with China, and he writes to Bouvet of his "zeal for the advancement of the glory of God and of the felicity of humanity, both by the propagation of the Christian religion and by growth of solid sciences, which give us means to admire the advantages of wisdom and the power of the author of things, and to better assist mankind" (W 64–65). The same vision of science grounds Leibniz's push for founding learned societies. He begins his draft of the constitution founding the Berlin Society of Sciences:

---

[18] G. W. Leibniz, *Political Writings*. Trans. by Patrick Riley (Cambridge: Cambridge University Press, 1988), p. 151.

For the spread of the Honor of God and also for the preservation and promotion of the right faith, true respect of God, good Morals and even the entire common well-being in every standing, it is most necessary that the minds of Men are enlightened through good sciences and useful studies, encouraged to realization and wonder at the perfections and work of God, and thus improved and led to Love and respect of God as the source of all good, but also held back from idleness and evil, and finally made more easily to serve God and the Fatherland, as well as themselves and . . . their other neighbors.[19]

Through study and science, minds improve better to recognize and wonder at nature, and thus to love and respect its Creator. This knowledge of nature leads to right religion, good morals, and even the benefit of all humankind. This progression from science to religion to virtue underlies and explains Leibniz's motto appearing throughout the founding documents of the Berlin Society – *propagatio fidei per scientias*.

The promotion of science, however, is not without dangers. Leibniz recognized that the rise of science also gave rise to a threat – materialism. In a letter to Bouvet, Leibniz explicitly recognizes overcoming materialism as the main problem in convincing the modern Chinese to accept Christianity (W 64). The main strategy of the critics of Chinese philosophy was to portray them as materialists. Thus Leibniz emphasized to the Jesuits not only that they should introduce science to the Chinese, but that they should introduce his own philosophy with it, because it defeats materialism (W 64, cf. W 56). In Europe, Leibniz sets up an opposition between the moderns, primarily Cartesians, and the ancients, and parallels this opposition to an opposition between science and religion (e.g. W 64). Leibniz claims that his own philosophy avoids these conflicts, which is why it should be introduced to the Chinese alongside science. Thus he writes to Verjus that he can contribute by "the establishment of a solid philosophy in which piety and truth are equally accounted" (W 56). Ironically, Leibniz wants his philosophy to do for China just what Needham proposed that Chinese philosophy had done for Leibniz. The need for piety and Leibniz's own philosophy should not be taken as a weakening or mitigation of the introduction of science. He does not present a compromise between the two, nor does he admit any conflict between them. On the contrary, the central focus of the *Theodicy*, in which Leibniz outlines his theory of natural theology, opposes Bayle's claim that science or reason conflict with theology. Science properly done leads to God.[20] We could just as well say that theology properly done requires science, as we need science more fully to witness God's

---

[19] Brather, *Leibniz und Seine Akademie*, p. 94.   [20] Cf. Grosholz, "Plato and Leibniz," p. 268.

perfection. The opposition between science and theology reveals itself as an opposition between *bad* science and theology. Leibniz brings together Cartesianism and Scholasticism not by adding something to science but by showing that science properly carried out requires this union. Leibniz does this primarily through his idea of force and his criticism of the Cartesian theory of motion, and we find the idea of force at the center of Leibniz's hopes to introduce his philosophy into China. He explains: "And by this means I believe to have rehabilitated the philosophy of the ancients or the school in which Theology is surely so useful, without at all departing from modern discoveries nor mechanical explanations, because mechanics even supposes the consideration of force and it has been found that nothing is more proper than force in the phenomena of bodies to give an opening to the consideration of spiritual causes" (W 64, cf. W 140). He repeats the same explanation to Verjus in explaining the use of his philosophy for China (W 56). Through these explanations, Leibniz portrays the introduction of his philosophy as part of the overall project of introducing science to the Chinese, all with the goal of leading to natural theology. Through the concept of force, science defeats materialism. This movement suggests the passage from Francis Bacon, with which Leibniz begins the "Confessions of Nature against Atheism": "casually sampled philosophy leads away from God but that drunk more deeply, it leads back to him" (A I, 1, 489; L 109).

One final problem to consider is the relationship between Leibniz's natural theology and revealed theology. When Bayle pushes the conflict between faith and reason, his primary focus is on the conflict between reason and the mysteries of the Christian religion. Leibniz summarizes his own response to this charge: "For after all, one truth cannot contradict another, and the light of reason is no less a gift of God than that of revelation" (PD 29; H 91). Leibniz addresses the conflict between reason and faith using the distinction between necessary truths and contingent truths, emphasizing the impossibility of conflict between faith and necessary truths. In knowing necessary truths, we express the order of ideas in God, an order God himself cannot violate. Leibniz goes so far as to write "one must take care never to abandon the necessary and eternal truths for the sake of upholding Mysteries, lest the enemies of religion seize upon such an occasion for decrying both religion and the Mysteries" (PD 22; H 88). There can, however, be conflicts between truths of faith and contingent truths, or, rather, they can appear to conflict (PD 3; H 75). The conflict is between religion and false knowledge of facts (T 122). As we have seen, our system of existential, contingent truths never captures the full order of the universe, which only God can know. We only attain knowledge of general principles, which Leibniz calls God's customs (DM 7; AG 40; DM 16; AG 48–49). God's specific decrees, however, can contradict these general maxims, so that, no matter how regular a law of nature appears, we can never know for sure that it will always hold. The provisional nature of existential truths leaves room for the possibility of miracles. In the *Theodicy*, Leibniz emphasizes the incomprehensibility of the Mysteries. To comprehend [*comprendre*] something is to have an adequate idea of it: "it is not enough that one have some ideas thereof; one must have all the ideas of everything that goes to make it up, and all these ideas must be clear, distinct, adequate" (PD 73; H 114). If we cannot comprehend an idea, if the idea is not adequate, we can draw no necessary conclusions. Thus the Mysteries can neither be proven nor disproven through necessary demonstration. Any objection brought against articles of faith would be merely probable and based on experience, and in a conflict between a probable argument and faith, faith can win.

The existence of the super-natural should not be taken as much threat to science. In practice, Leibniz is loathe to bring in miracles as an explanation for natural phenomena. God operates by rules, and though for reasons we cannot comprehend he may sometimes go against these general rules, he does so only exceptionally. Leibniz criticizes both Newton and Malebranche on the grounds that their systems call for a state of perpetual miracles, the former for allowing attraction at a distance and the latter for the doctrine of occasionalism. In addition, the role of miracles in our knowledge is itself circumscribed by reason. On the one hand, if what appears as an article of faith conflicts with our knowledge of necessary truths, then the necessary truths must win and we must admit that what appeared to be an article of faith really was not. On the other hand, reason must itself judge the truth of scripture and miracles: "reason judges as natural interpreter over other interpreters" (A VI, 4, 2362). Leibniz explains this use of reason in detail in the "Examen Religionis Christianae." Reason judges the truth of scripture partly by bringing the structure of necessary truths to it, and partly by judging the reliability of the miracles and prophecies used to support it. In the "Preliminary Discourse" to the *Theodicy*, Leibniz says that faith can be seen as a variety of experience, since it depends on the experiences of the church fathers (PD 1). Reason must judge and interpret these experiences just as it would any other. Ultimately the full body of knowledge based on probabilities about existential truths would incorporate scripture, based on the probability of its truth, in accord with experience and the judgment of reason.

In accounting for how we learn from other cultures, we have seen that both Leibniz's interests and his way of interpreting and engaging Chinese thought follow from a complex account of the integration of reason and experience. Leibniz's theory of natural theology follows this same foundation, depending on the structure of innate ideas common to all minds as reflections of the mind of God, and on some existential truth as a link to this particular, embodied world we share. Once a common existential truth is found, argument can proceed by analysis of the ideas of the things recognized. The common ground of existential truths, which Leibniz finds already present in classical Chinese thought, can be called natural theology. This natural theology comes from experience, although its recognition and structure depend on our possession of reason and the relevant ideas. While not universally recognized, natural theology is relatively common because of the commonalities of our experience, expressing the same universe. In its most primitive form, experience of the world leads to wonder, which leads us to look for some cause beyond matter, that is, to God. Our idea of God becomes more determinate as our knowledge of the universe becomes more determinate. Knowledge of this existing universe is science, in its broadest sense, so the common ground of natural theology follows from the common ground of science. Thus, through our knowledge of experience, we are led to an idea of God, and through our knowledge of necessary truths, we can refine this idea of God and examine what it entails, for example, the existence of a Heaven and Hell. The knowledge which results from these two processes cannot contradict revealed truths based on faith, because both faith and reason come from God.

This dual foundation for cross-cultural understanding suggests an answer to the question sometimes raised: why was Leibniz so interested in China in particular? The idea of natural theology is that it can be discovered by any people. Leibniz himself suggests at times that natural theology is fairly widespread, as he writes to Bouvet, "I have always had a tendency to believe that the ancient Chinese, as the ancient Arabs (witness the book of Job) and perhaps the ancient Celts, (that is to say Germans and Gaulians) have been far from idolatry, and rather adorators of a sovereign principle" (W 189). Nonetheless, he shows an interest in China much more than in any other place. Some circumstantial factors condition this preference, including, for example, the bias of his sources, the position of China on the opposite side of Asia, and the nature of the Chinese language, but we can now see a more fundamental reason. The development of natural theology comes with the development of knowledge. Thus China, which Leibniz calls the other center of "culture and refinement" (NS 1), would more likely have this natural theology and the common ground with Europe necessary for communication, understanding, and exchange. The connection between the most developed knowledge and the most common ground with Europe may seem obvious, but the connection with natural theology is not. Leibniz's approach contrasts two alternatives. One would view all knowledge without the help of revelation and grace as a corruption or "splendid sin." Thus the accomplishments of the Chinese would be at best irrelevant and at worst a source of prejudice, vanity, and ignorance. This position roughly corresponds to that of the opponents of accommodation in the Rites Controversy. The second alternative would take civilization as a corruption of nature. This view is brought up hypothetically by Philalethe in the *New Essays*. If there really are universal innate ideas, he argues, these should be clearest in the simplest and most natural people. Knowledge and civilization should lead us away from and obscure these ideas. Leibniz rejects this consequence of innate ideas, because having an actual thought of something requires two things: that one possess the idea of it (which all do); and that one come to discover it through some experience. The actual grasp of an innate idea depends on culture, or, as Leibniz calls it in the *New Essays*, the "natural history of mankind." Apperception of innate ideas requires reasoning and the systematic experience of nature. China, whose knowledge appeared to Leibniz as the most highly developed outside Europe, would also be most likely to have discovered those ideas which lay the basis for natural theology. This common ground of existential truths allows understanding and learning.

INTERPRETATION AND ACCOMMODATION

Through all of his writings, Leibniz strongly and consistently supported the position of accommodation in the Rites Controversy. The information coming from his Jesuit sources was naturally colored to favor accommodation, so it is not surprising that Leibniz would take up their cause. At the same time, the Rites Controversy had practical consequences for Leibniz, who believed that without accommodation the mission and the opportunity it presented for cultural exchange would be lost. Even if the mission itself were not lost by a decision against accommodation, Leibniz's Jesuit sources would certainly suffer. Leibniz, however, did not take up accommodation simply from expediency or the biases of his sources. The Rites Controversy centered on two separate questions: were the rituals directed toward ancestors and Confucius religious? Could the words *Shang Di* and *tian* be used to refer to God? Both of these questions turn on issues of interpretation: how should we interpret the meaning of these rituals? What do *Shang Di* and *tian* mean? In supporting accommodation, Leibniz either argues for specific interpretations of the relevant issues, or more broadly about how the issues should be interpreted. These arguments follow from, and reinforce, the hermeneutic principles discussed earlier. Before looking at these specific arguments, we should examine the broader foundation for accommodation in Leibniz's philosophy.

The possibility of natural theology goes hand-in-hand with respect for non-Christians, just as Aquinas' doctrine of natural theology was intended to accommodate the pagan thought of Aristotle. Given Leibniz's theory of natural theology, it is not only possible but quite natural that non-Christians would have some knowledge or intimation of God. In addition, for Leibniz, reason not only leads to God, but also to virtue, freeing virtue from dependence on revelation. This lays another foundation for accommodation: just as experience and reflection would lead the Chinese to the idea of a God who provided the reason for things, so would experience and reflection lead them to act virtuously, to emulate that harmonious and good principle. Given this basis, Leibniz's evaluation and praise of Chinese ethics follows naturally: "Hence the Chinese do not attain to full and complete virtue. This is not to be expected except by Heaven's grace and Christian teaching. Yet they temper the bitter fruits of vice, and though they cannot tear out the roots of sin in human nature, they are apparently able to control many of the burgeoning growths of evil" (NS 5). In fact, Leibniz thought they did this better than the Europeans, who had revealed religious truths.

The central role of reason in knowledge of God and in virtuous action directs Leibniz's philosophy toward accommodation. This contrasts with philosophers who place revelation and grace, both of which seem to have been given mostly to Europe, in the central role. A second reason leading to accommodation is our ability to grasp God's goodness. In examining the use of final causes, we noted that God's goodness entails that God not condemn innocents and virtuous pagans, supporting a position of accommodation. Regarding pagans, Leibniz writes, we must hold to the Scholastic maxim, "Quod facienti quod in se est, non denegatur gratia necessaria" – one who does what they can will not be denied the grace they need (T 95). He concedes that salvation requires knowledge of Jesus and that there have been countless pagans who lacked this knowledge, but he rejects the following as a false dilemma – such a person must either be saved without Christ or else be damned (T 95). For example, Leibniz replies, God could grant grace in ways we do not see, giving knowledge of Christ in one's dying moments (CD 111). Thus, those who have stood outside the range of Christianity and have missed its message can still come to the clemency and justice of God (CD 113). In the Rites Controversy, one of the main groups that lined up against the Jesuits and accommodation were the Jansenists and others in the Augustinian tradition. In the *Theodicy*, Leibniz comments directly on that group. He objects to the idea that unbaptized children or those who have never heard of Christ are necessarily condemned. He also objects to the claim that pagan virtues and actions are but "splendid sins." These theologians, he writes, "disparage man so much that they wrong the providence of the Author of mankind" (T 259; H 285). These passages from the *Theodicy* argue for a general position of accommodation – that pagans can be saved and that they can have virtue – directed against the Augustinian opponents of accommodation. In the *New Essays*, Leibniz turns this general argument directly to the Rites Controversy. Again he criticizes those Augustinians who believe in the damnation of unbaptized children. He then adds:

This attitude may have influenced the dispute which a number of over-zealous teachers had with the Jesuit missionaries in China: the latter had suggested that the ancient Chinese had had the true religions of their time, and true saints, and that there was nothing idolatrous or atheistic in the teachings of Confucius. Rome seems to have been more reasonable in not wanting to condemn a very large nation without understanding it. (NE IV, xviii; RB 501–02)[21]

Leibniz concludes with a pointed remark – we are lucky that God is more philanthropic than these men.

Besides these philosophical reasons rooted in natural theology and the goodness of God, Leibniz's accommodation depends on practical views of compromise in the Church, developed in his writings on Church reunification. He explains this view in the *Examen Religionis Christianae*, with regard to the use of images in Christianity, warning that someone who wants to root out evil must take care not to destroy the Church at the same time (A VI, 4, 2407–08). He then quotes a passage from Augustine: "there is a difference between that which we teach and that which we endure; there is a difference between that which we must prescribe and that which we must emend, and until we emend, we are compelled to tolerate" (A VI, 4, 2407). This idea of tolerating bad practices for the greater good of the Church underlies Leibniz's call in the *Novissima Sinica* for a unified missionary effort, in which all would teach the core principles necessary and sufficient for salvation, while tolerating differences on other matters. Leibniz extends the same toleration that he promotes toward Catholics and other sects of Christianity to the new Christians in China.[22] Leibniz would

---

[21] Translation modified.
[22] See Leibniz's notes to a letter from Gerhard Meier (A I, 14, 655).

compromise matters of religious practice and doctrine for the greater good of introducing Christianity into China, for the exchange of knowledge that the missions allowed, and for the good of harmony within the Church itself.

The strongest example of Leibniz's willingness to compromise in China was not even considered in the Rites Controversy, the question of polygamy. Early in his writings, Leibniz expressed fear that the mission would fail because the Chinese would not give up polygamy. Around 1690, he repeats several times in his correspondence that the Chinese should be allowed the imperfection of polygamy if necessary for their conversion.[23] He gives his clearest opinion in the *Examen Religionis Christianae*, under the sacrament of matrimony. There he writes that the Church should forbid polygamy in Europe:

But what should we say of those nations of infidels, if what could convert them to Christianity were an indulgence for long rooted polygamy, and if that appears to be the refusal or sole reason against such a good? It seems to me safer to leave the decision to the great Pope. But I would like to say that if it seemed useful to the Pope to concede the Chinese the right to polygamy in order to be able to lead them to the Christian faith (it is well known that this law of Christianity, which was contradicted by the oldest of its people, is considered one of the prime impediments to the faith), he would do nothing contrary to Christian doctrine. (A VI, 4, 2445)

Monogamy did indeed pose one of the biggest obstacles for conversion among the Chinese, not only because men did not want to give up their concubines but also for the social disruption the dismantling of families would entail. For many potential converts, rearranging their polygamous family system was the final obstacle the missionaries had to convince them of. Nonetheless, polygamy was a point that the Jesuits themselves would not accommodate. In advocating the accommodation of polygamy Leibniz goes beyond his sources, showing his greater flexibility.

For all these reasons, Leibniz was committed to promoting accommodation, both toward China and toward Christian factions within Europe. As the Rites Controversy centered on questions of interpretation, Leibniz argues for accommodation by employing what I have called his hermeneutic generosity. First, when the meaning is ambiguous, take the more favorable meaning. We do not know enough about the Chinese to decide against the rites, and, until we do, we should not condemn them. He writes:

---

[23] Leibniz carries on a discussion of the topic with Landgraf Ernst von Hessen-Rheinfalls, in letters from June, 1690 (A I, 5, 591), July 14, 1690 (A I, 5, 617), November 13, 1691 (A I, 7, 189), and December, 1691 (A I, 7, 231). See also the letter to Gerhard Meier, April 13, 1692 (A I, 7, 634).

As of now, I do not know if it is sufficiently clear what in fact is the authentic doctrine of the Chinese literati (especially of the classical ones), officially approved, based on their classical texts. In any event, one can hardly evaluate it properly in Europe until Chinese literature is no less familiar than the Rabbinical or Arab, so that it is possible for us to read their books and judge them critically, something that could indeed be done in Christendom. (Cult 8)

Until then, we should give the rituals the most favorable meaning we can (Cult 9). Leibniz employs the same principle in the question of terms. In the remarks sent to Des Bosses, he writes of the difficulty of determining what the ancient Chinese believed. With all of our history, criticism, and philosophy, he says, we still argue about the meaning of Plato, Aristotle, and Augustine. In China, we lack these tools, and the Chinese themselves seem to lack systematic form and vocabulary in philosophy (Remarks 5, 7). For these reasons, "as a general rule, nothing prevents us from thinking well of the ancient doctrines until we are compelled to proceed in any other way" (Remarks 5). In the *Discourse*, Leibniz explicitly reasons – it would be enough for the favorable interpretation of the ancients to be sustainable, since the moderns are ambivalent, but in fact these interpretations are more than sustainable (Discourse 1). Leibniz's method throughout the *Discourse* begins with some favorable evidence, and then shows that the objections and counter-evidence are inconclusive. In these arguments, the meaning of "favorable" shifts slightly from Leibniz's earlier generosity, by which an ambiguous text was given the most reasonable meaning. In these cases, the bias leads directly toward interpretations that will encourage exchange or harmonize with Christianity.

Leibniz's accommodation claims that a mistake in favor of accommodation is not so serious and is preferable to risking the entire mission. We have already seen him give this view regarding polygamy, and he gives a similar view in a letter to Annibal Marchetti (March [?]1702; LBr 603, Bl 6–7). In the previous letter, Marchetti had tried to convert Leibniz to Catholicism. Leibniz replies with a criticism of Catholicism in matters of ritual, namely, that some in Italy go so far as to approach idolatry, worshiping the creation rather than the Creator. He adds:

But nonetheless I favor your progress in China, for it is better for a corruption of Christian doctrine to be introduced there than nothing at all. Moreover, I hope prudent men of yours will make effort in the new church being established, so that abuses (which they themselves often identify) are for a good part avoided. (LBr 603; Bl 6–7; quoted in Bodemann, *Der Briefwechsel des Gottfried Wilhelm Leibniz*)

In this passage, we again see Leibniz considering issues of tolerance within Europe and toward China in the same terms, although here he will tolerate more in China. In "De cultu Confucii civili," he says that as long as the doctrines of Confucius are ambiguous, we should give them the best interpretation. He cites Paul's interpretation of the Athenian altar to an unknown god as a precedent (Cult 8).[24] He concludes: even if our interpretations are wrong, "certainly no pious deception would be more innocent, since danger to those mistaken and offense to those who teach is absent" (Cult 9).

One last principle supporting accommodation is Leibniz's focus not only on what the Chinese really intend, but also on how the Chinese doctrines can be interpreted. This move corresponds to the hermeneutic principle mentioned in the first section of this chapter: when a text is contradictory, we should take the good and eliminate the bad. Leibniz ends his argument for the accommodation of the rites with a plea for the missionaries to teach the neophytes what the ceremonies should mean and what spirit should underlie them (Cult 13). In making this last point, Leibniz differs from most other participants in the Rites Controversy. The question was usually what is the spirit behind the rites. Leibniz instead asks if, under the interpretations and guidance of the missionaries, Christians can perform the rites with an acceptable spirit. He writes in the remarks to Des Bosses that one cannot invent new terms, but must purify old ones (Remarks 2). So in the *Discourse* Leibniz not only tries to show that the doctrines are pure, but also to emphasize that they can be purified. Leibniz notes that Sainte-Marie himself says the Chinese contradict themselves, giving qualities of both God and matter to *li*. Rather than condemn the Chinese completely, why not cling to what is good and refute what is bad? (Discourse 11). In a similar way, Leibniz points out the presumptuousness and practical danger of condemning these ancient doctrines, and adds that, facing these consequences, "it is reasonable to inquire whether we could give it a proper meaning" (Discourse 3). One final example concerns the existence of souls after death. Leibniz writes that, in spite of the materialistic interpretations of the moderns, the evidence that the ancients believed in souls "allows enough of an opening for knowledgeable missionaries to enlighten them and to clear up their confusion" (Discourse 58). With some common ground, Leibniz believes it will not be too difficult to lead the Chinese to suitable views. All these statements show that Leibniz's accommodation intersects a hermeneutics concerned more with how a "good" doctrine can

---

[24] The passage he refers to is Acts 17: 22–34.

be interpreted out of Chinese philosophy than with the details of what particular individuals think or have thought. Leibniz bends the material to his needs, and encourages the missionaries to do the same.

We should now examine briefly what particular interpretations this approach yields. Leibniz expounds his view on accommodating the rites most clearly in the short essay sent to Verjus, entitled "De cultu Confucii civili." He begins by defining a religious cult: "we attribute to he whom we honor a superhuman power, capable of granting us rewards or inflicting punishments upon us. It matters little whether this power is in the being worshipped, as with the gods of the Gentiles, or rather in being able to intercede with God, as the saints for most Christians" (Cult 2). The question of rites is, do the Chinese rites honor super-human powers with the hope of reward? Leibniz answers that the rites are so ambiguous that they could be purely civil, especially since the Chinese are known to be excessive in ceremonies (Cult 3). In an essay sent to Des Bosses on the same theme, Leibniz writes, "However, we know that no people are more given to ceremonies than the Chinese, and their customs should not be judged by ours. Worship depends not so much on rites as on feelings" (Remarks 4). We have already seen ritual propriety [*li*] is one of the central Confucian virtues. Ricci conveyed this to Europe:

The ancient kingdom of China derived its name from the universal practice of urbanity and politeness, and this is one of the five cardinal virtues esteemed by them above all others and treated at length in their writings. . . . Indeed they make so much of urbane ceremonies that a great part of their time is wasted in them. To one acquainted with their customs, it really is a source of regret that they do not rid themselves of this external show, in which they far surpass all Europeans.[25]

Even if the Chinese believe that they benefit from the rituals, these benefits do not necessarily result from the beings they honor. Benefits may directly result from the virtuous behavior exhibited in following the rites, or benefits may come directly from God, pleased that people honor those who deserve it, just as God rewards those who honor their father and mother. Lastly, even if superstition has crept into the rites among some of the common people, this does not make the rites themselves superstitious or idolatrous, unless these superstitions are officially sanctioned. With this comment, Leibniz specifically refers to Kangxi's affirmation of the Jesuit interpretation of the rites, which denied all superstition.[26]

---

[25] Ricci, *China in the Sixteenth Century*, p. 59.
[26] Kangxi's pronouncement in favor of the Jesuit position was paraphrased to Leibniz in a letter from the Jesuit missionary Jean de Fontaney, from September 15, 1701, who said that the emperor declared that by the word *Ciel* [*tian*] the Chinese understand a sovereign, intelligent being who governs heaven and earth (W 146). For Kangxi's position, see p. 31.

The *Discourse* contains Leibniz's detailed and extensive arguments for accommodating the Chinese terms for God. The bulk of the *Discourse* is an attempt to explain a set of Chinese terms as a coherent natural theology compatible with Christianity. We have already encountered most of the terms: *Shang Di* – Lord on High, the closest concept to an anthropomorphic god; *tian* – Heaven or nature, perhaps a conscious being but more likely a guiding force immanent in the universe; *li* – the order or principle by which a dynamic universe develops; *qi* – the active material force which is ordered by *li*. Two other words Leibniz considers are *tian dao* and *tai ji*. *Tian dao* combines the same word *tian* with the well-known word *dao*, meaning "way" or "path," a word translated by Couplet as "Lex sive Ratio." *Tian dao* preserves the same ambiguity as *tian*, in that it could mean the "Way of God" or "the path of nature." *Tai ji* is usually translated as the "Great Ultimate." Matthews' dictionary gives "the Absolute – the ultimate principle of Chinese philosophy." *Tai ji* connects closely to *li*, usually referring to *li* in its totality or origin, but different philosophers render the precise relationship differently.[27] Leibniz takes all of his citations of Chinese thinkers from Longobardi and Sainte-Marie, saying that, by taking passages from his opponents, he will avoid accusations of bias. These citations themselves, however, are often contradictory, taken from a mix of sources from widely different eras. With this approach, the question of what the terms mean is like asking what "God" means in Western philosophy, using unidentified fragments from Augustine, Spinoza, and Nietzsche. Given these sources, the "Chinese" belief in spirits or an anthropomorphic deity cannot be answered. The ancient writings alone are compiled from many authors and many sources over a long period of time. As we have seen, the earliest texts seem to recognize the existence of spirits and to recognize *Shang Di* and perhaps *tian* as some kind of ruling god, but the texts are vague and somewhat contradictory. Confucius is notoriously reticent on the subject, refusing to discuss spirits.[28] The terms *Shang Di*, *tian*, and *tian dao* all come from these classical texts, with varying meanings. In the

[27] The *li xue* Confucian Chen Chun writes "The Great Ultimate is so called because, being the master of heaven and earth and the ten thousand things all converge on it and extend to the highest degree and do not go any further. As it is scattered to become heaven, earth, man, and things, each of these is balanced and well distributed without any deficiency . . . . The Great Ultimate simply means the sum total of the principles [*li*] of heaven, earth, and the ten thousand things" (Wing-Tsit Chan [trans.], *Neo-Confucian Terms Explained, by Ch'en Ch'un, 1159–1223* [New York: Columbia University, 1986], p. 118). Later he writes: "The Great Ultimate is the wondrous functioning of the undifferentiated reality. It evolves from nonbeing to being and then from being to nonbeing again. At bottom it is only the undifferentiated substance . . ." (*ibid.*, p. 188).

[28] A famous passage from the *Lun Yu* is: "Zigong said, 'We can hear about the Master's cultural accomplishments, but we do not hear his words on our nature [*xing*] or the way of *tian* [*tian dao*]'" (5.13). See also 6.22 and 7.21.

time of Leibniz, belief in spirits was usual among the common people, and
this belief was not taken to contradict the ancient texts. Nonetheless, the
dominant philosophical school, which controlled the examination system
choosing government ministers, was that of the *li xue* Confucians. We have
already seen that the metaphysics of that school centered on *li* and *qi*. *Tai ji*
was another a common term at the time, given various definitions, but taken
as some aspect of *li*. These terms, *li*, *qi*, and *tai ji*, were not used in these
senses in the classical texts. When Longobardi concludes that the Chinese
are atheists and materialists, he bases this claim on his interpretation of
the orthodox Neo-Confucian school. While "atheist" and "materialist" may
be peculiar to a Western context, Longobardi was correct in saying that the
li xue Confucians did not recognize a conscious anthropomorphic god. As
he and others claimed, of philosophical positions familiar to Europeans,
the later Confucians would most resemble Spinoza or the Stoics.

In setting up the background of Chinese thought in chapter 1, I described three relevant time periods in the development of Chinese thought:
the projected ancient period around the classics like the *Yi Jing*, connected
by Bouvet and others to the Biblical Patriarchs; the period of classical
Confucianism in the Warring States period, beginning with Kongzi himself; and the period of later Confucian responses to Buddhism, known as
"Neo-Confucianism." In both his immediate sources like Longobardi and
Sainte-Marie and in his broader sources like Couplet and Bouvet, Leibniz encountered ideas from all three of these periods without sufficient
means of separating and dating them. The enormous difficulty of making
sense of these writings was complicated further by the tendency of Confucians to justify their own views through a connection to the past. *Li xue*
philosophers supported their doctrines with the classical texts, speaking of
Shang Di, *tian*, and the spirits but interpreting them in terms of their more
naturalistic metaphysics. Although Leibniz's sources did not sufficiently
distinguish themselves into different time periods, Leibniz realized that
their differences and conflicts could only make sense in terms of historical
change. His interpretation becomes relatively successful because he takes
the morass of citations he finds and divides them into three systems. One
is that of the modern literati, the *ru*, whom Leibniz considers probably
to be atheists and materialists, in conflict with the doctrines of genuine
Confucianism. The second system is the superstitions and inaccurate formulations of the common people. The third is the system of the ancients,
which Leibniz takes to be an admirable natural theology, compatible with
Christianity. Because the citations come from so many different sources,
they often contradict one another. Leibniz's method takes what is positive

in the citations and attributes them to the ancients, and then weakens what is negative, either by showing the ambiguity of the text or by attributing it to the modern atheists or the superstitions of the common people. "Strengthen" and "weaken" here mean to make more or less compatible with Christianity. What strengthens Leibniz's argument is the equation formed by Neo-Confucians themselves between their own modern metaphysical terms and the ancient more theistic ones. Longobardi emphasizes this equation as well, arguing that, since *li* for the moderns is a material principle immanent in the universe, and since the *li xue* Confucians say that *li* is the same as *Shang Di*, *Shang Di* must also be a material principle. Leibniz reverses this argument using the more religious, god-like *Shang Di* of the ancient texts to suggest that *li* also is god-like. He then combines this interpretation with his interpretations of the modern texts, in which he shows that *li* is a prime mover. *Shang Di* and *li* taken together then form an acceptable idea of God (Discourse 28). Leibniz arrives at a coherent system which he considers to be ancient, unknowingly mixing ancient and modern terms and sources. As absolute, the universal spirit is called *li* or order; as operative in creatures, it is called *tai ji*; as governing, it is called *Shang Di* (Discourse 36). All three are ways of talking about God. In another passage he makes his conclusion clear:

What we call the light of reason in man, they call commandment and law of Heaven [*tian ming*]. What we call the inner satisfaction of obeying justice and our fear of acting contrary to it, all this is called by the Chinese (and by us as well) inspirations sent by the Xangti [*Shang Di*] (that is, by the true God). To offend Heaven [*tian*] is to act against reason, to ask pardon of Heaven is to reform oneself and to make a sincere return in word and deed in the submission one owes to this very law of reason. For me I find all this quite excellent and quite in accord with natural theology. . . . It is pure Christianity, in so far as it renews the natural law inscribed in our hearts – except for what revelation and grace add to it to improve our nature. (Discourse 31)

Leibniz responds, then, to the second question of the Rites Controversy by showing that the ancient Chinese recognized God under the name *Shang Di* and *tian*, and also under the names *li* and *tai ji*. The last two were not even considered as names for God in the Rites Controversy, showing Leibniz again extending accommodation further than his Jesuit sources. This conclusion emphasizes the fact already mentioned, that the question of terms was not just a question of translation, but a more fundamental question: did the Chinese honor the God of Christians under the names *Shang Di* and *tian*? Leibniz answers that they did. His interpretation of the ancient Chinese philosophy also turns out to look suspiciously like his own philosophy. This similarity plays into his advice to introduce philosophy to the Chinese in order to lead them gradually to Christianity, and that the philosophy to introduce should be Leibniz's own.

LEIBNIZ AS INTERPRETER

This project began with my initial surprise at how well Leibniz understood Chinese thought, given all the barriers he faced – no knowledge of Chinese, no tradition of interpretation to rely on, no knowledge of the thought of other cultures, and biased, fragmented sources. Although Leibniz makes many mistakes, his interpretation of Chinese philosophy has received praise, even from sinologists, and particularly in comparison to his contemporaries and limited sources. David Mungello refers to "Leibniz's remarkable understanding of Chinese culture."[29] Julia Ching and Willard Oxtoby go further, referring to his "very perceptive and astonishingly accurate interpretation of the Neo-Confucian concepts of li and ch'i [*qi*]," claiming that "Leibniz remains even now the greatest Western philosopher who understood the most of China and her philosophy."[30] A serious evaluation of Leibniz's interpretation would first require an authoritative explication of Chinese philosophy, with which to compare Leibniz's own interpretation: such an endeavor far exceeds the scope of this book. The approach would hardly be fair to Leibniz as well, given the limitation of his sources. The question has some relevance, however, if we wish to consider the value of Leibniz's philosophy for cultural exchange and comparative philosophy now. In concluding this chapter, then, I will make some remarks on the successes and failures of Leibniz as an interpreter of Chinese thought.

The failings of Leibniz's approach to China can be discussed along two lines. One is his inability fully to escape the Euro-centric views of his time. Leibniz's openness to other cultures is difficult to evaluate, as he was far ahead of most of his contemporaries, yet in most ways remains unacceptably behind our time. Leibniz advocates some of the principles that would become the stereotypes of orientalism, such as the belief that orientals were inferior in their ability to reason, or that Europeans could go into oriental lands and teach the people about their own culture, as Leibniz and Bouvet thought they would teach the Chinese the true meaning of the *Yi Jing*. Yet, Leibniz does explicitly and publicly argue for the general equality of Europe and China, and he emphasizes repeatedly that Europe needs to learn from China, even in such central matters as ethics. His fear that the

---

[29] Mungello, "Die Quellen," p. 233.   [30] Ching and Oxtoby, *Moral Enlightenment*, pp. 12, 15.

Chinese might learn all of Europe's knowledge and then become superior to the Europeans perhaps reveals parochial concerns of a European, but it also shows his respect for the Chinese and his lack of confidence in European superiority. In spite of his explicit openness, however, Leibniz remains deeply Euro-centric in that he never questions such things as the belief in a conscious, good Creator of the universe. This level of Euro-centrism remains assumed partly because of Leibniz's extreme confidence in his own thinking. Facing a conflict between his own thought and the thought of another, he almost always decides that he is right. His way of being "generous" to the other is to show that they actually agree with, or anticipate, his own views. In other words, it is difficult to distinguish Leibniz's Euro-centrism from his ego-centrism. In this approach, I believe Leibniz betrays the fallibilism his epistemology demands. In fairness to Leibniz, though, he was a step ahead of most of his contemporaries, who were sure that they were right *and* dismissed others as incapable of having anything relevant to say about this truth.

The main reason, though, that Leibniz does not question his deepest philosophical views is that he fails to recognize the radicality of cultural difference. This failure to recognize difference is the second major failing of Leibniz's approach. Leibniz's theory that we express the same universe and the same innate ideas leads him to see Chinese thought as too similar to his own. This tendency is reinforced on the practical side as Leibniz is so accommodating to Chinese thought. In his reluctance to say that Chinese thought is wrong, he hesitates to admit any differences with his own philosophy. The tendency to see Chinese thought as too similar to his own can be illustrated with an example we have already seen – Leibniz's argument to convince the Chinese of the existence of Heaven and Hell. Leibniz argues:

But perhaps they will not always ridicule it if they consider that this supreme substance – which on their own grounds is the source of wisdom and justice – could not act less perfectly on the spirits and the souls which it creates, than a wise king in his realm acts upon his subjects whom he did not create of his own will, and whom it is more difficult for him to govern since they do not depend on him absolutely. (Discourse 65)

Leibniz adds that a wise king punishes and rewards justly, so God must also do so. Leibniz argues here that the Chinese have not realized the consequences of the beliefs they already hold, so that they could be easily convinced by making these consequences explicit. We should first note that Leibniz was wrong – the Chinese were not easily convinced by such arguments. The reason is not because they could not realize the consequences of their beliefs, but because Leibniz misinterpreted their beliefs. In some sense, *li* is the source of "wisdom and justice," but not in the way that God is supposed to be the source of wisdom and justice in Leibniz's view. *Li* is not a conscious Creator of anything, so the analogy between *li* and a king fails. This lack of a conscious Creator is one of the most fundamental differences between Chinese philosophy and Western philosophy in the time of Leibniz. In this case, then, Leibniz interprets poorly, and his opponents who claimed that *li* was like Spinoza's God were more correct. What leads Leibniz to this misinterpretation? His conviction that Spinoza is wrong, and his desire to give the Chinese as much credit as possible. Leibniz's generosity leads him to identify Chinese philosophy too closely with "the truth," i.e. with his own philosophy. Another consequence of this assumed commonality is Leibniz's belief that a "commerce of light" will be easy, if only we dedicate ourselves to it. We see this confidence in Leibniz's fear that China will learn everything from Europe and then break off contact. There is something appealing about Leibniz's wish that China would learn the advantages of Europe and Europe would learn the advantages of China, and a new synthesis of both would appear, but experience has shown how difficult such exchange is. The idea of knowledge as a quantity which can simply be added to another quantity of knowledge now seems naïve, just as the image of an Egyptian pyramid crowned with a European steeple now appears ridiculous.

The aim of this interpretation of Leibniz has been to show how, in theory and in practice, he avoids the position of Descartes and Spinoza by requiring our universal innate ideas to emerge only through our concrete embodied experience. In spite of the pluralism that results from this position, Leibniz still assumes more similarity or universality than now seems justified. Leibniz recognizes a level of cultural limitation and cultural diversity, and this drives him toward cultural exchange, but his practice misses the fundamental cultural differences in how knowledge is structured and organized that prevent a simple exchange of knowledge from taking place across cultures. On the positive side, Leibniz's over-estimation of the ease of exchange was a fortunate error, in that it fueled his enthusiasm for exchange. Nonetheless, missing the radical differences of Chinese philosophy kept him from realizing how much he could have learned. For example, the Chinese had a long tradition of thinking through a universe without a conscious director and of developing non-substance based theories of the self. Leibniz was not even able to see these differences, partly because of his hermeneutic method biased toward similarity. This limit kept him from ever considering Chinese thought as an alternative, as it kept him from realizing that some of his deepest beliefs were peculiarly European. He was never forced to choose between his certainty in his deepest views and his commitment to cultural pluralism. Leibniz's assumption of too great similarity and ease of exchange does not necessarily undermine his method or the philosophical foundations we have examined so far. Every monad expresses the universe from a different perspective; Leibniz simply fails to realize how different those perspectives are. Leibniz's practice under-estimates his own finitude, but his system allows for it.

So far I have taken it for granted that we should evaluate Leibniz's interpretation by judging its accuracy by comparison with the best interpretations we have now. Accuracy, however, is not Leibniz's main goal. Consider one of Leibniz's hermeneutic principles of generosity: if a text is ambiguous or our knowledge of it is insufficient, we should take the most favorable interpretation. If the goal is accuracy, this principle is remarkably bad. Leibniz's hermeneutic principles choose the most favorable interpretation over the most likely interpretation, forcing us to question his real goal. In fact, Leibniz's immediate goal is not accuracy but giving a favorable view of China. Placing a political goal ahead of accuracy in questions of interpretation may make Leibniz seem strangely postmodern, but he clearly does so. Leibniz's stance is less radical than it seems, however, since his ultimate goal is more accurate knowledge of the universe and rationality that we share. The means to that goal is the political task of interpreting in a favorable light. If Leibniz's immediate goal is not accuracy but generosity, then the fact that he occasionally sees Chinese philosophy as too similar to his own is not necessarily a fair reproach. If the goal is to encourage exchange through a "principle of generosity," then Leibniz is quite successful. One reason such a generosity might be a valid goal of interpretation would be to counteract a widespread hostility or skepticism toward what is interpreted. In Leibniz's time, there was a general prejudice against non-European cultures, so that a conscious principle of generosity might be justified. Even now, a strong argument for a principle of generosity can be made, at least in exchange between different cultures. Given our long history of undervaluing non-Western cultures, a conscious presupposition in favor of the other culture, as Leibniz makes, seems justified, perhaps even as a moral imperative.

The main justification for Leibniz's principle of generosity, however, is that it encourages further exchange. On one side, the conviction that the other has something worth while to say leads us to continue to interact with the other in the face of the inevitable frustrations that cross-cultural interaction brings. For this goal, Leibniz's principle of generosity – that it is better to err in favor of the other than against the other – is appropriate. If we decide wrongly in favor of the other, our error will most likely be corrected as we further pursue exchange. If we err against the other and break off contact, our error will never be corrected. Such a split worries Leibniz, and history has justified his concerns. Given the presupposition that we can learn something worth while from any culture, even a correct judgment against the other can be dangerous if it causes us to dismiss further exchange. Taking the full context of Leibniz's writings on China, the main motivation for his principle of generosity is to convince other Europeans that China is worth learning from. If his interpretations are inaccurate, so be it. Errors will be corrected through further exchange. This principle of generosity serves a function not just for the interpreter but also for those interpreted. Leibniz used generosity as a hermeneutic principle because he believed that any other approach would be offensive to the Chinese themselves. In this sense, the principle of generosity is also a principle of respect, best seen in the contrast between Leibniz and many of the other interpreters of China, who took it for granted that the Chinese were wrong about everything. Leibniz's principle served a practical purpose, as an approach meant to make the Chinese more receptive to his own thought, but it shows a basic level of respect for the other. Underlying this hermeneutics is something like the presupposition described by Charles Taylor: "all human cultures that have animated whole societies over some considerable stretch of time have something important to say to all human beings."[31] Taylor concludes his essay with the claim that perhaps we have a moral duty at least initially to address other cultures on the basis of this presupposition.[32] I think Leibniz would agree.

---

[31] Charles Taylor, "The Politics of Recognition." In *Campus Wars: Multiculturalism and the Politics of Difference.* Ed. by John Arthur and Amy Shapiro (Boulder: Westview Press, 1995), p. 259.
[32] Ibid., p. 261.

CHAPTER 5

Leibniz and cultural exchange

At the time Leibniz wrote his most complex work on Chinese philosophy, the decision against the Jesuits and accommodation was already made. In 1704 Pope Clement XI decided against the Jesuits; his decree was published in China in 1707 and in Europe in 1709. Leibniz did not know it, but this decision was to remain the Church's position until the twentieth century. Kangxi was offended and issued a decree requiring missionaries to accept the position of accommodation if they wished to remain in China. The Jesuits evaded either the pope or the emperor for as long as they could, but, as the pope's decision stood firm, more and more missionaries were forced to leave. In 1724, Kangxi's son, Yongzheng, banished all missionaries except those necessary for astronomy. A long period of distance between Europe and China followed, lasting until hostilities broke out in the nineteenth century; hostility and forced concessions continued into this century. As the historical opportunity for exchange with China was lost, the philosophical landscape also shifted. The eclectic but avid Renaissance interest in other cultures had given way to gradual indifference among seventeenth-century philosophers, with the exception of Leibniz. Even so, it remained a time in which Leibniz could call for missionaries from China without creating too much commotion. Although Leibniz, Descartes, Locke, and Spinoza remain Euro-centric, all four make claims for the equal abilities of peoples from all cultures. This equality coupled with practical indifference transitioned into more explicitly racist philosophies and the need to theorize European dominance of other people. We remain in the legacy of the latter movement. A "commerce of light" sounds a bit silly now, but Leibniz's point remains astonishingly relevant. The force driving globalization is still the commerce of goods, and where the exchange of ideas happens, it still tends to be unidirectional. We need look no further than academic philosophy. Academic philosophers around the world know Plato, Aristotle, and Kant, yet few European or North American philosophers could even name three non-Western philosophers. It remains very common for a new Ph.D. in philosophy to have learned nothing of the thought of any other culture. This lack of philosophical exchange should be surprising, and should draw our attention. We now have the material means to carry out with ease the exchange Leibniz envisioned three hundred years ago. The lack of exchange must be attributed more to lack of will than to lack of means. Such lack of interest was perplexing even in Leibniz's time, when it was commonplace to think the West had been singularly blessed with the gift of revelation, and it was only a small step further to conclude that European culture and philosophy were similarly blessed. Today's philosophical climate, however, makes the lack of interest even harder to understand. It is difficult to imagine any philosophical system now that would justify not turning to the philosophies of other cultures. No *a priori* reason indicates that Western philosophy is so superior to all others as to make philosophical exchange useless. At the same time, we lack sufficient knowledge to make such a judgment *a posteriori*. It could be that philosophical exchange with other cultures is either useless or impossible, but we could only make such a conclusion after exerting a tremendous amount of effort – effort yet to be made. In contrast, many factors in contemporary philosophy urge us toward exchange with other cultures. The recognition that all knowledge comes from a particular perspective naturally suggests that we consult other perspectives. The recognition of a connection between thought and language and between thought and environment leads us to consult thought that has grown up in different languages and different environments. Fallibilism forces us to leave our fundamental beliefs in question and to consider other alternatives. All of these factors – the recognition of perspective, the connection between thought and language, and a principle of fallibilism – were recognized in Leibniz's philosophy and drove his promotion of cultural exchange.

I hope I have already offered Leibniz's call for cultural exchange and shown him as one model of an engaged intellectual promoting exchange. He puts it well in a letter to Peter the Great:

Although I count many years of service in administration and law, and though I have been consulted for a long time by great princes, I nevertheless consider the arts and sciences as more elevated, and capable of increasing the glory of God and the welfare of mankind, for it is especially in the sciences and knowledge of nature and art that we see the wonders of God. . . . I should regard myself very proud, very pleased and highly rewarded to be able to render Your Majesty any service in a work so worthy and pleasing to God; for I am not one of those impassioned patriots of one country alone, but I work for the well-being of the whole of mankind, for I consider heaven as my country and cultivated men as my compatriots . . . [1]

---

[1] Wiener, *Selections*, pp. 596–97; Leibniz, *Lettres et opuscules inédits* . . . Ed. by A. Foucher de Coreil, vol. VII, pp. 506–15.

I have argued for the interdependence of Leibniz's practical support for exchange and his broader philosophical system. Because of this connection, I believe Leibniz offers not just a role model and some strong rhetoric but that his philosophical system has value in supporting and explaining cultural exchange. Given the current poor state of intellectual exchange across cultures and Leibniz's own primary commitment to practice rather than speculation, it would seem a betrayal to his project not to offer some reflections on Leibniz's significance for cultural exchange today. Of course, the explanation for the current rejection of a "commerce of light" is more historical and social than philosophical. Nonetheless, contemporary ignorance of non-Western thought is bound with real philosophical issues, particularly issues of relativism and the balance between similarity and difference. These same issues drive the conflicts around multi-culturalism, taking place between two poles. The first claims the objective superiority of Western culture; while the second claims that no culture can claim superiority, denying trans-cultural norms by which cultures could be judged. Both these extremes hinder the goal of learning from another culture. In the first case, if we presuppose that Western culture is superior to others, we have no reason to undertake the effort of learning from another culture. This is the implicit position of those who claim that "philosophy" is unique to the West, in so far as that proposition is accompanied by the claim that philosophy is particularly good. The second position, however, is scarcely better. If we have no criteria by which to judge that the other culture might be better, we have no incentive to struggle with engaging and learning from that culture. If all cultures are equal, why bother? Both of these positions are partly caricatures, but the conflict points the direction for a theory of interpretation and cultural exchange which will have to negotiate between relativism and universalism. Our beliefs must be flexible enough that we are open to learning from other cultures, yet fixed enough to supply some criteria by which to judge both our own beliefs and those of the other culture. I believe this is just what Leibniz's system supplies. Leibniz's theory yields a system of knowledge based on probabilities. On the one hand, this knowledge is relativistic, in that everything is up for grabs and even our most secure knowledge is only extremely probable. Leibniz himself accepts this claim, at least regarding all existential truths beyond the existence of God and the existence of the self. Even the existence of the outside world is only extremely probably, which would make any theory about what in particular exists also only probable. On the other hand, we can still make well-grounded judgments, because all of our experience expresses a universe and a structure of ideas that are independent of either of our perspectives. When beliefs conflict we can appeal to our experience which expresses a universe we share, though our access to the universe is limited in a way that keeps us from settling any conflict beyond doubt. Leibniz's portrait of different monads expressing the same universe thus answers the tension between similarity and difference in cultural exchange or comparative philosophy. Leibniz's theory avoids these two alternatives with his doctrine of expression, which entails that there is no knowledge not partly relative to our embodied perspective but also no knowledge not grounded in a shared reality. Nothing is placed out of question as absolute, and nothing is placed beyond discussion as completely relative. By eroding the separation between what is universal and what is relative, Leibniz avoids the positions taken by other early modern philosophers. In practice, Leibniz occasionally fails to hold this middle ground, sliding away from the more relativistic side. Nonetheless, the theory as I have described it follows from Leibniz's philosophy.

Three aspects of Leibniz's system particularly found cultural exchange. First, all human beings relate through two common realms. One is the common world of experience, including aspects of the natural world and the commonalities of embodiment. The other is what Leibniz discusses as the set of innate ideas, expressing the understanding of God. This theological account is hardly acceptable now, but Leibniz has in mind some common way of structuring experience based on the principle of non-contradiction, which, in the *New Essays*, Leibniz calls an instinct. The status of this common realm is perhaps most easily naturalized in a Kantian direction, as transcendental structures which make experience possible, but they could just as well be naturalized as common psychological structures, more like Hume's principle that all knowledge of experience depends on the assumption that the world will remain consistent. The existence of these common realms guarantees that we can learn about our own experience from exchange with others, and it explains why we have enough common ground to make communication possible.

The second crucial aspect of Leibniz's philosophy for cultural exchange is that our relationship to both of these common realms is best characterized as expression rather than re-presentation. In both relationships, although there is no necessary similarity between what is common and our own experience, certain relationships or patterns are maintained and reproduced. Some of these relationships are expressed only vaguely, while others are grasped more clearly and distinctly. This relationship of expression eliminates perspective-free knowledge, making it crucial for Leibniz's pluralism. On any issue, we can benefit from other perspectives, and on most issues comparing perspectives is required. The limitations of perspective extend to our experience of our bodies and the natural world, as well as to our experience of common structures of consciousness, our innate ideas. Thus, even if there were fixed, universal categories or structures, they could never be grasped as such, but would be mediated through signs and the contingencies of experience.

The third important aspect of Leibniz's system is that consciousness and the process of understanding take place through the intersection of the expressions of these two common realms. Leibniz must make this claim if he is to avoid splitting our experience, but it describes well the process of cross-cultural understanding. This process consists in the dialectical interplay of ideas and categories, some of which are held in common and some of which vary, with particular experiences, some of which are held in common and some of which vary. We have seen this interplay in Leibniz's own process of interpreting Chinese thought, but we can see it more clearly by applying it to an example. Let me use a personal example, an extreme version of a kind of encounter common when in another culture. I was on a long, long train ride across China, sharing a bench seat with an older Chinese man. I woke up in the morning with the old man tugging on my shoulder. He smiled and said something in a dialect I could not understand. I answered, "I don't understand." He spoke some more, but I understood nothing. He then made a gesture toward his mouth as if he were eating something imaginary. In spite of our lack of common language, I thought he was referring to eating. I shook my head and moved my hand in front of my mouth – I had nothing to eat and hadn't planned on eating any breakfast. He seemed to understand. He took out a strange looking dried fish and offered it to me. I say he "offered it," but really he extended it and gestured toward me. I again shook my head, politely refusing. He smiled and offered the fish again. Eventually I said thank you and took it. So I ate the fish. He said some more incomprehensible things, and I tried to explain who I was in Chinese, but he did not understand. In the end we just smiled. When I finished the fish, he offered some fried bread, and after the same ritual of polite refusal, I ate some of his bread. We sat out the remainder of the trip, occasionally nodding and smiling to one another.

To say that we communicated depends on what we mean by "communication." Our experiences of the situation must have been radically different. He was offering his normal breakfast, while I was eating something bizarre. I have little idea what he was thinking or why he offered to share his food. Nonetheless, we reached some level of understanding. When he extended the fish toward me, I knew he was offering it to me to eat, not asking me to keep it as a good luck charm. I also knew he wasn't just giving me a chance to admire his breakfast. I even understood his initial gesture as a reference to eating. Similarly, he understood my initial gesture as one of refusal, and then that I accepted the fish. I hope he understood that I was happy to eat it. The crucial question is, how was such understanding possible? How can we best explain it? I choose this example precisely because it assumes so little intersection of our two cultural worlds. I did not understand his offer because I had previously learned that this was the way rural Chinese offered breakfast. I had never learned his "language," neither his spoken language nor his body language. If we really did not share any culture or set of interpretations, it seems that the only thing that would allow us to reach an understanding would be commonalities as human beings embodied in a natural world. In Leibniz's terms, we express a shared world. We could thus both gesture toward the same fish. Naturally, the fish carried different meanings for each of us, although we both knew it could be eaten and we were probably both thinking that this was going to make a good story when we got home. In no sense would I say that we had the *same* experience of the fish, but this is only to say that there is no objective grasp of this shared reality – we each express it from a different perspective. Expression requires as well that we could never settle a dispute about what meaning the fish should have "objectively," because we always only express it from a certain perspective. Similarly, no unit of meaning passed from his mind into mine, which is only to say that minds do not interact by passing ideas through windows. Nonetheless, the appearance of the fish as a common ground in both of our expressions allowed us to reach some understanding. Our reliance on a shared world goes beyond gesturing toward the dry fish. We could both see that a night of restless sleep had just passed, that I appeared to have no food of my own, and so on. Moreover, the encounter presupposed a broader knowledge of the world based on our own separate experiences. We both assumed that we would need food from time to time, and that the way we consume food is through our mouth. Of course, cultures are no longer entirely isolated from each other, but I could have had a similar exchange with someone whose culture had developed in complete isolation from my own, and I suspect the first Jesuits who entered China established communication in just this way.

This example supports the claim that we express the same universe, but does it show that we express a shared structure of ideas? Such an objection depends on a naïve separation of experience from how experience is conditioned by consciousness. Leibniz himself believes the two are inseparable. Taking the rational structure which we both express in a minimal sense, we can see it at work in our similar use of analogy. I assumed that the Chinese man was referring to eating when he made a certain gesture. This assumption was not the product of any explicit reasoning, but depends on an implicit analogy, made instinctively. From my experience, I believe that things that look and act like human beings move their mouths in a particular way when they eat. He looks and acts like a human being, and is moving his mouth in that particular way. Therefore he is probably referring to eating. The Chinese man relies on the same kind of implicit analogy in assuming that, after a night of sleep, I would want something to eat. The ability to draw such analogies is just what Leibniz means when he says that we all express the same totality of innate ideas.

So far I have been describing this Leibnizian theory as it explains understanding between two people in a concrete situation, but it applies just as well to understanding philosophy. I will again begin with an example, taking two well-known stories from the Confucian philosopher Mengzi. In context, both are meant to establish his claim that human nature tends toward the ethical social relations. In the first example, Mengzi speaks to King Hui of Liang, who asks if he is capable of being a great leader. Mengzi says that he is, giving the following story. One day the king happened to see an ox dragged to a sacrifice. On seeing the terror of the ox and hearing its pitiful cries, the king was moved and called for the ox's life to be spared. Mengzi claims that this spontaneous feeling of sympathy for the ox is the sprout of the virtue of benevolence [*ren*] (1A7). In the second story, Mengzi makes the same point. Anyone, he claims, who saw a helpless child about to fall into a well, would react with fear and concern for the child, even if no one were watching and there was no hope for reward, showing again that all people have a basic feeling of commiseration which can grow into the virtue of benevolence (2A6).

What is striking about these examples is that they seem so easy to understand. Mengzi's argument has lost little of its persuasiveness after nearly 2,500 years of time and transportation halfway around the world. How would Leibniz explain this easy understanding? The ground for this understanding is our common perception of the same universe. I have experienced very few of the same things that Mengzi experienced, but I have experienced similar patterns, so that, while we never saw the same child, we both have seen children. I have seen a few wells, although they must be different from those Mengzi refers to. I know a feeling at seeing a suffering animal. In addition, though, this understanding requires the ability consistently to draw consequences from ideas. So if I first think that the feeling Mengzi refers to is something more like indignation, I will see what consequences follow from this. I find that the virtue of benevolence develops from this feeling, and, if this feeling is indignation, then this connection would seem contradictory. Recognition of that contradiction leads me to reinterpret the feeling, perhaps connecting it with something like sympathy. The process of understanding requires this dialectical movement between ideas and experiences. Let me emphasize again that our experience of seeing a child about to fall into a well – supposing that we were even around an open well – is never the same as Mengzi's. In fact, my experience would never ever be the same as yours. Every person experiences differently, but that is why Leibniz says we all *express* the same reality. The power of the example is that Mengzi created the stories in complete isolation from Western cultures. Cultural overlap cannot account for our ability to understand his argument. That is, we do not have similar feelings because we are all under one cultural sphere which has taught us to feel a similar emotion. The only explanation for the similarities seems to be that we express the same universe. Note that this process also accounts well for misunderstanding, particularly as we discuss more abstract concepts. For example, Leibniz first connects *tian* with his own idea of God, then he applies to *tian* the consequences he derives from his idea of God. If he had had better texts and had been a more careful reader, he might have realized that the Chinese deduce different consequences from *tian*. The consequences suggest that *tian* matches our idea of "nature" better than our idea of "God." Further reading might bring out a new idea, a variation on the idea of nature, allowing new kinds of deductions.

I have described this process in Leibniz's terms very loosely, setting aside obvious problems like the relationship between thought and language and how well consciousness can be described in terms of ideas. My point is that Leibniz's combination of two commonalities united in one consciousness through expression captures well the balance between cultural differences and similarities, and explains the way these similarities and differences come together to allow understanding. This ability to account for cross-cultural understanding is one reason we should take Leibniz's theory seriously. In addition, we could make a pragmatic argument based on the consequences of this theory. If we *express* the same reality, we must always be aware of the limits of our perspective and we must recognize the potential good in other perspectives. We could never with certainty privilege one perspective over others. This side of the theory leads toward tolerance. At the same time, because we express the same reality, we have some ground on which to evaluate the perspective of the other. Thus we can decide that our view is probably better, but we can also decide that the view of the other is probably better. A strict relativist or skeptic could give a weak foundation for tolerance, but not a justification for learning from another culture, since there would be no way to establish that the new culture was worth learning from. Leibniz's theory then drives us toward learning from other cultures.

Finally, Leibniz's system and promotion of exchange coincides with a promotion of harmony. If what allows understanding is our experience of this same universe, then the best way to increase mutual understanding is to increase mutual experience. Leibniz himself does not explicitly draw this conclusion, but it follows from his theory. His focus on China in particular was based on his belief that the Chinese – as the other center of *"cultus ornatusque"* – had more experience in common with the Europeans. Monads can approach each other's perspectives by coming to share more similar points of view, and that comes from increased interaction and exchange. In other words, when there seems to be a gap between our understandings, or a conflict between different interpretations, the way to bridge between them is to return to experience and test the interpretations. This answer sounds a lot like science, which we have seen underlies Leibniz's approach to cultural exchange. In a world where cross-cultural understanding is crucial, it is equally crucial, then, to increase cross-cultural communication and interaction. Perhaps we do not need the Chinese to come and teach us natural morality, as Leibniz wished, but this kind of direct exchange and interaction itself promotes an ethics of harmony. In close connection with this need for shared experience is Leibniz's belief that knowledge and experience bring people together. Within a concrete situation, our expression of a shared world brings us together into a shared understanding, but Leibniz goes further, claiming that knowledge in general, even produced in isolation, tends to bring us together. In abstract terms, through reflection and knowledge, we transcend our own particular place in the universe, and participate in something more universal. This belief that knowledge from different perspectives tends to converge leads to Leibniz's extreme confidence in the ease of cultural exchange and in his theory of natural theology. Natural theology assumes that experience leads peoples living in complete isolation toward similar conclusions in understanding the universe. For Leibniz, it means not only that people in different cultures would develop similar sciences, but also similar views of ethics and God. This tendency toward convergence now seems a little naïve, but the product of this belief is a faith in open, respectful interaction with other cultures. We can have this open attitude because the perspective of another culture naturally complements our own perspective, leading to a greater understanding of the world we share. This process is just how Leibniz describes the need for the two complementary cultures of Europe and China to come together to form a more complete expression of the universe. Because our views are not simply different and irreconcilable, other cultures are not simply opposed and threatening. This faith in a shared world then leads to Leibniz's drive for cultural exchange. Such a faith might serve us well late in this age of globalization.

Bibliography

Ahn, Jong-Su. *Leibniz's Philosophie und die chinesische Philosophie*. Konstanz: Hartung-Gorre Verlag, 1990.

Aiton, E. J. *Leibniz: A Biography*. Boston: Adam Hilfer Ltd., 1985.

Aiton, E. J., and Eikoh Shimao. "Gorai Kinzo's Study of Leibniz and the I ching Hexagrams." *Annals of Science*, 38 (1981), pp. 71–92.

Aquinas, Thomas. *Introduction to St. Thomas Aquinas*. Trans. by Anton C. Pegis. New York: Modern Library, 1948.

Summa Contra Gentiles. Trans. by Anton C. Pegis. 4 vols. Notre Dame: University of Notre Dame Press, 1975.

Faith, Reason, and Theology. Trans. by Armand Maurer. Toronto: Pontifical Institute of Mediaeval Studies, 1987.

Augustine. *The City of God*. Trans. by Marcus Dods. New York: Modern Library, 1993.

Bak, Sang Hwan. *Chinesische Philosophie bei Leibniz. Ein Vergleich der Naturkonzepte*. Gießen, 1992 [Dissertation].

Baruzi, Jean. *Leibniz et L'organisation religieuse de la terre d'apres des documents inédits*. Paris: F. Alcan, 1907.

Bayle, Pierre. *Mr. Bayle's Historical and Critical Dictionary*. Trans. by P. des Mazeaux. London: Routledge/Thoemmes Press, 1997 (repr. from 1736).

Berger, Willy Richard. *China-Bild und China-Mode*. Köln: Böhlau Verlag, 1990.

Beurrier, Paul. *Speculum christianne religionis in triplici lege naturalii, mosaica et evangelica*. 1663.

Birmingham, David. *Trade and Empire in the Atlantic, 1400–1600*. London: Routledge, 2000.

Bodemann, Eduard. "Leibnizens Plan einer Societaet der Wissenschaften in Sachsen." *Neues Archiv fur saechische Geschichte v. Alterskunde*, 4 (1883). pp. 177–214.

Der Briefwechsel des Gottfried Wilhelm Leibniz. Hildesheim: Georg Olms Verlagsbuchhandlung, 1966.

Brather, Hans-Stephan. *Leibniz und Seine Akademie*. Berlin: Akademie Verlag, 1993.

Brauen, F. "Athanasius Kircher (1602–1680)." *Journal of the History of Ideas*, 43 (1982), pp. 129–34.

Breger, Herbert. "Maschine und Seele als Paradigmen der Naturphilosophie bei Leibniz." *Zeit und Logik bei Leibniz.* Ed. by Carl Friedrich von Weizsäcker and Enno Rudolph. Stuttgart: Klett-Cotta, 1989.

Broad, C. D. *Leibniz: An Introduction.* Cambridge: Cambridge University Press, 1975.

Brown, Stuart. "Leibniz as Platonist and Academic Skeptic." *Skepsis,* 9 (1998), pp. 111–38.

Burgelin, Pierre. "Théologie naturelle et théologie révélée chez Leibniz." *Leibniz, 1646 – Aspects de l'Homme et de l'Ouevre.* Paris: Editions Aubier-Montagne, 1968, pp. 1–20.

Burkhardt, Hans. *Logik und Semiotik in der Philosophie von Leibniz.* München: Philosophia Verlag, 1980.

Chan, Albert. "Late Ming Society and the Jesuit Missionaries." In Oh and Ronan, pp. 153–72.

Chan, Wing-Tsit (trans.). *A Sourcebook in Chinese Philosophy.* Princeton University Press: Princeton, NJ, 1963.

    (trans.). *Neo-Confucian Terms Explained, by Ch'en Ch'un, 1159–1223.* Columbia University: New York, 1986.

    Chu Hsi and Neo-Confucianism. University of Hawaii Press: Honolulu, 1986.

    Chu Hsi: New Studies. University of Hawaii Press: Honolulu, 1989.

Ching, Julia, and Willard Oxtoby. *Discovering China.* Rochester: University of Rochester Press, 1992.

    (trans.). *Moral Enlightenment: Leibniz and Wolff on China.* Monumenta Serica Monograph Series, Vol. XXVI. Nettetal: Steyler Verlag, 1992.

Collani, Claudia von. *Die Figuristen in der Chinamission.* Frankfurt: Verlag Peter D. Lang, 1981.

    Joachim Bouvet, S. J. Sein Leben und Sein Werk. Nettetal: Steyler Verlag, 1985.

    (trans.). "Das Problem des Heils der Heiden." *Neue Zeitschrift für Missions Wissenschaft,* 45 (1989), pp. 17–35, 93–109.

Confucius. *Confucian Analects, The Great Learning and the Doctrine of the Mean.* Trans. by James Legge. New York: Dover Publications, 1971.

    The Analects of Confucius, A Philosophical Translation. Trans. by Roger Ames and Henry Rosemont. New York: Ballantine Books, 1998.

    The Original Analects: Sayings of Confucius and his Successors. Trans. and ed. by E. Bruce Brooks and A. Taeko Brooks. New York: Columbia University Press, 1998.

Couplet, Phillippe, *et al. Confucius Sinarum Philosophus.* Paris, 1686.

Cook, Daniel, and Henry Rosemont, Jr. "The Pre–established Harmony between Leibniz and Chinese Thought." *Journal of the History of Ideas,* 42 (1981), pp. 253–67.

    Writings on China. Chicago: Open Court, 1994.

Couturat, Louis. *La Logique de Leibniz.* Hildesheim: Georg Olms Verlagsbuchhandlung, 1961.

Dascal, Marcelo. *La Sémiologie de Leibniz.* Paris: Aubier Montaigne, 1978.

Leibniz: Language, Signs and Thought. Philadelphia: John Benjamins Publishing Company, 1987.

"Leibniz and Epistemological Diversity." *Unità e Molteplicità nel Pensiero Filosofico e Scientifico di Leibniz*. Ed. by A. Lamarra and R. Palai. Leo Olschki, 2000, pp. 15–37.

"One Adam and Many Cultures: The Role of Political Pluralism in the Best of Possible Worlds." *Leibniz and Adam*. Ed. by Marcelo Dascal and Elhanan Yakira. Tel Aviv: University Publishing Projects, 1993.

Dascal, Marcelo, and Elhanan Yakira (eds.). *Leibniz and Adam*. Tel Aviv: University Publishing Projects, 1993.

DeFrancis, John. *The Chinese Language, Fact and Fantasy*. Honolulu: University of Hawaii Press, 1984.

Dunne, George H. *Generation of Giants: The Story of the Jesuits in China in the Last Decades of the Ming Dynasty*. Notre Dame: University of Notre Dame Press, 1962.

Eisenkopf, Paul. *Leibniz und die Einigung der Christenheit*. Munich, 1975.

Eno, Robert. *The Confucian Creation of Heaven: Philosophy and the Defense of Ritual Mastery*. Albany: SUNY Press, 1990.

Etiemble, R. *Les Jésuites en Chine (1552–1773), la querelle des rites*. Paris: Julliard, 1966.

Eze, Emmanuel. *Race and the Enlightenment: A Reader*. Cambridge, MA: Blackwell, 1997.

Foucault, Michel. *The Order of Things*. New York: Vintage Books, 1970.

Franke, Wolfgang. *China und das Abendland*. Göttingen: Vandenhoek and Ruprecht.

Fung, Yu-lan. *A History of Chinese Philosophy*, Vol. 1. Trans. Derk Bodde. Princeton: Princeton University Press, 1952.

Gernet, J. *Christus kam bis China*. München, 1984.

Godwin, Joscelyn. *Athanasius Kircher. Ein Mann der Renaissance und die Suche nach verlorenem Wissen*. Trans. by Friedrich Engelhorn. Berlin: Edition Weber, 1994.

Graham, A. C. *Disputers of the Tao: Philosophical Argument in Ancient China*. La Salle: Open Court Press, 1989.

Grosholz, Emily. "Leibniz and the Two Labrinths." *Leibniz and Adam*. Ed. by Marcelo Dascal and Yakira. Tel Aviv: University Publishing Projects, 1993.

"Plato and Leibniz against the Materialists." *Journal of the History of Ideas*, 57 (1996), pp. 255–76.

Grosholz, Emily, and Elhanan Yakira. *Leibniz's Science of the Rational*. Studia Leibnitiana Sonderheft 26. Stuttgart: Steiner Verlag, 1998.

Guerrier, Woldemar. *Leibniz in seinen Beziehungen zu Russland und Peter dem Grossen*. Hildesheim: Gerstenberg, 1975.

Hamann, Guenther. "G. W. Leibnizens Plan einer Wiener Akadamie der Wissenschaften." *Akten des II. Internationalen Leibniz Kongress*. Bd. 1. Wiesbaden, 1973, pp. 205–27.

Heidegger, Martin. *The Metaphysical Foundations of Logic.* Trans. by Michael Heim. Bloomington: Indiana University Press, 1984.

Heinekamp, Albert. "Das Problem des Guten bei Leibniz." *Kantstudien* 98. Bonn: H. Bouvier, 1969.

Herbert of Cherbury. *De Veritate.* Trans. by Meyrick H. Carré. London: Routledge/Thoemmes Press, 1992.

Heuvel, Gerd van den. *Leibniz in Berlin.* Berlin, 1987.

Ho, John. *Quellenuntersuchung zur Chinakenntnis bei Leibniz und Wolff.* Hong Kong: Lai Hing and Company, 1962.

Hsia, Adrian (ed.). *Deutsche Denker über China.* Frankfurt am Main: Insel Verlag, 1985.

Ishiguro, Hide. *Leibniz's Philosophy of Logic and Language.* Ithaca: Cornell University Press, 1972.

Ivanhoe, Philip J. *Confucian Moral Self Cultivation.* Indianapolis: Hackett Pub., 2000.

Ivanhoe, Philip J., and Bryan W. Van Norden (eds.). *Readings in Classical Chinese Philosophy.* New York: Seven Bridges Press, 2001.

Jensen, Lionel. *Manufacturing Confucianism: Chinese Tradition and Universal Civilization.* Durham, NC: Duke University Press, 1997.

Jolley, Nicholas. *The Light of the Soul: Theories of Ideas in Leibniz, Malebranche, and Descartes.* Oxford: Clarendon Press, 1990.

(ed.). *The Cambridge Companion to Leibniz.* Cambridge: Cambridge University Press, 1995.

Karlgren, Bernhard. *Analytic Dictionary of Chinese and Sino-Japanese.* Taipei: Ch'eng-Wen Publishing, 1966.

Kaulbach, Friedrich. "Subjektivität, Fundament der Erkenntnis und Lebendiger Spiegel bei Leibniz." *Zeitschrift für philosophische Forschung,* 20/3–4, pp. 471–95.

Klopp, Onno. "Leibniz's Plan der Grunding einer Societat der Wissenschaften in Wien." *Archiv fur österreichische Geschichte,* 40 (1869), pp. 157–255.

Kircher, Athanasius. *Oedipus Aegyptiacus.* 3 vols. Rome, 1652–55.

China Monumentis qua sacris qua profanes, nec non variis naturae & artis spectaculis, aliarum rerum memorabilium argumentis illustrata. Amsterdam, 1667.

Kulstad, Mark. *Leibniz on Apperception, Consciousness, and Reflection.* München: Philosophia Verlag, 1991.

Lach, Donald. *The Preface to Leibniz' Novissima Sinica.* Honolulu: University of Hawaii Press, 1957.

Asia in the Making of Europe. 2 vols. Chicago: University of Chicago Press, 1965–70.

Lai, Y. "The Linking of Spinoza to Chinese Thought by Bayle and Malebranche." *Journal of the History of Ideas,* 2 (1985), pp. 151–78.

Le Comte, Louis. *Nouveaux mémoires sur l'etat présent de la Chine.* 2 vols. Paris, 1696.

Le Gobien, Charles. *Histoire de l'édit de l'empereur de la Chine, en faveur Religion Chrestienne.* Paris, 1698.

Leibniz, G. W. *Vivi illustris Godefridi Guil. Leibnitii epistolae ad diversos.* Ed. by Christian Kortholt. 4 vols. Leipzig, 1735.

Sammlung einiger vertrauten Briefe . . . zwischen G. W. Leibniz und Daniel Ernst Jablonski. Ed. by Johann Erhard Kapp. Leipzig, 1745.

Lettres et opuscules inédits de Leibniz. Ed. by A. Foucher de Coreil. Paris: Ladrange, 1854.

Bericht des Secretars der Brandenburgischen Societaet der Wissenschaften. Ed. by Adolf Harnack. Berlin, 1897.

Neue Beitraege zun Briefwechsel zwischen D. E. Jablonski und G. W. Leibniz. Ed. by Johann Kvacala. Jurjew, 1899.

Leibniz Selections. Trans. by Philip Wiener. New York: Charles Scribner's Sons, 1951.

Selections. Trans. by Philip Wiener. New York: Scribner, 1951.

Theodicy. Trans. by E. M. Hubbard. London: Routledge and Kegan Paul, 1951.

Theologisches System. Trans. by Carl Haas. Hildesheim: Georg Olms Verlagsbuchhandlung, 1966 [1860].

Opuscules et Fragmens Inédits de Leibniz. Ed. by Louis Couturat. Hildesheim: Georg Olms Verlagsbuchhandlung, 1966.

Gottfried Wilhelm Leibniz: Zwei Briefe über das binäre Zahlensystem und die chinesische Philosophie. Ed. by R. Loosen and F. Vonessen. Stuttgart: Belser-Presse, 1968.

Die Hauptschriften zur Dyadik von G. W. Leibniz. Ed. by Hans Zacher. Frankfurt am Main: V. Klostermann, 1973.

Discourse on the Natural Theology of the Chinese. Trans. by Daniel Cook and Henry Rosemont. Monographs of the Society for Asian and Comparative Philosophy. No. 4. Honolulu: University of Hawaii Press, 1977.

Leibniz and Ludolf on Things Linguistic. Trans. by John Waterman. Berkeley: University of California Press, 1978.

Das Nueste über China. Trans. by H. G. Nesselrath and H. Reinbothe. Koln: Deutsche ChinaGesellschaft, 1979.

L'être et la Relation, avec trente-cinq lettres de Leibniz au R. P. Des Bosses. Ed. by Christiane Fremont. Paris: Librairie Philosophique J. Vrin, 1981.

New Essays on Human Understanding. Trans. by Peter Remnant and Jonathon Bennet. Cambridge: Cambridge University Press, 1981.

Discours sur la théologie naturelle des chinois: Plus quelques écrits sur la question religieuse de Chine. Ed. by Christiane Fremont. Paris: L'Herne, 1987.

Political Writings. Trans. by Patrick Riley. Cambridge: Cambridge University Press, 1988.

Leibniz Korespondiert mit China. Ed. by Rita Widmaier. Frankfurt am Main: V. Klostermann, 1990.

G. W. Leibniz's Monadology: An Edition for Students. Trans. by Nicholas Rescher. Pittsburgh: Pittsburgh University Press, 1991.

Moral Enlightenment: Leibniz and Wolff on China. Trans. and ed. by Julia Ching and Willard Oxtoby. Monumenta Serica Monograph Series, Vol. XXVI. Nettetal: Steyler Verlag, 1992.

Writings on China. Trans. by Daniel Cook and Henry Rosemont Jr. Chicago: Open Court, 1994.

Briefe von G. W. Leibniz an den Astronomen Gottfried Kirch aus den Jahren 1702–1707. Ed. by Johannes Imelmann. Berlin, 2000.

Leinkauf, Thomas. *Mundus Combinatus. Studien zur Struktur der barocken Universalwissenshcaft am Beispeil Athanasius Kichers SJ (1602–1680)*. Berlin, 1993.

Li, Wenchao, and Poser Hans (eds.). *Das Neueste über China, G. W. Leibnizens Novissima Sinica von 1697*. Stuttgart: Studia Leibnitiana Supplementa 33, Steiner Verlag, 2000.

Lin, Jinshui. "Chinese Literati and the Rites Controversy." In Mungello (1994), pp. 65–82.

Locke, John. *A Letter Concerning Toleration*. Ed. by James H. Tully. Indianapolis: Hackett, 1983.

Longobardi, Nichola. *Traité sur quelques points de la religion des Chinois*. Paris, 1701.

Luk, Bernard Hung-Kay. "A Serious Matter of Life and Death, Learned Conversations at Foochow in 1627." In Oh and Ronan, pp. 173–206.

Lundbaek, Knud. *T. S. Bayer (1694–1738): Pioneer Sinologist*. London and Malmö: Curzon Press, 1986.

Malebranche, Nicholas. *Dialogue Between a Christian Philosopher and a Chinese Philosopher on the Existence and Nature of God*. Trans. by A. Dominick. Iorio. Washington DC: University Press of America, 1980.

Mates, Benson. *The Philosophy of Leibniz: Metaphysics and Language*. New York: Oxford University Press, 1986.

Martini, Martino. *Sinicae historiae decas prima res a gentis origine ad Christum natum in extrema Asia*. Munich, 1658.

Matthews, R. H. *Matthews' Chinese-English Dictionary*. Cambridge, MA: Harvard University Press, 1966.

McRae, Robert. " 'Idea' as a Philosophical Term in the Seventeenth Century." *Journal of the History of Ideas*, 26 (1965), pp. 175–90.

Mengzi. *The Works of Mencius*. Trans. by James Legge. New York: Dover Publishing, 1970.

Mercer, Christia. *Leibniz's Metaphysics: Its Origins and Development*. New York: Cambridge University Press, 2001.

Merkel, Franz Rudolf. *G. W. Leibniz und die China-Mission*. Leipzig: JC Hinrichs'sche Buchhandlung, 1920.

Miscellanea Berolinensia. Berlin, 1710.

Minamiki, George. *The Chinese Rites Controversy from its Beginning to Modern Times*. Chicago: Loyola University Press, 1985.

Montaigne, Michel de. *Complete Works of Montaigne*. Trans. by Donald Frame. Stanford University Press, 1958.

Müller, Kurt. *G. W. Leibniz und Nicolaas Witsen*. Berlin, 1955.

Mungello, David. *Leibniz and Confucianism: The Search for Accord*. Honolulu: University of Hawaii Press, 1977.

"Malebranche and Chinese Philosophy." *Journal of the History of Ideas*, 41 (1980), pp. 551–78.

"Die Quellen für das Chinabild Leibnizens." *Studia Leibnitziana*, 14 (1982), pp. 233–43.

Curious Land: Jesuit Accommodation and the Origins of Sinology. Wiesbaden: Franz Steiner Verlag, 1985.

(ed.). *The Chinese Rites Controversy: Its History and Meaning.* Monumenta Serica XXXIII. Nettetal: Steyler Verlag, 1994.

Naert, Emilienne. "L'Idée de Religion Naturelle selon Leibniz." *Leibniz, 1646–1716. Aspects de l'Homme et de l'Ouevre.* Paris: Editions Aubier-Montagne, 1968.

Needham, Joseph. *Science and Civilization in China.* Cambridge: Cambridge University Press, 1954–.

Ng, On-cho. *Cheng-Zhu Confucianism in the Early Qing: Li Guangdi (1642–1718) and Qing Learning.* Albany: SUNY Press, 2001.

Oh, Bonnie, and Charles Ronan (eds.). *East Meets West: The Jesuits in China, 1582–1773.* Loyola University Press: Chicago, 1988.

Perkins, Franklin. "Ideas and Self-Reflection in Leibniz." *Leibniz Society Review*, December 1999, pp. 43–63.

Peterson, Willard. "Another Look at Li." *Bulletin of Sung and Yuan Studies*, 18 (1986), pp. 13–32.

"Why did They Become Christians? Yang T'ing-yün, Li Chih-tsao, and Hsü Kuang-ch'i." In Oh and Ronan, pp. 129–52.

Pichler, Aloys. *Die Theologie des Leibniz.* 2 vols. Hildesheim: Georg Olms Verlagsbuchhandlung, 1965, repr. of 1864 edn.

Pinot, Virgile. *La Chine et la formation de l'esprit philosophique en France (1640–1740).* Geneva: Slatkine, 1971.

Pombo, Olga. *Leibniz and the Problem of a Universal Language.* Munster: Nudus Publikationen, 1987.

Raudzens, George. *Empires: Europe and Globalization 1492–1788.* Phoenix Mill (UK): Sutton, 1999.

Ricci, Matteo, and Nicholas Trigault, *China in the Sixteenth Century: The Journals of Matteo Ricci, 1583–1610.* Trans. by Louis Gallagher. Random House: New York, 1953.

Riley, Patrick. *Leibniz' Universal Jurisprudence.* Cambridge, MA: Harvard University Press, 1996.

Ritter, Paul. *Leibniz Ägyptischer Plan.* Darmstadt: Otto Reichl Verlag, 1930.

Robinet, André. *Malebranche et Leibniz: Relations personnelles, présentées avec les textes complets des auteurs et de leurs correspondants revus, corrigés et inédits.* Paris: Librairie Philosophique J. Vrin, 1955.

Iter Italicum. Firenze: L. S. Olschki, 1988.

Roy, Oliver. *Leibniz et la Chine.* Paris: J. Vrin, 1972.

Rule, Paul. *K'ung-tzu or Confucius? The Jesuit Interpretation of Confucianism.* Boston: Allen & Unwin, 1986.

Rutherford, Donald. *Leibniz and the Rational Order of Nature.* Cambridge: Cambridge University Press, 1995.

Said, Edward. *Orientalism.* New York: Pantheon Books, 1978.

Schickel, Joachim. "I Ching: Logisches anzumerken." *Große Mauer, Große Methode: Annäherungen an China.* Stuttgart: Ernst Klett Verlag, 1968, pp. 231–84.

Schmitt, Charles. "Perrenial Philosophy: From Agostino Steuco to Leibniz." *Journal of the History of Ideas,* 27 (1966), pp. 505–32.

Shi, Zhonglian. "Leibniz's Binary System and Shao Yong's Xiantian Tu." *Das Nueste über China.* Ed. by Wenchad Li and Hans Poser. Stuttgart: Franz Steiner Verlag, 2000.

Sivin, Nathan. *Medicine, Philosophy and Religion in Ancient China: Researches and Reflections.* Brookfield, VT: Variorum, 1995.

Science in Ancient China: Researches and Reflections. Brookfield, VT: Variorum, 1995.

Spence, Jonathon. *The China Helpers: Western Advisers in China, 1620–1960.* London: Bodley Head, 1969.

Emperor of China: Self-portrait of K'ang-Hsi. New York: Alfred A. Knopf, 1975.

The Memory Palace of Matteo Ricci. New York: Viking Press, 1984.

Spinoza, Benedict de. *A Spinoza Reader.* Trans. by Edwin Curley. Princeton University Press, 1994.

The Letters. Trans. by Samuel Shirley. Indianapolis: Hackett, 1995.

Theological-Political Treatise. Trans. by Samuel Shirley. Indianapolis: Hackett, 1998.

Political Treatise. Trans. by Samuel Shirley. Indianapolis: Hackett, 2000.

Spizelius (Spitzel), Theophil. *De re literaria Sinensium commentarii.* Antwerp, 1660.

Stich, Stephen (ed.). *Innate Ideas.* Berkelely: University of California Press, 1975.

A Summary Account of Leibnitz's Memoir addressed to Lewis the Fourteenth Recommending to that Monarch the Conquest of Egypt . . . London: Hatchard, 1803.

Schwartz, Benjamin. *The World of Thought in Ancient China.* Cambridge, MA: Belknap Press of Harvard University Press, 1985.

Taylor, Charles. "The Politics of Recognition." *Campus Wars: Multiculturalism and the Politics of Difference.* Ed. by John Arthur and Amy Shapiro. Boulder: Westview Press, 1995, p. 259.

Tillman, Hoyt. "A New Direction in Confucian Scholarship." *Philosophy East and West,* 42 (3) (1992), pp. 455–74.

Trapnell, William. *The Treatment of Christian Doctrine by Philosophers of the Natural Light from Descartes to Berkeley.* Oxford: The Voltaire Foundation, 1988.

Van Kley, Edwin S. "Europe's Discovery of China and the Writing of World History." *The American Historical Review,* 76 (1971), pp. 358–72.

Vitkus, Daniel J. "Early Modern Orientalism: Representations of Islam in Sixteenth and Seventeenth-Century Europe." *Western Views of Islam in Medieval and Early Modern Europe.* Ed. by David R. Blanks and Michael Frassetto. New York: St. Martin's Press, 1999, pp. 207–30.

Walker, D. P. *The Ancient Theology: Studies in Christian Platonism from the Fifteenth to the Eighteenth Century.* Ithaca: Cornell University Press, 1972.

Walravens, Hartmut. *China Illustrata. Das europäische Chinaverständnis im Spiegel des 16. und 17. Jahrhunderts.* Weinheim: Acta Humaniora, 1987.

Watson, Richard. *Representational Ideas: From Plato to Patricia Churchland*. Boston: Kluwer Academic Publishers, 1995.

Widmaier, Rita. *Die Rolle der Chinesischen Schrift in Leibniz's Zeichentheorie*. Wiesbaden: Franz Steiner Verlag, 1983.

"Gottfried Wilhem Leibniz' Streben nach Harmonie zwischen China und Europa." *Western Learning and Christianity in China: The Contribution and Impact of Johann Adam Schall von Bell*. Ed. by Roman Malek. Nettetal: Steyler Verlag, 1998.

Wilhelm, Helmut. *Change: Eight Lectures on the I-ching*. New York: Pantheon, 1960.

Wilhelm, Richard, and Cary Baynes (trans.). *The I-ching or Book of Changes*. Princeton: Princeton University Press, 1961.

Willett, Cynthia (ed.). *Theorizing Multiculturalism. A Guide to the Current Debate*. Malden, MA: Blackwell Publishing, 1998.

Wimmer, Franz. *Interkulturelle Philosophie. Bd. I, Geschichte und Theorie*. Wien: Passagen-Verlag, 1990.

"Intercultural Philosophy." *Topoi*, 17/1 (March 1998), pp. 1–13.

Wu, Yi. *Chinese Philosophical Terms*. New York: University Press of America, 1986.

Yates, Francis. *Giordano Bruno and the Hermetic Tradition*. Chicago: University of Chicago Press, 1964.

Yoke, Ho Peng. *Li, Qi and Shu: An Introduction to Science and Civilization in China*. Seattle: University of Washington Press, 1985.

Young, John Dragon. "Chinese Views of Rites and the Rites Controversy, 18th–20th Century." In Mungello (1994), pp. 83–110.

Zempliner, Artur. "Gedanken über die erste deutsche Übersetzung von Leibniz' Abhandlung über die chinesische Philosophie." *Studia Leibnitiana*. 2 (1970), pp. 223–31.

"Leibniz und die chinesische Philosophie." *Studia Leibnitiana Supplementa*, 5 (1971), pp. 15–30.

Zürcher, Erik. "Jesuit Accommodation and the Chinese Cultural Imperative." In Mungello (1994), pp. 31–64.

Index